DICTIONARY OF

Music Production

AND

Engineering

TERMINOLOGY

For
Jennie and Nate, my loving parents;
Arthur and Lillie Mayer;
and Mr. John Hammond, Sr.

—— DICTIONARY OF ——

Music Production

AND

Engineering

—— TERMINOLOGY ——

Wayne Wadhams

with illustrations by Robin Coxe-Yeldham

SCHIRMER BOOKS
A Division of Macmillan, Inc.
NEW YORK

COLLIER MACMILLAN PUBLISHERS
LONDON

Schirmer Books
A Division of Macmillan, Inc.
866 Third Avenue, New York, N.Y. 10022

Collier Macmillan Canada, Inc.

Library of Congress Catalog Card Number: 87-30998

Printed in the United States of America

printing number
1 2 3 4 5 6 7 8 9 10

Library of Congress Cataloging-in-Publication Data
Wadhams, Wayne.
    A dictionary of music production and engineering
terminology.

    1. Music trade—Dictionaries.   I. Title.
II. Title: Music production and engineering terminology.
ML102.M85W3 1987   338.4'778'0321   87-30998
ISBN 0-02-872691-X

Contents

Preface

It has been my pleasure and privilege to work with brilliant minds in many areas of the entertainment industry. In some twenty-three years since I naively formed a band to help defray the costs of a college education, I have enjoyed a random walk through fields as diverse as writing and performing (live and on vinyl), writing and producing jingles for radio and television spots, and producing motion pictures and television programs and TV spots themselves. While I haven't reached the very top of each field, my career has given me a depth and breadth of experience that is fairly unique.

Along the way, several colleges and universities have asked me to guest lecture on, or to design individual courses in, filmmaking, sound recording, and business topics ranging from music publishing to limited partnerships for entertainment ventures. One often learns how well he really knows a subject by how well he can teach it to others. I have accepted these engagements as periodic opportunities to test and expand my own knowledge. Beyond all that, I have had so much fun in learning about the entertainment industries that I can't resist passing some of this knowledge along.

In 1982 I was asked by the President and Provost of Berklee College of Music to undertake a comprehensive study of the entire music production industry, with the goal of making recommendations about the kind and extent of theoretical, technical, and business training in recording and production that would best help Berklee graduates take responsible positions in the industry. After surveying a wide cross-section of professionals in music, film, and video production, from New York to Los Angeles, I recommended and later supervised the design and construction of a new department and major, with six recording studios— something quite unique in music education. Now called Music Production and Engineering (MP&E), this department has been up and running and fully-enrolled since 1983.

College-level textbooks in the entertainment production fields are scarce. Even more scarce are up-to-date glossaries of the terms the versatile music producer or engineer must know in order to serve his clients and work efficiently with collaborators. This volume began as a five-part glossary intended for use only in the MP&E department. Then, several friends in the industry asked for copies. Later, a few of them suggested that it be expanded and made, shall we say, more precise. A year later, voilà!

Because this is, to my knowledge, the first book of its type, I have no doubt blundered on one or more bases. However, with no model from whose mistakes to learn, this is inevitable. I can only hope it will find an audience broad enough, and one whose use of it will be frequent enough, to justify future editions. These, with input from all, can only improve.

Acknowledgments

The contributors to this book have given freely since January of 1983. I list them in order of their involvement—Peter Fink, who wrote a major chunk of the glossary for the MP&E curriculum at Berklee, from which this book ultimately sprang. And Susan Huete, Kevin Dixon, Tom Ketterer, and Elise Snoddy, who edited that early tome.

The professionals teaching at Berklee who asked for additions and revisions to the text, and later reviewed the sections of the entire work pertaining to their individual specialties—Bill Gitt, Robin Coxe-Yeldham, Michael Szakmeister, Andy Edelstein, Keith Maynard, Bud Billings, Don Wilkins, David van Slyke, Joe Hostetter, and Gerald Gold. Also, let me not forget to thank the hundreds of students who have field-tested the various editions, and whose need for a more complete one has spurred me on.

The preparation of the final edition would have been impossible without the aid of Anthony Marvuglio, former student, patient collaborator, and word-processing virtuoso. And for patient guidance in the (to me) new craft of preparing a reference work, thanks to Maribeth Payne, my senior editor.

For encouraging me to broaden the scope and market of this volume to embrace the many industries whose vocabularies are now represented, from Berklee College I thank Lee Berk, President of Berklee College; Don Puluse, Chairman of the MP&E Department and Music Technology Division; Warrick Carter, Dean of the Faculty; and Bruce MacDonald, Director of Development.

And finally, my thanks to those in education and industry whose generous input became the blueprint upon which the MP&E curriculum was built. A very incomplete list of these friends must include Michael Berniker, Larry Blake, Dr. Richard Bobbit, Fred Bouchard, Gary Burton, Mickey Eichner, Robert Feiden, Ethel Gabriel, Kevin Gavin, James Gianopulos, Michael Gibbs, Mr. John Hammond, Sr., Mikey Harris, Rickey Leacock, Bruce Lundvall, Arif Mardin, Lennie Petze, Doreen Riley-Courtright, Deac Rossell, David Schwartz, Allen D. Smith, David Sonenberg, Esq., Joseph Tarsia, and Robert Walters.

I dedicate this book to Mr. Robert Share, former Provost of Berklee College of Music, who first brought me in to the college to make a few "suggestions," and under whose guidance the MP&E curriculum and department sprouted and took sound educational form, until his untimely passing in 1984. If the love of humanity and music is an art form, Bob was a consummate artist. His, indeed, was a love supreme.

Key to Letters
Beside Definitions

(A) = ADVERTISING.   A term used by ad agencies, jingle producers, and other subcontractors.

(B) = BUSINESS, including legal, accounting, investment, banking, contractual, and related terms.

(C) = COMPUTERS.   Hardware, software, and programming terms for business and creative users.

(D) = DIGITAL RECORDING.   Professional or home systems, concepts, circuits, etc.

(E) = ENGINEERING.   A technical term used in recording studios, studio design, acoustics, maintenance, etc. Scientific and mathematical terms.

(F) = FILM (or motion pictures).   A term used in film-making pre-, post-, or during production itself, or in film distribution.

(G) = GENERAL INFORMATION.   A musical term or slang term—something *all* producers of music know and use.

(I) = INTERLOCK or SYNCHRONIZATION of multiple machines: audio, video, or film. Concepts and equipment.

(J) = JARGON, JOKES—and funny descriptive terms—actually in use, or invented for your amusement.

(P) = MUSIC PUBLISHING.   Copyright, licensing, composer royalty payment, and related terms.

(R) = RECORD INDUSTRY.   Terms relating to production, sales, promotion, artist and producer agreements, mastering and duplication of records, CDs, etc.

(S) = SYNTHESIZERS.   Concepts, circuits, controls, waveforms, and interfaces with other studio equipment.

(U) = UNION.   Scale wage payments, benefits, working conditions for AFM, AFTRA, and other musical and technicians' unions.

(V) = VIDEO (or television).   Creative, functional, and technical terms—from scripting to syndication.

Introduction

Something quite unique has occurred in sectors of the music and entertainment industries long thought to be entirely separate. A decade ago, television directors began directing theatrical motion pictures. Conversely, motion picture cameramen and technicians were asked to apply their arts to the television medium. Rock and pop records began appearing in more and more soundtracks. On the heels of commercial success, recording artists and producers were asked to create jingles for network television spots and scores for feature films, television specials, and miniseries. Composers and writers for one medium discovered new markets in other media. The music and entertainment industries began to merge.

More recently, the technologies on which these industries are based have been drawn together like two galaxies whose gravitational attraction plots a collision course. In this case, however, the uniting force has been the rapid development and deployment of computer software and hardware in almost every area of entertainment technology. Ten years ago the personal computer did not exist. Chips were not available at any cost for use in the design and building of recording console automation systems; for audio/video synchronization and interlock systems; for digital recording systems for sound and image; for motion picture and video editing systems; for electronic music composition and synthesis and video animation systems, not to mention the interfacing of such systems with one another. There were no computer programs for motion picture and video production budgeting, word processing, royalty calculation and payment, etc. Now all of these systems and operations are commonplace, and the entertainment industries are changed forever—and for the better.

Who Needs This Book?

I have written with four specific types of readers in mind. First, there are creative minds: composers, musicians, singers, scriptwriters, and copywriters, who will benefit by understanding the vocabulary of the technicians and engineers who bring their creations to life in recording studios, sound stages, and on location. This volume may thus help to demystify high-tech and put it at the service of ideas.

Second, this volume serves professionals in one area of entertainment production who need quickly to learn the vocabulary of another specialty. For example, the record producer asked to produce a jingle for a TV spot will know better what has been asked of him, and work much more efficiently with those in advertising, if he understands the basic terminology of that profession. In these contexts, I hope this book will prove a clear and accurate teacher and translator.

Third, for the professional continuing in his own field, I intend this as a readable and functional dictionary. It is not intended to replace comprehensive and highly technical reference works such as Tremaine's *Audio Cyclopedia* or the *Focal Encyclopedia of Film and Television Techniques*. Nor can any mere dictionary hope to impart an organized and rigorous body of knowledge. Thus, this volume is no substitute for the proven values of audio textbooks such as Woram, Eargle, Pohlmann, Runstein, or the various Tonmeister handbooks; nor can it replace standard texts on the arts and crafts of musical arranging, motion picture and television production, and the like. However, familiarity with the daily tools and operation of a profession can distance one from the precise definitions of the concepts and equipment that underlie that profession. In this context, I hope these definitions will be crisp and clear refreshers of material already in daily use.

Finally, there are the many students and apprentices preparing to enter one or another of the professions embraced by the entertainment industry. All things are mastered one at a time, but it is almost inevitable that many of today's aspiring engineers will move into production of records, jingles, or scores. Many student composers will likewise find it necessary to negotiate agreements to write and/or produce for various media. Almost all will eventually avail themselves of the computer-based technologies that have spurred the grand unification just described.

What is Included?

Decisions about which terms to include and which to omit have been difficult. However, my goal is to define (1) any terms used by professionals making music for any type of client in any medium, and (2) words and idioms that will aid professionals in related fields when working with or representing music makers. (The latter group might include entertainment attorneys, managers and agents, etc.). A composer scoring a film doesn't need to know the optical principle on which zoom lenses are designed. He does need to know what a zoom shot is, what it looks like on-screen, and what emotional quality the shot may convey in the context of the finished film. Without these understandings, he cannot read a script or view the film as a member of the creative team, using his art on behalf of goals that the director must communicate to every participant in the project.

Then there is the sticky question of which models and brands of equipment to "define." In general, I have included a definition whenever a particular piece of equipment or trademarked name is *the* standard device or process of its type, used almost universally for that specific function; or where the device's name is used almost synonymously with its function. For example, "Sel-sync," an Ampex trademark, is used by engineers everywhere to indicate tape playback via the record head. Similarly, many engineers and producers call almost any noise gate a Kepex. These uses are technically incorrect, but professionals set the standard in any industry, not dictionaries. Apologies to any manufacturers who disagree with current decisions on this matter. Time alone will tell how these "standards" fare.

How Is the Book Organized?

The guiding principle on which the entries were organized and alphabetized is common usage, not grammatical or stylistic conformity. Acronyms are tossed around freely in the entertainment industries. Company names, unions, job titles, specific pieces of equipment, and some multiword processes are all shortened or "acronamed" for speedy and efficient communication. In consulting many sources, I found many acronyms published alternately with and without periods between the letters. Therefore, the alphabetizing has been done on a letter-by-letter basis. The only rule I can deduce from experience is that acronyms such as ASCAP, which can be pronounced as a word, are most often written without periods. Company names, devices, and processes ranging from AGC (Automatic Gain Control) to VCO (Voltage Controlled Oscillator) also seem to appear without punctuation. Since it would be difficult for a novice to guess the words for which ASCAP stands, definitions of terms that most often appear as acronyms are located at the alphabetical listing of that acronym. If you cannot find a specific term or organization listed under its full name, check under the acronym.

Aids to Understanding

You will note that beside each term defined is one or more capital letters. Each one of these letters corresponds to one of fifteen categories, professions, or topic headings to which the defined terms belong. Those terms whose meaning is identical in more than one profession are preceded, logically, by more than one letter. On the other hand, if two or more of the definitions of a term are used in the same field, the letter appearing above the first in this sequence applies to them all. (See "EQUALIZER" for a good example.)

A complete "key" to the letters and their corresponding meanings appears before the text. For quick reference, one-word equivalents for each letter are listed across the bottom of each pair of pages. Those who need to quickly survey or review the terminology of any field can find the relevant definitions in a single scan through the book.

There are also about one hundred illustrations, drawn lovingly by Robin Coxe-Yeldham. Some terms, even with the clearest verbal explanation, can be misunderstood without a crisp visual image. This is especially true of terms describing the function, operation, and maintenance of generic types of industry-standard equipment. For this reason, we have refrained from showing specific brands and models of even the most popular equipment. Instead, the illustrations convey essential and most common features, controls, components, etc., so that the purpose and general use of each genre of device or procedure will be clear. It must be left to the reader to apply this knowledge to any specific equipment or situations as he encounters them in the course of his work.

The Style and Format of Definitions

Early on in writing the book, I decided to heed the words of my grade school English teachers. A word is only yours after you use it in a sentence three times. Thus, definitions herein are written in complete sentences. You won't have to refer to a table of grammatical abbreviations, etc. It is my feeling that technical concepts and processes are difficult enough to convey in words alone, so why compound the problem with verbal shorthand. In addition, I have tried to demonstrate how terms and their various forms are used in industry context, supplying examples, showing conjugated forms and idioms in which they appear, etc. I trust the reader will gladly spend a few extra seconds to absorb a thorough explanation and (hopefully) to carry off a lasting imprint of the knowledge gained.

A Few Words of Caution

Please bear in mind that the vocabulary of the entertainment industries is growing and changing even as you read these words. Many old war-horses of professional jargon have bitten the dust. New terms pop up all the time, and—here's the tricky part—many terms have completely different meanings in different geographical areas, sometimes even at separate companies or studios within the same city! What one New York advertising firm calls a "window" is a "donut" to another. Across the country the same type of spot may be called the "hole"!

This kind of confusion can arise where the same word, abbreviation, or acronym is used in more than one industry. AM is both a radio term and the acronym for two separate job descriptions in the advertising profession. To *assume* that one knows the intended meaning of such terms, especially in a contractual context, can prove embarrassing at best, highly unprofitable at worst! Similarly, the noun and verb forms of the word "track" have distinct and mutually exclusive meanings in almost every field from video to engineering to record promotion. Be careful to find the meaning you need—and in the right field, too.

For those among you with a bent toward mathematical precision, acoustic or audio research, custom circuit design, or the natural desire to reprove the laws of physics, a table of Standard Units and Measures follows the main text. This table will not find daily use with most readers. Yet, I have not found a complete listing of these conversion factors and equations under one cover. So here they are, for the first time listed on the same pages.

If this volume can provide a bridge between people working in all areas of music production and their clients, collaborators, subcontractors, employees, and legal and business representatives, I will have more than achieved my goals. Precise communication is itself an art form not to be undervalued in a world of ever-increasing speed and confusion. I look forward to seeing how this volume fares in the real world, and to keeping future editions apace with the careers and aspirations of the creative minds for whom it is written.

-A-

A.A.A.A. (or AAAA) American Association of Advertising Agencies. (*See* FOUR As.)

A and B ROLLS (F) Rolls consisting of camera-original film (negative or reversal) and opaque leader, spliced together and ready for printing. Segments of the original footage corresponding exactly to the shots in the edited work-print are cement-spliced alternately into A or B rolls. Opaque leader is spliced in between each segment of original, its length matched to that of the shot appearing in the opposite roll. Because the opaque leader is cut precisely at the frame line, it over-laps and masks the scraped and spliced end of the original. In 16mm films, this prevents the splices themselves from appearing in answer or release prints. Optical effects such as fades and dissolves can be made without intermediate stages of photographic duplication (as is normal in 35mm), simply by having camera-original in A and B rolls simultaneously and providing separate exposure control instructions to the printer for each roll at these footages. For superimposition of titles or more complex effects, C, D, E, and other rolls can be added. All rolls are sequentially printed onto the same strip of print

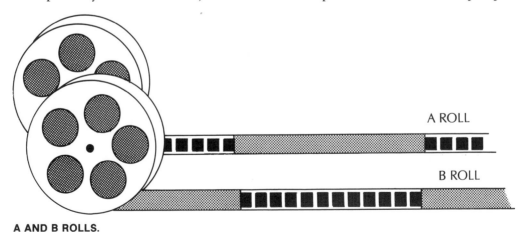

A ROLL

B ROLL

A AND B ROLLS.

---

or internegative stock, giving the desired composite effects. The process of making composite prints from A and B rolls is also called CHECKERBOARD PRINTING. (See SYNC BLOCK)

A&R Artists and Repertoire. **1.** The department in a record company
(R) that selects the performing groups or artists who will be signed to the label, what songs or compositions each artist will record, and who will work with the artist in the production, arranging, and performance of this material for the recording of master tapes. The A&R person's responsibilities can be greater or lesser, depending on how complete the artist's creative team is at the time of signing. **2.** The process of making such selections.

A&R ADMINISTRATION **1.** The department at a record company
(R) that (a) monitors the costs in the making of various artists' master tapes; (b) makes payments to recording studios, musicians, singers, and others rendering services in connection with these tapes; and (c) usually calculates and pays royalties to the artist, producer, and any others sharing in the profits from records, cassettes, CDs, and the sale of flat-fee licenses for other use of the master tapes. Also, the process of monitoring costs in any recording project and actually making payments to studios, musicians, and singers, etc. Members of this department are normally accountants fully trained in the relevant union contracts and benefits, etc. A separate accounting department takes care of general operating and overhead expenses for the com-

pany. **2.** The process of performing all the functions described above.

A-B **1.** To compare two recorded programs or sound sources, usually
(E) by switching from one to the other. For example, a compressed signal may be A-B'ed with the uncompressed signal, or one copy of a master tape compared with another, each played on separate machines. Because the louder of two programs will be preferred by most listeners, the volume of each source is normally adjusted until both are equal.
(G) **2.** To compare the "sound" or peformance of two functionally similar devices—e.g., amplifiers, speakers, compressors, etc.—by sending the same signal source to each and listening alternately to their outputs. Again, for a fair comparison the output levels should be matched.

ABOVE-THE-LINE Those expenses in a motion picture, video, or jingle
(F,V,A) budget that cannot be predicted from union wage scales or other published sources of prices, fees, rates, and the like. The price of acquiring and rewriting the screenplay, director's and producer's payments, and composer's and other negotiated payments are all above the line, along with fees and salaries of featured "stars." Sidemen's wages or bit players would be a part of the below-the-line budget for a production. (*See* BELOW-THE-LINE; NEGATIVE COST.)

ABSORPTION COEFFICIENT In acoustical measurements, the deci-
(E) mal number that indicates the proportion of sound striking a surface

---

(A) = Advertising • (B) = Business & Law • (C) = Computers • (D) = Digital • (E) = Engineering & Scientific •
(F) = Film • (G) = Music & General • (I) = Interlock & Sync • (J) = Jokes & Jargon • (P) = Music Publishing •
(R) = Record Industry • (S) = Synthesizers • (U) = Unions • (V) = Video

that is absorbed by that surface. Specified either as an average for a group of selected standard frequencies, or individually for one or more frequencies or bands. (*See* SABINE.)

ACA (or ACN)   Active Combining Amplifier or Active Combining Network. (*See* COMBINING AMPLIFIER; COMBINING NETWORK.)

ACADEMY LEADER   The familiar visual "countdown" that precedes the first shot of a motion picture. Symbols and numbers on the academy leader are used for aligning A and B rolls and the optical track for composite printing, for aligning the workprint and edited soundtracks for mixing, and for timing the "change-over" from one reel of film to another during projection. Named after the Academy of Motion Picture Arts and Sciences, which sets all format standards.
(F)

ACCESS   To transfer data to or from a storage device— e.g., a floppy or hard disk, etc.
(C)

ACCESS TIME   The time required to retrieve data from or write data into any selected memory address.
(C)

ACCOUNTANT   A specialist in the financial organization of businesses. He sets up books, tracks cash flow, profit and loss, and prepares tax statements and payments. This is especially important in the music and entertainment industries, since income sources may be worldwide and can extend for many years on an individual song, album, score, jingle, motion picture, or video
(G,B)

program. (*See* SPREADSHEET; BOOKKEEPER; BOOKS.)

ACCOUNT EXECUTIVE (A.E.)   The person at an advertising agency whose primary job is to maintain close relations with and supervise all work done for a specific client company. One person may act as A.E. for several small clients, or be the A.E. for only one product brand manufactured by a large account. The A.E. often designates the media mix by which an ad or whole campaign will reach the client's market.
(A)

ACCOUNT MANAGER   See AM.

ACCOUNT SUPERVISOR (A.S.)   The A.E.'s boss. A small agency may not have an A.S. At a larger agency, the A.S. might oversee all work done for General Foods, for example, while several A.E.s beneath him oversee work done for separate brands of cereal that the parent company manufactures.
(A)

ACETATE   1. A reference phonograph disc that is cut on a mastering lathe as a test copy or "proof" of the lacquer master disc from which records will ultimately be pressed. Because the acetate's surface is very soft, it can be played only a few times before stylus wear reduces the high-frequency information in the grooves. (*See* LACQUER; SUBSTRATE; TEST PRESSING.) 2. Short for vinyl acetate. The soft plastic compound applied to the aluminum disc or substrate used in making an "acetate" as defined above. (*See* VINYL.) 3. Short for cellulose acetate. A plastic chemical compound formerly used as the base
(R)

(A) = Advertising • (B) = Business & Law • (C) = Computers • (D) = Digital • (E) = Engineering & Scientific •
(F) = Film • (G) = Music & General • (I) = Interlock & Sync • (J) = Jokes & Jargon • (P) = Music Publishing •
(R) = Record Industry • (S) = Synthesizers • (U) = Unions • (V) = Video

for recording tape, but replaced by polyester or mylar after about 1965. Acetate-based tape was long preferred for professional use because it breaks under tension, rather than stretching as mylar does. However, acetate curls and becomes brittle with prolonged storage—not desirable qualities for recording tape. (*See* MYLAR.)

ACN   Active Combining Network. (*See* COMBINING NETWORK.)

ACOUSTIC BAFFLE   Any partition
(E)   placed between two sources of sound, or between a sound source and a microphone, to prevent sound from passing through. The baffle may consist of layers of felt or any cloth used to prevent high frequencies from reaching a microphone, one or more sound blankets, or a movable "wall" section with interior layers of sound-absorbent material. The latter type is used to isolate separate instruments in recording studios.

ACOUSTIC LABYRINTH   1. A type
(E)   of design for the body or housing of highly directional microphones that enhances the rejection of off-axis sources. Two or more concentric tubes in front of (and sometimes around) the capsule create a compact series of folded pathways through which all sounds approach the diaphragm. Those arriving on-axis reach the capsule via these paths in phase coherence. Sounds arriving off-axis, due to the different lengths of the pathways, reach the diaphragm out of phase and are partially or fully cancelled. The design engineer can specify the path lengths to achieve desired amounts of cancellation in various bands and for specific angles of incidence. Shotgun mics have acoustic labyrinths built into their long, tubular bodies. **2.** A type of speaker enclosure in which sound waves emanating from the rear of the woofer cone travel through a long, folded interior path before coupling with the outside. This extends bass response considerably.

ACOUSTIC LENS   A device placed in
(E)   front of a high-frequency speaker that disperses or directs the sound in a desired pattern. Normally used to increase the angle of dispersion, either horizontally, vertically, or both.

ACOUSTIC SUSPENSION SYSTEM   A
(E)   type of loudspeaker enclosure designed so that the internal volume of air resists the movement of the woofer cone at specific frequencies. Since most small woofers have resonant frequencies in the 60–

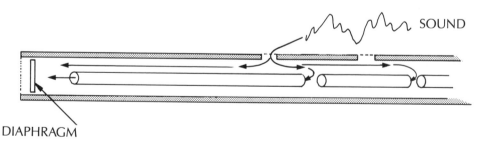

ACOUSTIC LABYRINTH. Sound entering from sides and rear arrive at diaphragm out of phase.

150–Hz range, acoustic suspension enclosures are often used to suppress this band and effectively extend the bass response of "bookshelf" systems. However, since the enclosure damps the speaker's low-mid output, acoustic suspension systems are relatively inefficient. (*See* EFFICIENCY; BAFFLE.)

ACOUSTIC TREATMENT (E) Any sound-absorbent material used (a) to prevent sound from passing through a wall, or (b) to control reverberation or echoes within a room. Also, the sum of all such materials by which a room is made to achieve certain acoustic specifications.

ACOUSTICS (G) 1. The science that studies the behavior of sound and methods for its control in various environments. 2. The qualities of a specific room, studio, hall, or outdoor location that determine its effect on sounds delivered from a source to a listener or microphone.

ACQUIRED MASTER (R,U) In the AFTRA Code of Fair Practice, any master tape a signatory obtains for release from an independent producer, usually via a master purchase or license agreement.

ACTION (F,V) (G) 1. Everything that happens on-screen in a motion picture or video production. 2. The director's command to the actors to begin doing and saying what is specified in a particular shot of a script—e.g., "Action!". (*See* SPEED!) 3. The keyboard and associated parts of an acoustic or electric piano, organ, or synthesizer that transmit energy from the player's fingers to the strings or other sound-generating components.

ACTIVE COMBINING AMPLIFIER *See* ACN.

ACTIVE COMBINING NETWORK *See* ACA.

ACTIVE DEVICE (E) Any electronic signal processing device that requires AC or DC current to power its operation, and that generally includes an amplifying stage after its primary processing circuit, allowing the output level to be matched to the input level. (*See* PASSIVE DEVICE.)

ACTIVE SENSING (S) A MIDI code signal and reception system that lets slaved devices know if all the MIDI cables are still properly connected. Without this system, if a cable is dislodged while one or more synth notes are depressed, those notes will sound continuously, ruining the performance.

A-D CONVERTER (Read "A to D"). See ANALOG-TO-DIGITAL CONVERTER.

ACT OF GOD (B) An unforeseeable disaster that prevents one from fulfilling contractual responsibilities or normal duties. In most cases floods, hurricanes, tornadoes, and other acts of God release people from penalty for non-performance. They may or may not be covered by insurance policies.

ACTUALS (A) Advertisements using real, unstaged testimonials to sell the product. Actuals are popular and effective for print ads and broadcast spots.

AD (or A.D.) 1. Assistant Director. His primary duty is to direct the on-

(F,V) screen actions of bit players and extras in large or complex scenes. The AD may also preside over rehearsals of the entire cast until they have their lines and basic blocking memorized. **2.** Art Director or Advertising Director.

ADI   See AREA OF DOMINANT IN-FLUENCE.

ADDITIVE SYNTHESIS   The process of creating complex tones or patches by combining simpler ones—e.g., a group of sine waves.
(S)

ADDRESS   The number correspond-
(C)   ing to a specific location in memory.

ADDRESS BITS   In SMPTE time code, a group of data bits within each SMPTE word that contains time, sync, or location information defined by the user rather than by the time-code generator.
(I,V)

ADDRESS TRACK   In 1″, C-Format, and ¾″ U-matic videotape formats,

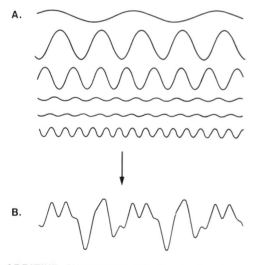

ADDITIVE SYNTHESIS. (A) Randomly chosen amounts and phases of a fundamental and its second through sixth harmonics; (B) The complex wave created by combining the above waveforms.

(I,V) a narrow analog track recorded near one edge of the tape at the same time picture is originally recorded on the tape. This track contains control data (not SMPTE code) that cannot be insert-edited later, although a separate and parallel "control track" is accessible for later insert-editing. The ½″ video formats have no address track. Hence, all control data goes to the control track. There is some confusion, even in the industry, about the naming of these tracks in various formats. (*See* FORMAT (illustration); CONTROL TRACK.)

AD LICENSE   A special-purpose license issued by a publishing company, record company, or other copyright holder to any company desiring to use a song or recorded performance in a jingle or spot. The license can be written for one spot, a campaign (with limited time period), or may allow blanket use by the licensee.
(A,P)

ADMINISTRATION   The portion of the music publisher's responsibilities with which he exercises legal control over copyrights and the monies that accrue as his compositions are used; signing of all licenses (and negotiating those whose rates are not statutory); registration of compositions with ASCAP, BMI, the Harry Fox Agency, etc.; collection and distribution of monies to co-publishers and the composer(s). (*See* PUBLISHING COMPANY; SUBPUBLISHING.)
(P)

ADO   Ampex Digital Optical. A video image-processing device manufactured by Ampex Corporation that allows complex manipulation of multiple live or taped video im-
(V)

ages. The ADO can create real-time split-screen displays of video images from many sources, with the capability of zooming any of these up to full-screen, rotating or flipping them horizontally or vertically, etc. (*See* MIRAGE.)

ADR
(V)
Automatic Dialogue Replacement. A technique and electronic device used in video post production for speedy "looping" of badly recorded dialogue.

ADSR
(E,S)
Attack, Decay, Sustain, Release. The four sections of every sound's envelope. (*See* ATTACK; ENVELOPE.)

ADT
(A,E)
Automatic Double Tracking. Generic name for a number of techniques used in jingle studios to quickly give the impression that vocals have been double tracked. ADT can be done by tape and/or short digital delays, sometimes with slow flanging. Some manufacturers make dedicated ADT modules for rack-mounting.

ADVANCE
(B)
Generally, any money a company pays to an artist, producer, or independent contractor as an inducement for him to sign a deal. A producer who has paid the bills in the making of a master tape will normally get a recoupment advance from the record company, reimbursing him for his expenses. An artist may receive an advance to cover expenses while in rehearsal for recording, to help with touring costs in the promotion of records, or just to "persuade" him to sign. Advances made to recording artists are charged-back to their royalty account.

ADVERTISING
(A)
Specific messages placed in the media whose purpose is to inform, convince, or motivate a specific audience to buy and use a product or service, to vote for a certain candidate, to contribute to a specific charity, etc. This audience is called the "market" or "target audience."

ADVERTISING AGE
(A)
The primary trade journal for the advertising industry, charting activities in all areas from production to media buying, and Neilsen ratings to network programming trends and preferences.

ADVERTISING AGENCY
(A)
A company that designs and prepares advertising messages (either for printed media, radio or television broadcast) and secures or purchases actual ad space or broadcast time for these messages. The agency will generally submit to its clients two bids, one for creating and preparing the ads, and a second for a recommended "media buy" by which an ad or campaign will reach the public. Generally, the commissions an agency makes on media buys for its clients provide the bulk of its net income, since the design phase for an ad campaign may cost only $100,000, while the total amount spent on a media buy may be $1 million to $10 million, or even more.

ADVERTISING DIRECTOR (A.D.)
(A)
The person in charge of advertising for an agency's client company. As the ad manager's boss, the A.D. generally has the power to approve the budgets for all creative services and media buys.

ADVERTISING MANAGER (AM)
(A) The person in charge of specific areas or media for the advertising of a client company. Small companies may have one person acting as ad manager and ad director. Larger companies may have separate A.M.s for print, radio, etc.

A.E.   See ACCOUNT EXECUTIVE.

AES   See AUDIO ENGINEERING SOCIETY.

AFM
(U) American Federation of Musicians. The labor union that represents professional musicians in all their client and employer relations—setting pay rates and working conditions; establishing and maintaining health, welfare, and pension funds; monitoring and collecting fees and other payments dues to members for their services, etc.

A.F.R.T.S.
(E,V) Armed Forces Radio and Television Standards. The separate military band of radio and TV broadcast frequencies, and some of its technical specifications or requirements for finished programming, are quite different from those used in producing programs for commercial radio and television. Check the A.F.R.T.S. guidelines brochures for details.

AFTRA
(U) American Federation of Television and Radio Artists. The labor union that represents professional singers and narrators in all their client and employer relations, setting pay rates, working conditions, etc. Since many narrators and singers also appear on-camera in motion pictures, video programs and commercials, AFTRA has effec-tively merged with SAG (The Screen Actors Guild). Many AFTRA members are also SAG members, and vice versa. Because of the analogous crossover of artists from live theater to film and video, AGMA (American Guild of Musical Artists) and the other theatrical performers' unions have affiliated with AFTRA.

AGAC
(P) American Guild of Authors and Composers. A third performing rights organization similar to ASCAP and BMI but much smaller. AGAC primarily represents modern classical or "serious" composers.

AGC   See AUTOMATIC GAIN CONTROL.

AGENT
(B,G) Any person who, acting on behalf of a second person or company, has the authority to enter into contractual agreements that are binding on the second party. One person may be a normal employee in one situation, an agent in another. For example, a recording engineer is an employee during sessions, but an agent if he orders recording tape on behalf of the studio owner.

AGMA
(U) American Guild of Musical Artists. A union representing singers and musicians who appear in stage presentations, particularly musicals, opera, etc. An AFL-CIO member organization.

AIDA
(A) Attention, Interest, Desire, Action. The four underlying goals of the advertising industry. A good ad commands attention, stimulates interest, kindles a desire for a product or service, and prompts action toward buying the product or ser-

---

(A) = Advertising • (B) = Business & Law • (C) = Computers • (D) = Digital • (E) = Engineering & Scientific •
(F) = Film • (G) = Music & General • (I) = Interlock & Sync • (J) = Jokes & Jargon • (P) = Music Publishing •
(R) = Record Industry • (S) = Synthesizers • (U) = Unions • (V) = Video

vice. (*See* MARKETING; PROMO-TION.)

AIRPLAY   The playing of a record on any of the broadcast media: AM or FM radio, network or local television, cable TV, etc.
(R)

AIRPLAY ROYALTIES   Royalties payable for airplay, usually collected from broadcasters by ASCAP, BMI, AGAC, or SESAC. These organizations then distribute these monies to publishers and/or composers whose works were broadcast. Also called broadcast royalties.
(R,B)

ALBUM FUND   A type of financial vehicle used for major record productions. When granted an album fund, the producer has the record company's guarantee that he may spend up to the entire amount of the fund in producing the record, without requiring any intermediate approvals for individual expenditures during the production. Hence, the record company cannot stop the project once the fund is established. The producer, however, is obligated to complete the project using only the money in the fund. He will most likely have to give up some of his points if he needs additional money for completion. There are many variations of this arrangement, depending on the artist's and producer's stature in the industry. (*See* APPROVED-BUDGET RECORD PRODUCTION.)
(R)

ALBUM-ORIENTED ROCK   See AOR.

ALGORITHM   An exact computational (or tone-generating and tone-processing) procedure, defined by
(C,S)

one or more equations, that reliably produces a desired answer, result, or sound output. A computer program is an extended algorithm, for example. (*See* READ-ONLY MEMORY.)

ALIASING   In digital recording, audible beating between the sampling frequency and high frequencies in the program material. For example, a 25-kHz tone present in the program would cause aliasing at 19 kHz in a digital system that samples at 44 kHz. $(44 - 25 = 19)$. A low-pass filter cutting off frequencies above 20 kHz in the input signal will eliminate aliasing. (*See* NYQUIST FREQUENCY; BRICKWALL FILTER.)
(E,D)

ALIGNMENT   1. In tape recording, the process of adjusting all parameters of the position and orientation of the tape heads and guides with respect to the tape path. 2. The adjustment or calibration of any parameter of an electronic circuit or device—e.g., program level, bias level, or equalization, to bring this parameter into conformance with an industry-wide standard.
(E)

TAPE HEAD ALIGNMENT: The adjustment of the positioning and angular orientation of the tape recorder heads to match industry standards. In the professional two-track format, these standards are defined such that the tape-to-head pressure is even across the tape width, the tracks are centered across the tape width, and high-frequency response is optimized by orienting the head-gaps at precisely 90 degrees with respect to the direction of tape travel. (*See* WRAP; TILT; HEIGHT; TANGENCY; AZIMUTH.) (Illustration next page.)
(E)

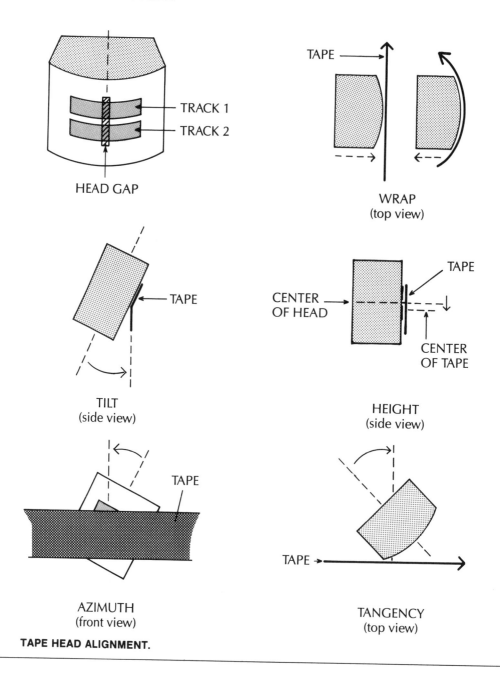

TRACK 1
TRACK 2
HEAD GAP

TAPE

WRAP
(top view)

TAPE

TILT
(side view)

CENTER
OF HEAD

TAPE

CENTER
OF TAPE

HEIGHT
(side view)

TAPE

AZIMUTH
(front view)

TAPE

TANGENCY
(top view)

TAPE HEAD ALIGNMENT.

ALL-IN DEAL   A type of master purchase agreement in which one party (the artist or producer) has paid all the expenses in producing the master tape. The record label pays that party one gross royalty rate, from which that party pays

(R)

all others who have a royalty interest in the tapes.

ALU   Arithmetic and Logic Unit. The portion of a CPU that actually performs arithmetic and other computational procedures.

(C)

AM

(A)

(E)

1. Account Manager or Advertising Manager. Use such acronyms with care, especially in contracts.

2. Amplitude Modulation. One of the two methods by which commercial radio broadcasts are made.

AMBIENCE TRACK   An edited roll of magnetic film (or one track of a multi-track tape) assembled by the sound editor in preparation for the final mix of a motion picture or video production, containing the series of room tones or ambient sounds of the various rooms, sets, and locations in which a film or videotape scene was shot. Upon request of the director, the sound editor may mix in sounds other than those present during the original shooting, either to change or intensify the "ambient" sound quality of the scene, or to imply the existence of another location adjacent to that visible on camera. (*See* ROOM TONE.)

(F,V)

AMBIENT NOISE   The environmental noise that is continuously present in any room or location. This may include truck noise coming through walls, heating or air conditioning noise, or any other sound that cannot be turned off.

(E)

AMC   See AMERICAN MUSIC CONFERENCE.

AMERICAN ASSOCIATION OF ADVERTISING AGENCIES.   See FOUR As.

AMERICAN FEDERATION OF MUSICIANS   See AFM.

AMERICAN FEDERATION OF TELEVISION AND RADIO ARTISTS   See AFTRA.

AMERICAN GUILD OF AUTHORS AND COMPOSERS   See AGAC.

AMERICAN GUILD OF MUSICAL ARTISTS   See AGMA.

AMERICAN MECHANICAL RIGHTS ASSOCIATION   See AMRA.

AMERICAN MUSIC CONFERENCE (AMC)   A trade organization that promotes the interests of music publishers, instrument manufacturers, etc.

(P,B)

AMERICAN RESEARCH BUREAU   See A.R.B.

AMERICAN SOCIETY OF COMPOSERS, AUTHORS and PUBLISHERS   See ASCAP.

AMERICAN STANDARD CODE FOR INFORMATION INTERCHANGE   See ASCII.

AMORTIZE   In accounting, to write off the total cost of something over a period of time. A tape recorder with a five-year life span, for example, may be amortized over five years, even if it only takes two years to pay off the loan with which it was purchased.

(B)

AMPEX DIGITAL OPTICAL   See ADO.

AMPLIFIER   An electronic device or circuit that increases the strength of a signal. In most amplifiers this is achieved by using the low-level input signal voltage as the model for or gate by which a more powerful signal is varied or allowed to pass to the output.

(E)

(A) = Advertising • (B) = Business & Law • (C) = Computers • (D) = Digital • (E) = Engineering & Scientific •
(F) = Film • (G) = Music & General • (I) = Interlock & Sync • (J) = Jokes & Jargon • (P) = Music Publishing •
(R) = Record Industry • (S) = Synthesizers • (U) = Unions • (V) = Video

AMPLITUDE MODULATION (AM)

(E) In radio broadcasting, the type of transmission in which the program signal level is used to control or modulate the instantaneous power generated by the transmitter. Also, the band of frequencies in which all AM stations broadcast their signals—from 580 to 1,600 kHz in the electromagnetic spectrum. (*See* FREQUENCY MODULATION (FM).

A.M.P.T.P.

(F,V) Association of Motion Picture and Television Producers, Inc. Represents major movie studios and television broadcasters in business dealings with technical and craft unions, etc.

AMRA

(R,P) American Mechanical Rights Association. An organization similar to the Harry Fox Agency, but much smaller. AMRA collects mechanical royalties and negotiates synchronization licenses mainly for modern classical or "serious" composers and their publishing companies.

ANALOG RECORDING

(E) Any method of recording in which the recorded waveform is a continuous representation of the original signal. Example: conventional magnetic recording, direct to disc.

ANALOG SEQUENCER

(S) A sequencer into which sounds for storage and later recall are fed as analog signals, via analog potentiometers.

ANALOG-TO-DIGITAL CONVERTER

(D) **(A-D)** In digital recording, the group of circuits that sample the analog waveform, measure its instantaneous voltage, and convert this decimal value to its binary equivalent, in preparation for storage on tape (or on floppy disk, in random access memory, etc.). (*See* DIGITAL RECORDING; SAMPLING RATE; QUANTIZATION; ALIASING; CLOCK.)

ANAMORPHIC

(F) Any process used in photographing motion pictures in which (by use of special lenses) the horizontal axis of the image is optically "squeezed" during shooting and expanded again during projection. This allows very wide-angle or panoramic shots to be filmed and shown, without changing the shape or dimensions of the frame of film in the camera and projector. Cinemascope and Panavision are the primary trade names for the process, although every film-producing nation has its equivalents—Tohoscope, for example, in Japan.

ANECHOIC CHAMBER

A room that is completely isolated from out-

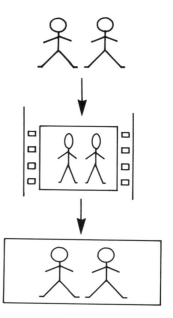

ANAMORPHIC.

(E) side sounds and the interior of which is as completely sound-absorbent as possible. The result is that no sound is reflected by any interior surfaces. Since the only sound transmitted is direct from the source to the receptor, with no addition from the interior or exterior environment, anechoic chambers are used to test the response of loudspeakers, microphones, etc.

ANSWER PRINT   The first composite print made from the edited picture negative (in 35mm) or the A and B rolls of a motion picture (in 16mm). Each shot is exposed, color-balanced, and effects performed, per the director's wishes. Further changes and corrections can be made in a second or third answer print, if necessary.
(F)

AOR   Album-Oriented Rock. A type of FM radio programming featuring popular groups, but not only their hit singles (as is the case with "Top 40" radio programming). AOR stations often broadcast one or both sides of entire albums.
(R)

APHEX AURAL EXCITER   A signal processing device manufactured by Aphex Corporation. The various Aphex models add a distinctive "presence" to input signals, but the internal design and what it actually does to signals is proprietary.
(E)

APPLICATIONS SOFTWARE   Any complex software the user buys to accomplish a repetitive job that is unrelated to the basic nature of his own goals. A word-processing program is a good example, since it is mathematically complex, but its internal operations are functionally irrelevant to the user who is writ-
(C)

ing letters or, for example, this book.

APPOINTMENT   1. The act of giving another person or company the right to control or administer the copyright of a musical composition or other copyrighted work. 2. Generally, the act of empowering another person or company to act on one's behalf. One may appoint a manager, booking agent, or other party who is empowered to handle specific portions or all of a person's career, financial holdings, estate, etc.
(P)
(B)

APPROVED-BUDGET RECORD PRODUCTION   The type of financial arrangement used by major record labels for the production of most records. The production budget is developed jointly by the producer and the label's A&R person. Once this budget is approved, the label still retains the right to authorize (or deny authorization for) the expenditure of monies for each item or service budgeted. The label can stop the project at any time, either if disatisfied with the partially completed master tapes, or if other circumstances within the company make it inadvisable to complete the project. There are many variations on this arrangement, depending on the artist's and producer's stature in the industry, etc. (*See* ALBUM FUND.)
(R)

APPV   Audio Post-Production for Video. The process of preparing the individual soundtracks and the final mix for a videotaped production.
(V)

A.R.B.   American Research Bureau. An audience-research and surveying company, similar to the Neilsen
(R,A)

(A) = Advertising • (B) = Business & Law • (C) = Computers • (D) = Digital • (E) = Engineering & Scientific •
(F) = Film • (G) = Music & General • (I) = Interlock & Sync • (J) = Jokes & Jargon • (P) = Music Publishing •
(R) = Record Industry • (S) = Synthesizers • (U) = Unions • (V) = Video

Organization, but specializing in radio station ratings. Using electronic circuit boxes wired to the radio receivers of test households, the A.R.B. surveys audiences four times a year in every metropolitan area. The resulting numerical ratings for each station, called Arbitrons, tell what percentage of the entire radio listening audience, on average, is tuned to that station. (*See* SWEEP WEEK.)

ARBITRATION CLAUSE   The clause in a contract that specifies how disputes will be settled, what outside parties will be used to resolve disputes, and whether such outside opinions will be binding on the parties to the contract itself.
(B)

ARBITRON   The radio station ratings published every three months by the American Research Bureau. (*See* A.R.B.)
(R,A)

AREA OF DOMINANT INFLUENCE (ADI)   The geographical area surrounding a major market, large city, or media center. Example: The Boston ADI, the Chicago ADI, etc. Expenditures for print, radio, or television advertising are often estimated for an entire ADI.
(A)

ARMED FORCES RADIO AND TELEVISION STANDARDS See A.F.R.T.S.

ARITHMETIC and LOGIC UNIT See ALU.

ARRANGER   The professional who, after receiving general instructions from the producer (or sometimes the artist or client), makes the actual decisions concerning how a piece of music will be performed
(U,G)

and by which instruments. Most professional arrangers prepare a conductor's score of the complete chart. A copyist will then copy individual parts or staves onto separate sheets of music paper for each musician. For large projects, arrangers are often assisted by orchestrators who specialize in writing for sections such as strings, brass, woodwinds, etc. The arranger usually conducts all the musicians whose parts he writes. The AFM lists scale wages for arrangers, plus à la carte charges for each operation performed in complex arrangements. (*See* ORCHESTRATOR.)

ART DIRECTOR   The ad agency employee who, working with the copywriter, develops the concept and overall style or "look" for new ads, spots, and campaigns, including the general specifications for any music to be produced. A member of the creative director's staff.
(A)

ARTIST   In recording contracts, the person or group of people who have signed an agreement to play, sing, speak (or otherwise make sounds) for the making of master tapes for records, cassettes, etc. Per legal convention, when capitalized this word refers to the specific artist named in the contract under discussion. (*See* ROYALTY ARTIST.)
(R)

ARTISTS and REPERTOIRE   See A&R.

A.S.   See ACCOUNT SUPERVISOR.

ASCAP   American Society of Composers, Authors and Publishers. Formed in 1908, ASCAP was the
(P)

---

first American performing-rights organization. It collects fees for broadcast of recorded compositions on radio and television, and for live public performances of music, and distributes payments to the copyright holders of these compositions. Owned by writers and publishers, it is a non-profit corporation, retaining only a small percentage of fees collected to cover the costs of surveying, accounting and collections.

ASCII (C)   American Standard Code for Information Interchange. The most common code used for transmitting text data from computer to computer, or to peripherals. The code employs 8-bit binary words, by which each letter of the English language, each Arabic numeral, and each commonly used symbol is uniquely designated.

ASPECT RATIO (F)   The numerical ratio of picture height to width. The original motion picture ratio of 3:4 was carried over into the specifications for television screens, and this ratio remains the international television standard today. However, most motion pictures are now shot and projected theatrically with a 1.85:1 ratio, called "widescreen." Cinemascope and similar anamorphic systems have a 2.35:1 ratio in 35mm motion picture production.

ASPERITY NOISE (E)   An increase in the noise level of a circuit or recording in a band immediately above or below a single frequency present in the program signal.

ASSEMBLY (F,V)   1. The first splicing together of shots in the order called for by the script. Shots are usually left full length, with dramatic overlap of action if filmed from different angles. (V) 2. Any sort of videotape editing session.

ASSEMBLY-EDIT (V)   The process of copying all tracks simultaneously (video, audio, sync, and control tracks) from the camera-original tapes onto a video master. Used mainly to construct a videotape rough cut, assembly editing is the opposite of insert editing.

ASSIGNMENT (B,P)   1. The legal process of turning the control of or proceeds from something over to another party or company. One might assign part or all of the publishing rights of a song to another publisher, or assign an already-existing contract to a third party for continued execution. (*See* APPOINTMENT; RECAPTURE; REVERSION; TRANSFER.) (E) 2. The sending of a signal to a desired tape recorder track or other destination, usually by a matrix of switches in each module of a recording console.

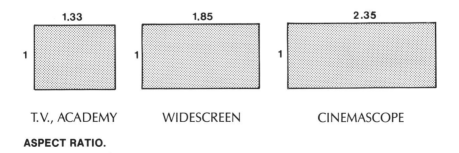

ASPECT RATIO.

(A) = Advertising • (B) = Business & Law • (C) = Computers • (D) = Digital • (E) = Engineering & Scientific •
(F) = Film • (G) = Music & General • (I) = Interlock & Sync • (J) = Jokes & Jargon • (P) = Music Publishing •
(R) = Record Industry • (S) = Synthesizers • (U) = Unions • (V) = Video

ASSISTANT DIRECTOR   See AD.

ASSISTANT ENGINEER   A studio employee whose responsibilities include setting up and tearing down for sessions, accomplishing signal routing, patching and other such operations, operating the tape machines (tape-op), and general "go-for" assignments, all at the request of the recording engineer in charge of the session.
(E)

ASSOCIATION OF MOTION PICTURE AND TELEVISION PRODUCERS   See A.M.P.T.P.

ASYNCHRONOUS   A data transmission mode in which intermittent groups of characters are sent, each group preceded, and followed by start and stop bits, respectively. Much slower than synchronous transmission mode.
(C)

ATR   Audio Tape Recorder. Often used by video engineers.
(E)

ATTACK   The first page of the envelope of a sound or signal, representing its initial transient or onset, followed by the decay, sustain, and release. Collectively referred to as the ADSR, these factors are all continuously variable signals produced by most synthesizers. (*See* ENVELOPE (illustration).)
(E,S)

ATTACK, DECAY, SUSTAIN, RELEASE   See ADSR.

ATTACK TIME   Generally speaking, the length of time any electronic device takes to fully respond to an incoming signal. Most often used to describe the time it takes a compressor, limiter, or expander to begin acting on the signal.
(E)

ATTENTION, INTEREST, DESIRE, ACTION   See AIDA.

ATTENUATION   A fixed or variable reduction in signal strength, which may in turn reduce the volume of sound heard.
(E)

ATTENUATION PAD (or PAD)   A resistive network or other circuit, generally passive, that is inserted in an audio line to reduce the signal level.
(E)

ATTORNEY IN FACT   See POWER OF ATTORNEY.

AUDIENCE SHARE   The percentage of all people listening to or watching broadcast programs at a particular time who are tuned in to a specific program. In television, similar to a show's Neilsen rating. (*See* ARBITRON.)
(A)

AUDIO ENGINEERING SOCIETY (AES)   The professional organization whose members report on new technological developments in audio, and bring together designers, manufacturers, and users of various equipment to establish international standards and promote the growth of the industry as a whole. The membership includes scientists, equipment companies, studio owners, engineers, distributors, etc. (*See* SPARS.)
(E,B)

AUDIO POST-PRODUCTION FOR VIDEO   See APPV.

AUDIO TAPE RECORDER   See ATR.

AUTHOR   The U.S. copyright laws use "author" to mean the writer of the lyrics and/or words to a musical
(G)

(A) = Advertising • (B) = Business & Law • (C) = Computers • (D) = Digital • (E) = Engineering & Scientific •
(F) = Film • (G) = Music & General • (I) = Interlock & Sync • (J) = Jokes & Jargon • (P) = Music Publishing •
(R) = Record Industry • (S) = Synthesizers • (U) = Unions • (V) = Video

work. Not the bookwriter of a musical drama.

AUTO-ASSEMBLY   In on-line editing, the process by which the edit-programmer produces the edited video master tape according to instructions on the computer-encoded edit decision list, (hopefully) without human intervention. This process is only used for broadcast programming in shows where all shots were flat-lit and uniformly exposed. Less-consistent footage demands scene-to-scene correction and other manipulation that is beyond the capability of a pure auto-assembly.

(V)

AUTO-INPUT   One of the electronic operating modes of a multi-track recorder. When auto-input is selected, all channels will remain in sel-sync playback mode until the machine is placed in record. Any channels that are in "ready" status will then begin recording and will automatically pass their input signals direct to their outputs. When recording is stopped, these channels return to sel-sync playback mode. Also called STAND-BY mode.

(E)

AUTO-LOCATOR   A device by which a tape transport system can be controlled to locate and go to specified positions on the recording tape. Auto-Locator is actually MCI's trade name for its device, but the term has been adopted generally to apply to all such devices, regardless of brand name or manufacturer.

(E)

AUTOMATIC DOUBLE TRACKING
    See ADT.

AUTOMATIC GAIN CONTROL (AGC)   A compression circuit that is often installed in the audio recording electronics of ENG and other semi-pro, and most home video cameras and portable VCRs. The compression is quite severe, which aids intelligibility of dialogue at the expense of natural dynamic range.

(V,E)

AUTOMATION, CONSOLE   A computerized mixdown-assist system pre-installed in or attachable to some consoles. In the "write" mode, the automation system produces a continuous record of all the actual fader settings and adjustments made by the engineer during a mix. Most automation systems allow the engineer to change or "update" what he did with any specific track faders, while remembering and recreating his previous manipulations of other tracks, thus progressively improving a mix until all the desired effects are achieved. The engineer's level changes are recorded and recreated by voltage-controlled amplifiers (VCA) in each input module of the console. This VCA-produced data can be recorded directly onto a track of the multi-track tape, giving a continuous record of all mixdown fader settings. Or the VCA outputs can be recorded onto a separate floppy disk. In the latter system, alignment of the fader data with the multi-track master tape is achieved by referring to a common SMPTE code recorded on the 2″ tape and floppy disk. Other systems for recording and reproducing the fader settings are also used.

(E)

AUXILIARY SLOT   A receptacle or multi-pin jack by which additional

(C) circuitry can be plugged into a computer to increase the memory or computational abilities of the basic machine.

AUXILIARY STORAGE (C)   Magnetic floppy disk, hard disk, or other storage that complements the limited space in RAM and ROM.

A-WEIGHTING   See WEIGHTING.

AXIS (E)   In microphones, the direction of maximum sensitivity, generally perpendicular to the surface of the diaphragm or ribbon. In loudspeakers, the line projecting through the center of the voice coil toward the listening area. This is usually the direction in which the speaker exhibits the best overall frequency response. (*See* MICROPHONE; POLAR PATTERN.)

AZIMUTH (E)   One of the five main parameters in tape head alignment, designating the vertical angle between the head gap and the direction of tape travel. When the head gap is exactly perpendicular to the tape travel, high-frequency response is maximized. (*See* ALIGNMENT, TAPE HEAD (illustration).

- B -

BACK COATING In magnetic recording tape, a thin coating applied to the non-oxide or back surface, (a) to reduce slippage between tape layers, (b) to prevent the accumulation of static charges, and (c) to minimize curling or wrinkling of tape after prolonged storage. (*See* MAGNETIC RECORDING TAPE (illustration).

(E)

BACKGROUND **1.** The name of a performance and payment category used in the calculation of fees by ASCAP, BMI, etc. for broadcast performances of songs or musical recordings. These fees are then paid to the publishers, composers and record companies who own the respective copyrights. (*See* USE WEIGHT.) **2.** The lowest payment category used by AFTRA in computing broadcast residuals due to singers for reuse of performances in radio and TV spots, etc.

(P,R)

(A)

BACK PLATE In a condenser microphone, the fixed, rigid capacitor element that is charged with an electric polarity opposite to that of the diaphragm. (*See* MICRO-

(E)

PHONE—by design and function (illustrations).)

BACKING TRACK(S) The prerecorded accompaniment a singer hears, generally through headphones, while overdubbing a lead or background vocal track. Also called a bed. Usually consists of RHYTHM TRACKS or BASIC TRACKS.

(E)

BACKTIMING Subtracting the length (in minutes and seconds) of a recorded segment from the time in a longer program at which the segment is supposed to end. If a 3-minute segment is to end a 30-minute program, backtiming will tell you to begin rolling the segment at 27:00.

(V,E)

BAFFLE **1.** Any loudspeaker enclosure or cabinet, or the surface on which a loudspeaker is mounted. (*See* ACOUSTIC SUSPENSION SYSTEM; BASS REFLEX ENCLOSURE; EFFICIENCY.)

(E)

FOLDED BAFFLE: A speaker enclosure the rear side of which is entirely open.

INFINITE BAFFLE: In theory, a speaker mounting surface so large that it completely separates the energy emitted by the front and rear surfaces of the speaker cone—e.g., a wall between two rooms. In practice, any speaker enclosure that is completely sealed and airtight, generally filled with absorbent material to prevent any of the internal sound energy from escaping, even through vibration of the walls.

2. An ACOUSTIC BAFFLE.

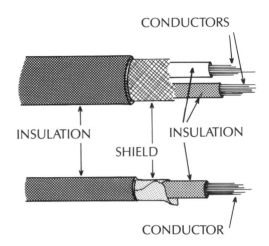

BALANCED LINE (2 conductors and a separate shield). UNBALANCED LINE (2 conductors, including shield).

BAILMENT (B)   In general, a temporary transfer of real property from one person to another, without transfer of title or ownership. For example, borrowing a record, leaving instruments overnight in a rented recording studio, checking a coat at a restaurant, etc. The person who owns the property is the bailor, the person accepting it the bailee. Consignment sales are considered bailments, since the record store accepts records for the purpose of selling them, but returns the same records if they remain unsold.

BALANCE (E)   The relative level or "volume" of two or more audio channels, recorded tracks, or any sound sources, when heard simultaneously.

BALANCED LINE (E)   An electrical cable with two conductors and a separate shield. When a signal is present, the conductors have the same potential with respect to ground, but opposite polarities. (See also UNBALANCED LINE.)

BALLISTICS (E)   In electric meters, a measurement of the speed and accuracy with which the indicator (e.g., a needle or series of LEDs) responds to changes in the quantity being measured. (See VU METER; METER, PEAK READING.)

BAND (R)   1. Strictly speaking, the wider, spiraled grooves that separate any two selections on a record. Colloquially, band is used to indicate any single selection on a record, cassette, or reel-to-reel tape or compact disc. Example: "Please replay band number six again."

(E)   2. A specific range of frequencies, either those characteristic of specific sounds or instruments, or those to be processed or otherwise treated electronically.

BANDWIDTH (E)   1. Strictly speaking, the arithmetic difference between the highest and lowest frequencies that are (a) passed by an electronic device, or (b) present in a specific acoustic sound or audio signal. Example: The bandwidth of a telephone is approximately 2.2 kHz—i.e., 2,400 Hz minus 200 Hz. The endpoints of a circuit's or system's bandwidth are those frequencies at which its response or output is attenuated by 3 dB. (*See* TURN-OVER FREQUENCY; CUT-OFF FREQUENCY.) **2.** Colloquially, the low and high frequencies of any specific frequency band. One might say, "The bandwidth of an electric guitar is 80 Hz to 8 kHz."

BARGAINING CHIP   In a contract negotiation, a specific provision or requirement that one party may delete, forego, or "trade-off" to the other party in return for a similar "favor." In a record contract, for instance, the label may offer a higher royalty if the artists agree to an extra year option. In this case, both items would be bargaining chips. In most cases, a deal is consummated before the parties trade chips—i.e., the chips are not deal-breakers.
(B)

BASE   In magnetic recording tape, the thin "ribbon" of polyester or other plastic material to which the oxide and back coating are applied. The base of most professional recording tapes is 1.42 mils thick. Width and length vary according to use. (*See* MAGNETIC RECORDING TAPE (illustration).)
(E)

BASIC TRACKS   The group of instruments or vocalists recorded first during a multi-track session. This group, perhaps including bass, drums, and standard rhythm section, will be played back through headphones to other instrumentalists who later "overdub" solos; lead or background vocals; or narration, percussions, strings, and other "sweetening" or sound effects. Also called the bed or rhythm tracks. (*See* BACKING TRACKS.)
(E,G)

BASS REFLEX ENCLOSURE   A type of loudspeaker enclosure with a hole or port in the surface on which the speakers are mounted, usually the front. Since this allows some of the energy from the rear of the speaker cones to project into the listening area, bass reflex systems have relative high efficiency. Sometimes called a vented enclosure. (*See* BAFFLE; EFFICIENCY.)
(E)

BASS TRAP   In room acoustics, an enclosed volume adjacent to the studio or control room, positioned where low frequencies are concentrated by the room's inherent shape and dimensions. A vent between the room and bass trap allows these lows to enter the trap, whose dimensions are selected to admit specific bands. The trap is filled with absorbent material to prevent low-frequency energy from re-entering the room.
(E)

BAUD RATE   In data transmission, the number of bits per second delivered to the output of a device, or which can be received by another device. In data transmission, sending and receiving devices must operate at the same baud rate. Called bps for short.
(C)

BEAMSPLITTER   A two-way, semi-transparent mirror embedded in an optical-grade prism. Used in some camera viewfinders to direct part of the incoming light to the eyepiece and the rest to the film or imaging tube. Also used in certain optical printers, etc.
(F,V)

BEATS PER MINUTE   See BPM.

BED   **1.** The background music or musical track used behind a nar-
(A)

rator or foreground dialogue in a radio or TV spot. A spot may begin with a vocal ID or front, after which the music continues as a bed, then returns to the foreground for a vocal tag. Also called rhythm tracks, basic tracks, backing tracks.

(R) (*See* DONUT.) **2.** Loosely, the rhythm tracks or complete instrumental tracks of a master tape, to which the vocals and solos will be added by overdubbing.

BEL

(E) The logarithm in base 10 of the ratio of two different levels of power—acoustic or electric. Since large apparent sound-level changes correspond to fractional portions of a bel, the decibel (1/10 bel) is used as the unit of level for sounds and audio signals. (*See* DECIBEL.)

BELOW-THE-LINE

(F,V,A) Those production costs in a budget that can be accurately estimated from published rental rates, dealer or manufacturer price lists, union scale wages and benefits payment schedules, etc. (*See* ABOVE-THE-LINE; NEGATIVE COST; LINE ITEM.)

BERNE UNION (or CONVENTION)

(P) The international agreement reached in 1886 by representatives of various European governments, who for the first time established the concept and standards of international copyright. This body of law, administered by the World Intellectual Properties Organization (WIPO), is still in effect. The United States was not at Berne, but does belong to the UCC (Universal Copyright Convention), a later meeting with similar goals.

BETACAM

(V) A professional videotape format employing the 1/2″ Beta format, but at an increased tape speed, which gives picture quality comparable with the 1″ C format. Betacam also allows separate recording of the Red, Green, and Blue picture information via RGB mode. This capability gives much better control of edge-cuts in special effects such as chroma-keying. Often called Beta for short.

BETAMAX

(V) A system used for 1/2″ color videotape recording, developed by Sony for home use only. Generally acknowledged to give higher picture quality than VHS. (*See* FORMAT, **5.**)

B-FORMAT

(V) A 1″ professional video format developed by Bosch Corporation in Germany. Although it is generally considered superior to the standard C-format, "B" equipment is used only in a few production and post-production facilities. The video master tapes made there must then be transferred to C-format for broadcast.

BI-AMPLIFICATION

(E) The process of electronically separating the bandwidth of a signal into two bands— low and high frequencies—then providing separate amplification for each of these bands. Tri-amplification separates the bandwidth into three, separately amplified bands, etc. These techniques are most often used in high-powered sound reinforcement systems, (a) to allocate amplifier power most efficiently, and (b) to prevent potentially damaging frequencies from reaching the bass, midrange, and treble drivers. (*See* CROSSOVER NETWORK.)

BIAS

(E) In magnetic tape recording, a very high frequency electric current that is mixed with program

---

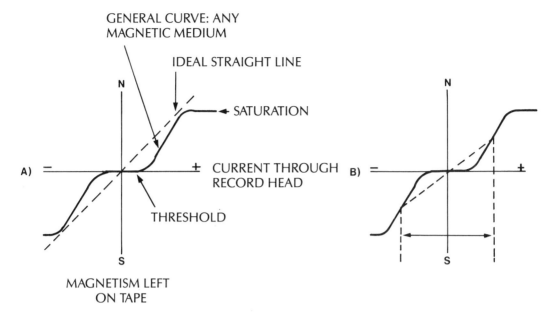

GENERAL CURVE: ANY
MAGNETIC MEDIUM

IDEAL STRAIGHT LINE

N

SATURATION

A) — CURRENT THROUGH
RECORD HEAD

THRESHOLD

S

MAGNETISM LEFT
ON TAPE

B) —   N   +

S

BIAS. (A) No bias; (B) High frequency AC bias: By switching rapidly back and forth between the upper and lower halves of the curve using a frequency above the audio range, an average of the two halves results, i.e., a straight line.

material as it goes to the record head. It affects the magnetic domains in the oxide such that the tape responds more linearly to various instantaneous amplitudes in the program material, thereby reducing distortion.

BIAS BEATS   An audible frequency
(E)   created when two bias frequencies are mixed, the arithmetic difference of whose frequencies is less than 20 kHz. If the difference is greater than 20 kHz, the bias beats will be above the range of human hearing.

BIAS FREQUENCY   The frequency
(E)   of the bias current, generally between 150 kHz and 200 kHz.

BIAS OSCILLATOR   In a tape re-
(E)   corder, the electronic circuit that generates a fixed bias frequency. The same oscillator is often used to drive bias and erase circuits.

BIAS TRAP   A low-pass filter that
(E)   prevents the bias frequency from reaching the record or playback electronics of a tape recorder.

BI-DIRECTIONAL MICROPHONE   A
(E)   microphone that is sensitive only to sounds arriving from the front and rear of the capsule, but not from the sides. Also called a figure-8 mic, because the polar pattern, viewed from the side or above, resembles a figure-8. Ribbon microphones are naturally bi-directional. Other types can be made to respond in this pattern. (*See* POLAR PATTERN (illustrations).)

BILLBOARD   The largest and most in-
(R)   fluential of the record industry trade magazines. It publishes weekly charts for rock, soul, dance, video tapes, compact discs, plus industry news, single and album

reviews, etc. (*See* REPORTING STATION.)

BIN
(F)
(E)
1. A barrel into which strips of film hang, suspended from a row of pins or small nails above. Also called editing bin. **2.** In tape duplication, the container or housing that holds a tape loop to be duplicated.

BIN CARD   A sort of giant "file card"
(R)
used in record store bins to set the records of one artist apart from those of the others. Usually has the artist's name (or sometimes a specific type of music—e.g., "New Age") at the top of the card in large, bold lettering.

BINAURAL RECORDING   A two-
(E)
channel recording technique in which two omni-directional microphones are placed a few inches on either side of an acoustic baffle, each mic recorded onto a separate tape track. The intent is to reproduce the hearing characteristics of human ears, including perceptions of the ambient and reverberant sound of the room as heard by sound receptors separated by one "head-width." (*See* X-Y MIKING; SPACED PAIR; BLUMLEIN PAIR.)

BINDER   A liquid or gelatinous me-
(E)
dium in which oxide particles are suspended while they are applied to recording tape. Usually consists of a solvent that evaporates, and an adhesive substance that, when dry, permanently bonds the oxide to the base. (*See* MAGNETIC RECORDING TAPE (illustration).)

BIPACKING   A method used in produc-
(F)
ing special effects for motion pic-
tures. Two strips of exposed film are run through an optical printer with their emulsions in direct contact. The combined images are photographed onto a strip of print film. The process is often used for making moving matte shots. The areas to be matted out on are filmed on a strip of high-contrast black and white stock, which is then bipacked with the background scene. The result has a "hole" in each frame where a foreground object or scene is later matted in by the same process.

BI-PHASE MODULATION   In SMPTE
(E)
code generation, the electronic process that produces the signal containing the SMPTE data itself. A 1.2 kHz square wave is momentarily modulated to 2.4 kHz with each new bit of location information coming from a source, which may be a crystal-controlled clock, a circuit deriving such information from the 60 Hz line feed, etc.

BIT   The smallest unit of information
(C)
that can be stored, transmitted, or processed by any digital circuit—e.g., a computer. Each bit is a "1" or "0" and corresponds to a single yes/no, on/off, or other similar decision. Abbreviated from BInary digiT.

BIT-PACKING DENSITY   In digital
(C)
recording (either audio or computational), the number of bits encoded per unit length of the recorded track on tape, compact disc, hard disk, or other storage medium.

BIT STREAM   **1.** The continuous se-
(D)
quence of data bits that represents the changing voltage in the original

---

program waveform or—if more than one channel of audio signal is incorporated into a single bit stream—waveforms. **2.** Any series of data bits being transmitted, processed, or stored. (C)

BITS PER SECOND   See BPS.

BLACK LEADER   Opaque leader used to fill the lengths between individual film shots in A and B rolls.

BLANKET LICENSING FEE   The annual amount paid by any specific radio station, TV station, restaurant, club, or concert hall to ASCAP and BMI. In return the "licensee" may use any songs in the ASCAP and BMI catalog, respectively. The fees can vary from about $100 a year for a small bar to $20 million for a TV network. (P,A)

BLANKET POLICY   A type of insurance policy that many producers and production companies carry. It covers losses due to a number of common problems that arise in the making of master tapes, films, videos, spots, etc.—e.g., damage to master tapes or original footage; loss in transit or shipping; damage to rented equipment, studios, etc. Each blanket policy will list the perils covered. Additional perils can be added by a separate floater. (B)

BLEEDING   Leakage of one sound or signal into another. Acoustically, one instrument can bleed into another instrument's microphone. Electrically and magnetically, adjacent conductors or recorded tracks can induce currents in their neighbors and bleed into them. For example, SMPTE code may bleed into an audio or video signal, or (E,V)

vice versa. Sometimes called bleed-through. (*See* CROSSTALK; FRINGING EFFECT.)

BLIMP   A soundproof housing that surrounds a motion picture camera to prevent its mechanical noise from registering on the soundtrack with dialogue or other desired sounds. A camera is "self-blimped" if soundproofing is incorporated in its basic design to such an extent that a separate housing is not necessary for most shooting. (F)

BLOCK (or DATABLOCK)   A unit of measure for large collections of data. Variously defined as 256 or 512 bytes of data. For example, one can say a certain program occupies 8 blocks of memory space. (C)

BLOCK BOOKING   The reservation of "blocks" of time in a recording studio schedule for a large recording project. A "block" may be all the studio's time for many days or weeks, in which case the session or project is called a "lockout." (B)

BLOCKING   The desired physical movements of actors, camera(s), and sometimes even microphones during a scene. Blocking instructions may be given verbally at the time of rehearsal or shooting or completely pre-diagrammed like football plays. For example, in a certain scene one actor's blocking may call for him to walk toward a table while the camera tracks left, turn left when another actor delivers a line, and collapse when the phone rings. (F,V)

BLOOP   The sound made by a splice as it is reproduced during projection or playback on an optical (F) sound reproducer. Blooping is the process of covering the splice with paint or tape so that it no longer creates a bloop when reproduced.

BLUELINE (or BROWNLINE) PROOF

(R,A) An inexpensive proof made by the printer and sent to the client before color separations or printing plates are actually made. Since the proof is blue (or brown) on white, its main value is in making sure all the photo-, graphic-, and line-art is present and in the right position (i.e., that the paste-up has not fallen apart or been damaged in shipment from the artist) prior to four-color printing.

BLUE SCREEN

(F,V) The process of photographing objects or actors located in front of a uniformly lit blue background of a standard color (called chroma-key blue in video). In an optical printer or video editing suite, a separately photographed background shot can be inserted into the blue screen shot wherever the blue color appears. Whatever was originally in front of the blue screen thus appears to be in the foreground of the new shot. (*See* CHROMA-KEY; MATTE.)

BLUMLEIN PAIR

(E) Two bi-directional microphones whose capsules are located on the same vertical axis, with one capsule aimed 45 degrees to the left of the center of a sound source, the other capsule aimed 45 degrees to the right of the center. The outputs of these two capsules, when summed, give a relatively constant voltage as a constant sound source circles 360 degrees around the pair. This affords a very natural stereo imaging and awareness of room ambience. The technique was developed by Alan Blumlein in 1930. (*See* M-S MIKING; SPACED PAIR; BINAURAL RECORDING.)

BMI

(P) Broadcast Music Inc. The second American performing rights organization to be formed. BMI functions much like ASCAP and competes with it for composer and publishing company members.

BOARD

(E) 1. Another word for the recording or mixing console.
(A,F,V) 2. Short for storyboard.

BOND, PRE-RECORDING

(U) A prepayment of part or all of the musicians' or singers' scale wages and benefits, which is required by the AFM or AFTRA in some cities, usually when booking sessions for a new record company or non-signatory.

BOOK

(G) In a musical stage play, film, or video production, the written script, including dialogue and

SOUND SOURCE

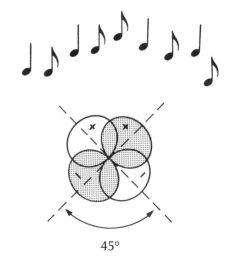

45°

BLUMLEIN PAIR.

lyrics—anything said or sung by the actors. The bookwriter is not to be confused with the author, the name often used in contracts for the lyricist of the show's songs.

BOOKING AGENT
(B)
A person or company who seeks and schedules live performances or appearances for soloists, groups, bands, orchestras, and other performing artists. Agents usually deal with only one type of hall or venue—i.e., some agents specialize in bars, others in college bookings, and still others in concert hall bookings, etc. Agents earn their living by taking a percentage of the gross receipts paid to the performer by the promoter or sponsor of the event.

BOOKKEEPER
(B,G)
A professional who can properly list income and expenses in "books" or financial ledgers, file receipts, and set up ledgers so that his client can best determine how to spend money and prepare necessary city, state, and federal reports, including tax forms. A company may have a bookkeeper on staff who prepares the books so that an accountant can quickly review them for financial planning or tax preparation. Bookkeeper and accountant are often used interchangeably.

BOOKS
(B,G)
The financial documents of a business. A set of ledgers that are necessary for filling out tax forms and other required reports of business activities. Books give accurate and easily accessible information about cash flow, profit or loss, and the general state of a business. They are usually produced by an accountant or bookkeeper from the original invoices, payment records, checkbooks, and receipts kept by the company's employees and officers. (*See* CASH FLOW; P&L.)

BOOM OPERATOR
(F,V)
A sound technician on a film or television crew who operates the microphone boom, moving the mic(s) into positions where the recordist determines he obtains the best sound quality. Also called a boom man.

BOOM STAND
(E)
A telescoping support arm that can be attached to a microphone floor stand, by which the position of the microphone can be adjusted horizontally and vertically—for example, to hold a mic in place over the strings of a grand piano.

BOOT
(C)
In computers, to load a user-selected operating system into the computer's working memory. This system will instruct the computer how to receive future data and programming commands from the operator, and how to arrange and store this data in memory.

BOOTLEG
(R)
To release on records or tape an unauthorized or illegally made recording of a performing artist. Also, to illegally reproduce and sell copies of a record or tape originally released legitimately on the label to which an artist is contracted. Also used to designate the bootlegged release pressing, cassette, or videotape itself.

BORROWING MONEY
(B,G)
A sometimes-necessary way of setting up a business or producing a speculative project. Since the percentage of independently produced records, motion pictures, and video produc-

---

(A) = Advertising • (B) = Business & Law • (C) = Computers • (D) = Digital • (E) = Engineering & Scientific •
(F) = Film • (G) = Music & General • (I) = Interlock & Sync • (J) = Jokes & Jargon • (P) = Music Publishing •
(R) = Record Industry • (S) = Synthesizers • (U) = Unions • (V) = Video

tions that earn their costs back is very low, potential lenders must be warned of the high risk in such ventures, especially if the borrower is personally incapable of repaying the loan in the event of a failure. A business that continually turns out product is much more likely to get a needed loan, simply because this company has more chances of financial success that will allow repayment per the loan agreement. (*See* LIMITED PARTNERSHIP.)

BOSCH   The German company that
(V)   manufactures, among other things, professional video and sophisticated video animation systems. The Bosch model 4000 allows the animator to draw or paint shapes on the video screen via light pen, to add apparent third dimensions to these, rotate the shapes or objects in space, zoom in or out of them, define and position light sources illuminating these solids, cast shadows onto backgrounds, and create detailed shading and other lighting effects on these digitally created images. All user-defined images and objects can be stored in computer memory, then recalled, combined, and manipulated in real-time or screen-time to make composite animated scenes. (*See* MIRAGE; PAINTBOX; DUBNER.)

BOUNCING TRACKS   The technique
(E)   of transferring one recorded track, or blending several previously recorded tracks, onto a single unused track on the same multi-track tape. The previously recorded track(s) may then be erased and reused. To maintain proper synchronization of the material on all tracks, bouncing is done in sel-sync mode.

BPM   Beats Per Minute. A measure-
(R)   ment used by disc jockeys to determine whether two rock or dance records will blend or mix together smoothly. BPM ratings are often printed by record companies on the labels of promotional copies sent to radio stations, record pools, and individual disc jockeys.

BPS   Bits Per Second. A measure of
(C)   data transmission rate. (*See* BAUD RATE.)

BREACH   The breaking or violation of
(B)   a law, right, promise, agreement, contract, etc. In legal parlance, one cures a breach with a remedy.

BREAKAGE ALLOWANCE   In record-
(R)   ing contracts, a 10% royalty reduction that exempted labels (prior to the introduction of non-breakable vinyl) from paying royalties on units that broke in shipment. The royalty base rate is usually the 90% that remains after the breakage allowance is deducted from 100% of units sold by the label. This reduction still appears in many contracts.

BREAKDOWN   1. A detailed listing of
(B,F,V)   expenses in one or more categories
(R)   of a larger budget. 2. In records produced primarily for dancefloor play, a lengthy instrumental section (sometimes enlivened with sound effects and recording tricks—delays, repeats, reversed sounds, etc.) inserted between vocal sections of a master tape. Typically, the breakdown will begin with four or eight bars of drums, only, then have equal sections in which other instruments or effects are added.

BREATH CONTROLLER   A mouth-
(S)   operated device that regulates an

---

output voltage according to the air pressure blown into it. The resulting voltage may vary the level, timbre, or other parameter of another signal, generally in a synthesizer.

BREATHING   An audible increase and decrease of the background noise level in an audio signal, usually caused by excessive level changes in compression or limiting. Also called pumping. (*See* COMPRESSOR (illustration).
(E)

BRICKWALL FILTER   A low-pass or high-pass filter that, in theory, should have infinite attenuation beyond the turnover frequency. Anti-aliasing filters, for example, should have brickwall characteristics.
(D,E)

BRIDGE   In a song, a third section, which connects the verse and chorus with some different musical and/or lyrical material, but not a solo. Also called release or C-section.
(G)

BROADBAND   Including a wide range of frequencies, generally the entire range of human hearing. One might refer to the broadband performance of an audio device with respect to some other parameter—noise, distortion, etc.
(E)

BROADCAST MUSIC INC.   See BMI.

BROADCAST ROYALTIES   Same as airplay royalties.

BROWNLINE PROOF   See BLUELINE PROOF.

BTX   A brand name and manufacturer of electronic devices that will maintain synchronization between two
(E,V,F)

tape recorders, tape recorders and a projector or video playback, etc. Used primarily to interlock one or more multi-track recorders to a video playback, for purposes of recording, overdubbing, or mixing music in sync with picture. The device uses the SMPTE code for electronic control of all machines. (*See* SMPTE CODE; SYNCHRONIZATION; SERVO-CONTROL.)

BUDGET   A listing of expenses planned in the upcoming production of a musical (or any) project. Major categories such as musicians, vocalists, studio time, materials, arrangers, copyists, etc. are generally broken down into listings of the length or amount of individual services necessary at each step, along with their expected costs. Every budgetary expense listed separately is called a line item. (*See* ABOVE-THE-LINE; BELOW-THE-LINE.)
(B,G)

BUFFER MEMORY   In digital circuits, an intermediate storage device (or memory) that can receive and dispense data at different rates, or merely hold data until the following device is prepared to accept it. Often used to adapt the output rate of one device—e.g., a computer—to the input rate of another—e.g., a printer. One use of buffer memories in digital recording occurs in error correction circuitry, where such a device holds data read from tape until it can be checked for accuracy, at which point it is decoded and reproduced. Buffers are also used to resequence data in de-interleaving, and to reduce wow and flutter in digital playback. (*See* REGISTER.)
(D,C)

(A) = Advertising • (B) = Business & Law • (C) = Computers • (D) = Digital • (E) = Engineering & Scientific •
(F) = Film • (G) = Music & General • (I) = Interlock & Sync • (J) = Jokes & Jargon • (P) = Music Publishing •
(R) = Record Industry • (S) = Synthesizers • (U) = Unions • (V) = Video

BUG   1. In computers, an error in a
(C)   program or other piece of software.
(E)   2. Any malfunction of or defect in
a mechanical or electronic device,
hopefully correctable by an appropriate maintenance person.

BULK   To bulk erase a tape.
(E)

BULK ERASER   A tape demagnetizer
that can erase an entire cassette,
(E)   reel of 1/4", or multi-track tape
without removing the tape from its
reel. Essentially a powerful electromagnet. Some bulk erasers have
circuits built in that automatically
fade the magnetic field up from
and ultimately back down to zero.
This eliminates "pops," "groans,"
and other erasure noise normally
left on tape if the eraser is suddenly turned on or off. Also called
a degausser.

BUMPERS   Small segments of music
in a television or film score that
(F,V)   usually precede a dissolve. In
television, normally used before
commercial breaks.

BURNED-IN TIME CODE   See
CODE WINDOW.

BURST ERROR   Any large-scale or extended sequence of erroneous data
(D)   or missing data. Burst errors can
be created by major dropouts, tape
splices, incorrect alignment of
playback heads with data tracks,
etc.

BUS (or BUSS)   A mixing circuit or
network that combines the output
(E)   of two or more channels. A recording console contains many buses—
e.g., a mixing bus, monitor bus,
channel bus, ground bus, distribution buses, etc.

(C)   DATA BUS: One or more
wires through which digital data is
transmitted. Parallel data grouped
in words of n-bits will require an
n-wire data bus. Multiplexed data
can be transmitted on a single-wire
bus.

BUS SELECTOR SWITCH   A two-or-
more position switch allowing sig-
(E)   nals to be routed to one or more
buses.

BUSINESS   The general procedure by
which a person or company or-
(B)   ganizes and controls all finances,
paperwork, and other matters pertaining to one-time or repetitive
operations, ventures, or productions. Also, the process by which a
person merchandises and actually
performs services or sells products
to clients, and (hopefully) collects
payment for them.

BUSINESS CARD   A card (about 2" ×
3") imprinted with a businessper-
(B,G)   son's name, company name, address, phone number, and other
information. Used to familiarize
others with the nature of one's ser-
vice(s) or product(s) and how to
reach him by mail and phone. A
good business card is designed to
project an image or view of oneself or the company that is positive, memorable, and (hopefully)
unique.

BUSINESS PLAN   A document prepared by someone desiring to raise
(B)   money in order to open a new
business, or to expand or issue
stock for an existing one. Includes
descriptions of what the business
will do or make, for whom, at
what price, known competitors,
and the anticipated costs of setup,
operation, and manufacture, with

detailed projections of cash flow and potential profitability, etc. All the facts necessary for a potential investor or lender to commit money to the business. Also called a prospectus.

BUY OUT
(B)
(B,F,V)
1. A business arrangement under which a composer, writer, or any creative talent who would normally receive a percentage of a production's profit agrees to accept a flat fee or one-time payment. 2. An amount paid to someone providing a service, with the agreement that no matter how long that service may take to perform (within defined limits), the buyer will pay only the agreed-upon amount. For example, film or video technicians may accept a buyout

figure for their daily wage on a particular production. The amount will be more than the normal scale; the "extra" amount replaces or "buys out" all overtime charges that would normally be due for each shooting day.

BYTE
(C)
A sequence of 8 bits of data, established as a standard parcel of information in computing because it can designate any of 63 possible items (2 raised to the 8th power, minus 1). This number is sufficient to uniquely specify any letter in the English alphabet, any single Arabic numeral, and a group of commonly used symbols. For that reason, the byte is used as the basis of the ASCII code.

-C-

CALIBRATION (E) The adjustment of a physical or electronic performance parameter of equipment to bring that parameter into conformance with a known standard. For example, one might calibrate the record or playback level, frequency response, tape tension, etc. of a recorder. (*See* ALIGNMENT.)

CALL (R) (F,V) 1. In recording sessions, the date, time, and place at which union musicians or singers hired for a recording session must be present and ready to perform. 2. The date, time, and place at which members of the cast and/or crew must be present on the set and ready to work or perform. There may be several different call times for different personnel, all noted on a call-sheet. For example, the set and lighting crew may have a 6 AM call, the camera and sound crew a 7 AM call, extras and bit players an 8 AM call, and the stars a 9 AM call. Such are the privileges of stardom. (*See* WRAP.)

CALREC SOUNDFIELD MICRO-PHONE (E) A brand and type of binaural stereo microphone used for critical recording of orchestral and choral music. Actually has six capsules to allow separate recording of L/R, Front/Rear, and Up/Down sound sources.

CAMCORDER (V) A video camera and recorder built into a single, hand-held piece of equipment.

CAMERA-READY (A,R) In the preparation of visual ads, album covers, or other materials to be printed, artwork that has all of the photographic, graphic, and typeset materials (i.e., pictorial-art and line-art) layed out in their final relative positions on a single surface and "pasted-up"—i.e., rubber-cemented in place. When the entire job is ready for shipment to the printer, it is camera-ready. Also called a paste-up.

CANADIAN ACADEMY OF RECORDING ARTS AND SCIENCES See CARAS.

CANADIAN MUSICAL REPRODUCTION RIGHTS ASSOCIATION See CMRRA.

**CANADIAN RADIO AND TELECOM-
MUNICATIONS COMMISSION**
See CRTC.

**CANADIAN RECORDING INDUSTRY
ASSOCIATION**   See CRIA.

CANCELLATION   The partial or com-
(E)   plete attenuation of an acoustic
sound or audio signal caused when
two sound waves or signals of identical frequency but opposite (or
nearly opposite) phase are combined.

CANNED   Slang for pre-recorded, not
(G)   live. Applied to music or visuals.

CAPAC   Composers, Authors and Pub-
lishers Association of Canada. The
(P,R)   largest performing rights organi-
zation in Canada, analagous to
ASCAP in the United States. PRO
CANADA, formerly BMI CAN-
ADA, is CAPAC's major com-
petitor.

CAPACITANCE   Electrically, any op-
(E)   position to a change in voltage.
Generally specified in units of
microfarads for most electronic
components and circuits.

CAPACITOR   An electrical component
that can store an electric charge
(E)   and that opposes changes in voltage, generally in direct proportion to the speed of those changes.
A capacitor thus may be used to
attenuate high frequencies while
allowing low frequencies to pass
relatively unhampered. Internally,
two electrodes or conductive plates
are located in close proximity.
When a charge is applied to one,
this induces an opposite charge in
the other. This charge in turn resists
any change in the first.

CAPACITY   Legally, the unrestricted
right and power to enter into a
(B)   proposed contract. The law applies different qualifications to the
capacity of various people, businesses, and their agents. Minors,
criminals, aliens, married women,
etc. have different restrictions
placed on their capacity.

CAPSTAN   In a tape transport, the
rotating spindle that actually pulls
(E)   the recording tape past the heads
at the desired, constant speed. The
capstan must be perfectly cylindrical where it is in contact with the
tape, and can be the extended
motor shaft itself, or be driven indirectly through gears, belts, or
pulleys. (*See* HEAD STACK.)

CAPSTAN IDLER   A rubber-coated
or soft-surfaced wheel that holds
(E)   the recording tape securely against
the capstan when a tape transport
is in the record or play mode.
Some transports have no capstan
idler, and rely only on friction between a soft-surfaced capstan and
the tape to maintain continuous
speed. Also called a pinch roller, a
pressure roller, or, in the U.K., a
puck. (*See* HEAD STACK (illustration).)

CAPSTAN MOTOR   The motor that
directly or indirectly drives the
(E)   capstan and thus moves the tape
past the heads. The capstan itself
may be the extended shaft of the
capstan motor, finely machined to
achieve proper tape speed when
the motor is operating at its normal
rpm rate.

CAPSULE   In a microphone, the diaphragm or actual sound receptor,
(E)   including, in various types of mics,

the moving coil, ribbon, permanent magnet, or fixed capacitor plate, and the housing in which these are mounted. (*See* MICROPHONE, by design and function (illustrations).)

CARAS   Canadian Academy of Recording Arts and Sciences. The Canadian organization analagous to NARAS in the United States.
(R,P)

CARRIER   The very high frequency wave (a) whose frequency is modulated by the program signal in FM radio broadcasting, or whose amplitude is modulated by the program signal in AM broadcasting, or (b) used as the source from which all output signals are derived in an FM synthesizer.
(S)

CART   A cartridge-loaded tape player used primarily in radio, in so-called "production" studios, and sometimes in motion picture and video mixing studios. Each commercial, regularly played song, or sound effect will be copied onto a separate leadered and tape-looped cartridge. When started or "hit," the cart begins playing instantly and continues playing until the end of the head-leader returns to the playback head. It is thus pre-cued for the next play.
(E,F,V)

CARTAGE   Money paid by the producer or client to union musicians for the transportation of bulky instruments or ancillary equipment to recording sessions. The AFM requires a $30 cartage charge for an orchestral harp and a $6 charge for each instrument or case that cannot easily be carried on public transit by the musician himself. A large drum kit, with perhaps six cases including
(U)

traps, might cost $36 in cartage. Cartage is billed at the time of the session, along with union wages and benefits.

CASH BOX   A record industry trade magazine, similar to *Billboard*.
(R)

CASH FLOW   The difference between money taken in and paid out by a business during a specified period of time, including a report of how this figure is determined. A positive cash flow indicates more money taken in than paid out; a negative cash flow indicates more money paid out than taken in. Large companies and seasonal businesses compile projected or actual monthly cash flows, detailing each category of cash in and cash out. An annual cash flow summary has thirteen columns, one for each month, with an extra column to total amounts taken in and paid out in each category.
(B)

CATALOG   **1.** The entire group of compositions or songs for which a writer or publisher owns or controls the copyrights. **2.** All the records that a record company has released, the rights to the master tapes of which may later be sold or licensed, either singly or as a group. **3.** A list of all the files or programs contained on a disk or other storage medium, or currently stored in a computer's working memory. From the catalog, a user selects the files on which he wants to work. Sometimes called a menu.
(P)
(R)

(C)

CATEGORY   **1.** The classification of a recorded vocal performance that determines the appropriate AFTRA payment and/or residuals scales by which the singers are paid for the
(A)

original session and any re-use or new use of the resulting master tapes. There are different categories for soloists and duos, groups of various sizes, singers who "step out," etc. **2.** Loosely, in the determination of broadcast royalties due to the copyright holder for the use of songs or recordings, any of the four use weights: background, theme, supertheme, or featured.

(P,R)

CATHODE RAY TUBE   See CRT.

CATTLE CALL   An open audition at which anyone can try out for parts in a film or show.

(F,V)

C.C.I.R.   Comité Consultatif International Radio. An international radio standards committee, whose recommended recording pre-emphasis and post-emphasis curves are standard on all recorders in most European and some other countries. (*See* N.A.B.)

(E)

CD   Compact Disc.

(R)

CD-I   Interactive Compact Disc. An internationally standardized data storage and reading format that allows various combinations of digital audio, text, still images, and limited amounts of real-time video images to be encoded on a compact disc. Philips and Polygram jointly developed the CD-I format. (*See* SCHEMA.)

(D,R)

CD-ROM   Compact Disc Read-Only Memory. A data storage format for compact discs that enables digital sound and or visual materials to be encoded on the disc. If visuals will accompany audio, the format allows enough memory for about

(B,R)

one still image for each 30 seconds of audio. As a publishing medium, CD-ROM offers book publishers vast storage capacity. The *Grolier Encyclopedia* was the first book available in this format, the entire printed edition fitting on a single CD. Random access availability of data and the enormous indexing capacity of CDs make this a great medium for printed matter. The total data storage capability of a single CD-ROM is about 550 megabytes.

CEMENT SPLICER   A splicer that bonds two pieces of motion picture film permanently by cementing two overlapping edges together. Used only on picture or prints with optical tracks, or in the assembly of A and B rolls, but never on workprint or magnetic film. (*See* HOT SPLICER.)

(F)

CENTER DETENT   A notched position in the range of a variable control, allowing the user to return the control precisely to that position. Used to denote "flat" position on tone controls, etc.

(E)

CENTER FREQUENCY   The frequency that is boosted or attenuated most by the operation of any peaking equalizer or other similar processing device or circuit.

(E)

CENTER TAP   In a transformer, the electrical midpoint of the windings, made accessible for external connection. Used, for example, in delivering power to balanced-line condenser microphones. A DC voltage is applied to the center tap of a transformer wired across the two conductors, thus charging both equally without having any net ef-

(E)

fect on the audio signal passing through them.

CENTRAL PROCESSING UNIT   See CPU.

C-FORMAT   The international standard for professional 1″ videotape equipment. Developed by Sony, and sometimes called S-format after that company's name. (*See* B-FORMAT; BETACAM; FORMAT, **5** (illustration).)
(V)

CHANNEL   A single signal or signal path, or, loosely, the circuit through which one signal passes. One may refer to a specific "channel" of a multi-track tape, to the left or right "channel" of a stereo audio signal, or to the corresponding amplifier and speaker "channels" that reproduce it.
(E)

CHANNEL ASSIGNMENT MATRIX   In a recording console, the group of buttons or switches by which the signal from any input channel can be assigned to one or more buses, and thereby be sent to one or more tracks of the multi-track recorder.
(E)

CHARACTER GENERATOR   An electronic device that "typesets" the written copy for use in titles, subtitles, or credits of video productions. The operator enters the copy at a standard typewriter keyboard. When the copy is in computer memory, the operator can use a variety of word-processing functions to "lay out" and "paste up" individual title cards, or produce a single display that will scroll up or down on the video screen and at any desired speed. The operator can usually select the colors of both the type itself and background (if
(V)

any). Some models offer a roster of even more complex effects. The finished "line-art" can then be edited into or superimposed on a video program like any pre-recorded shot, or superimposed over existing shots. Chyron, a well-known brand, is often used as the generic name for any generator.

CHARGE-BACK   An expense a record company incurs in the production or promotion of a specific record, and which can later be recouped from or charged back to the artist's royalty account. Advances to recording artists, production budgets for their master tapes and music videos, special packaging and promotion, and tour support are common charge-backs. The term is used analagously in film and video productions. (*See* RECOUPABLE; RECOUPMENT.)
(R,F,V)

CHART   **1.** A musical score or arrangement. The term is used both to designate the conductor's score, with all parts, or any individual instrumentalist's part—e.g., a drum chart, guitar chart, etc. **2.** A list of current hit singles or albums. *Billboard* magazine publishes national charts for each major musical market (i.e., pop, soul, country, music videos, compact discs, etc.), but every radio station has its weekly chart of local hits. Many stores also publish sales charts.
(G)

(R)

CHECKERBOARD PRINTING   See A and B ROLLS.

CHIP   **1.** In disc mastering, the thin thread of acetate lacquer that is carved out of the master disc by the cutting stylus. Also called swarf. **2.** The miniaturized signal-process-
(R)

(C)

ing heart of an integrated circuit, or any of the thumbnail sized data-storage or data-processing circuits in computers, digitally controlled devices, etc.

CHORUS **1.** A type of signal process-
(E) ing that slightly delays and, by rhythmic flanging, doubles the apparent number of players or singers heard in the signal. Chorusing also adds a vibrato to the resulting
(G) signal. (*See* ADT.) **2.** In normal song structure, a refrain or recurring section, generally containing the title or most memorable line(s) of the song—i.e., the hook.

CHROMA-KEY A keying process by
(V) which a video engineer can place a foreground subject against a background from another video source. The video engineer selects a solid color as the keying reference and uses this as the background color when photographing the subject. Wherever the SEG finds this color, it substitutes the corresponding area of the background scene—e.g., a street scene or mountain backdrop. One problem: If the subject has any of the keying color in his clothing or hand props, those areas will also be replaced by the new background. Similar to the bluescreen process in motion pictures. In black and white, the analogous process is called over-laying. Also called color separation overlay. (*See* KEY; BLUE SCREEN; MATTE.)

CINEMASCOPE See ANAMORPHIC.

CIRC Cross Interleaving Reed-Solomon
(D,C) Code. The combined error detection and correction scheme used

in compact discs and some other computer applications.

CISAC International Conference of Societies of Authors and Com-
(P,R) posers. The organization formed in 1926 that presides over issues concerning international copyright, especially with respect to piracy and new media for music reproduction—CDs, etc. CISAC is not a collections organization.

CLAM Slang for a mistake or wrong note played in a performance. For
(G) example, "You hit a clam in measure six."

CLAPSTICK (or CLAPPER) Originally, a pair of hinged boards that,
(F,V) when "clapped" together, provide a visible cue on film and a simultaneous sound cue on synchronous tape. By shooting and recording a "clap" during each take of a motion picture, the magnetic film and workprint can be aligned for proper synchronization. Modern clappers simultaneously flash a light for the camera and generate a short tone that can be sent directly to the recorder. The clapper is usually attached to a small blackboard or magnetic board on which information about each take can be displayed. This data will then appear in each take. Also called a slate. (*See* SLATE (illustration).)

CLICK TRACK A pre-recorded track of metronomic clicks used to en-
(E) sure (a) the proper tempo for music to be recorded, and (b) the desired timing for a particular spot, or segment of music. Typically, the click track will be recorded on one track of a multi-track tape, then played (in sel-sync) via cue

amp and headphones for the conductor (or one or more of the musicians), while the music being played is recorded on other tracks of the same tape.

CLICK-TRACK GENERATOR (E) An electronic device that produces time-keeping signals for a click track. Basically, an electronic metronome.

CLIENT (A) A person or company who hires an advertising agency, production company, or independent music producer. On small accounts or in local campaigns, the client may directly hire a producer or production company to make TV or radio spots. In this case, no agency is involved.

CLIPPING (E) Distortion from a power amplifier caused when transients in the input signal require more instantaneous output power than the amp can muster. Those peaks are flattened or "clipped." (*See* DISTORTION (illustration).)

CLOCK (A,F) 1. In recording sessions for jingles or film scores, a stopwatch. (E,D,S) 2. Any circuit that cyclicly triggers repeated processes in a digital circuit or device. For example, a very high frequency generated by a crystal is divided down to 44,100 Hz. This acts as the clock that triggers each cycle of the sampling circuits in compact disc players. Similar clocks control the sampling rate in synthesizers, digital delay lines, flangers, harmonizers, etc. (S)   MIDI CLOCK: The 31,250 Hz fixed-frequency oscillator that triggers the generation of each bit of MIDI code.

CLOSED-LOOP TAPE PATH (E) A tape transport system in which the section of tape passing by the heads is physically isolated from feed and take-up tension variations by two capstans and idlers—one before the headstack, another after. (*See* ISO-LOOP.)

CLOSE-UP.   See CU.

CMRRA (P,R) Canadian Musical Reproduction Rights Association. The Canadian organization that collects and distributes mechanical royalties. Analagous to the Harry Fox Agency in the United States.

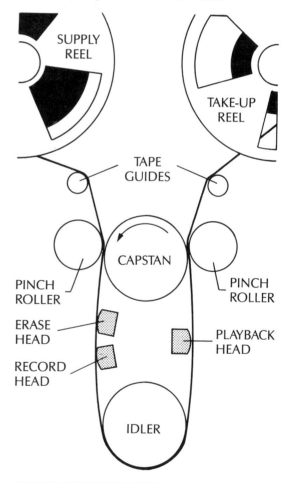

CLOSED-LOOP TAPE PATH.

CMX
(V,F)   A computerized video editing machine (made by CMX Corporation) that is capable of storing in hard-disk memory a large amount of video picture and corresponding sync sound (with burned-in SMPTE data). By specifying the starting and ending SMPTE location codes for each shot in a proposed sequence, the editor can instruct the machine to electronically assemble the sequence and play it almost instantaneously. The assembly is made entirely within the CMX memory, and requires no copyediting of the videotape footage. By substituting different SMPTE numbers for any shot, the editor can then try alternate takes, add to or shorten any shots, or completely reorganize the sequence until he is satisfied, previewing each update immediately. Fades, dissolves, and other simple effects can also be entered into memory. The CMX can then write the completed edit list onto a floppy disk (and print hard copy if desired), which can be used to instruct the CPU or edit programmer during an auto-assembly or on-line editing session. The final CMX assembly can also be recorded to tape to serve as a kind of workprint for the on-line session.

COCKTAIL PARTY EFFECT   The
(E)   ability of the human ear and brain to focus or concentrate on just one of a number of similar sounds of equal volume, all of which are heard simultaneously. Picking out and being able to understand one voice among all those talking at a party is the origin of this term.

CODE WINDOW   A display of the
(V,I,E) SMPTE time-code numbers, usually corresponding to each frame of picture viewed on a monitor. These numbers appear in a small box or "window" that replaces a portion of the program image, usually at the bottom right. Depending on the equipment used and the desires of the operator, the data in the window can be generated in real time from the source of SMPTE data (live, tape, etc.), or may have been recorded as a permanent part of the picture on this particular copy of a pre-recorded program. Such "burned-in" code is generally recorded onto copies of footage that will be used for off-line and CMX editing. The source of the SMPTE data in this case is the sync or control track of the original video footage.

COERCIVITY   The magnetic field
(E)   strength required to bring any specific type of recording tape, when fully saturated, to complete erasure. Measured in oersteds, and abbreviated H_c.

COHERENCE   The polarity relation-
(E)   ship between two complex sounds or signals being combined, measured at any desired instant. Total coherence indicates full reinforcement, while incoherence designates no correlation, or partial or total cancellation.

COHERENT SIGNALS   Two or more
(E)   complex sounds or signals that maintain similar polarity most of the time. They therefore generally reinforce each other.

COINCIDENT MICROPHONES   Two
(E)   or more microphones whose diaphragms are located vertically on the same axis. Sounds coming

toward them thus arrive at all the diaphragms simultaneously. Most stereo microphones are coincident in internal design.

COLD COPY   In narration for radio or TV spots, copy that is read without musical or other background sounds.
(A)

COLOR KEY   A set of positive acetate transparencies made from color separations for color printing, with one color of ink printed on each layer. By viewing through all the layers (when they are properly aligned, or "registered"), one can get a good idea of how the final color print will look. The key saves the printer from setting up a 4-color press just for a proof.
(A,R)

COLOR REVERSAL INTERMEDIATE
See CRI.

COLOR SEPARATIONS   A set of four black-and-white negative transparencies made by photographing the camera-ready artwork through colored filters, one for each of the three primary colors (red, blue, and green), the fourth separation recording only those areas of the artwork that are very dark or pure black (most line art, for example). The black separation is needed because printing inks are transparent, and even when all three primaries register at full density on their respective separations (indicating black at that point in the artwork), the corresponding point on the final print would appear only medium grey. The black separation thus gives a true black on the print, while adding contrast and apparent "depth." The separa-
(A,R)

tions are then used to make printing plates for each color.

COLOR TEMPERATURE   A number which expresses the relative amount of red and blue in any specific source of light by comparing its spectrum to that of an object heated to that temperature (in degrees Kelvin). For instance, at about 2,800°K (much hotter than molten iron), an object will give off light which has the color balance of a 60-watt bulb—i.e., a relatively high proportion of red compared to blue. The midday sun, however, has a color temperature of about 5,400°K, with a correspondingly higher percentage of blue light in its spectrum. Candlelight, much redder than incandescent, is down around 1,900° K, while an overcast sky, which filters out red in sunlight, gives a resulting color temperature as high as 20,000° K. (*See* TIMING: HAZELTINE; SCENE-TO-SCENE COLOR CORRECTION
(F,V)

COLORATION   An irregular emphasis or lack of certain frequencies or ranges in the overall frequency response of an originally acceptable sound or signal. Examples are heard in the off-axis sound received by cardioid microphones or a speaker that emphasizes or eliminates certain frequencies, either because of inherent design flaws or improper placement in the listening area.
(E)

COMBINING AMPLIFIER   An amplifier that combines two or more signals prior to sending them to a single audio bus, signal processor, tape recorder track, or other destination. Often called an ACA (Ac-
(E)

tive Combining Amp), although there are also passive versions.

COMBINING NETWORK   A passive resistive network in which two or more signals are combined before being sent to a single bus, signal processor, or other destination.
(E)

COMITE CONSULTATIF INTERNA-TIONAL RADIO   See C.C.I.R.

COMMAND   In computers, any single instruction by which the user tells the machine what to do. Opposite of a message.
(C)

COMMON LAW COPYRIGHT   A method of establishing proof of copyright ownership of a composition (or a book, script, or any intangible creation). By sending a copy of the work to yourself via registered mail and *not* opening the letter, you have a sealed, legally dated copy that can be used in case of a copyright conflict in the future. Once opened, however, the letter loses its protective value. The law recognizes ownership upon creation, but proving the date and authorship can be tricky if challenged. Sometimes called a poor man's copyright.
(P)

COMPACT DISC READ-ONLY MEM-ORY.   See CD-ROM.

COMPANDER   A contraction of the words COMpressor and ex-PANDER. Most noise-reduction systems are companders, compressing all or a portion of a signal during record, and expanding it in a precisely inverse manner during playback. (*See* COMPLEMEN-TARY SIGNAL PROCESSING.)
(E)

COMPETENT   In legal parlance, able to act responsibly in the execution of the terms of a contract. Of sound mind and body, etc.
(B)

COMPLEMENTARY SIGNAL PROCESS-ING   Any type of signal processing that performs two equal and opposite processes on the signal—one before recording, the other after playback. Noise reduction and tape recorder pre- and post-de-emphasis are good examples.
(E)

COMPLETION BOND   A guarantee of completion for a major motion picture or video production, usually required by investors in the project to cover the possibility of the producers' going over budget and running out of production funds. The bonding agent, if he accepts the project, charges about 3–6% of the total budget. If the primary budget runs out, he takes over the production, making, at his expense, any changes in script or personnel that are necessary to complete it. He may also acquire some or all of the producer's and/or director's points, especially if their contracts contained penalty clauses for going overbudget.
(F,V)

COMPOSERS, AUTHORS AND PUB-LISHERS ASSOCIATION OF CANADA   See CAPAC.

COMPRESSION, AIR   The squeezing together of air molecules during the first half of each complete cycle of a sound wave. It corresponds to the portion of the wave that appears above the axis when graphed. Opposite of rarefaction.
(E)

COMPRESSION DRIVER   A loud-speaker in which the vibrations of
(E)

(A) = Advertising • (B) = Business & Law • (C) = Computers • (D) = Digital • (E) = Engineering & Scientific •
(F) = Film • (G) = Music & General • (I) = Interlock & Sync • (J) = Jokes & Jargon • (P) = Music Publishing •
(R) = Record Industry • (S) = Synthesizers • (U) = Unions • (V) = Video

a relatively large cone or diaphragm are forced through a narrow "throat," at which point they are coupled to a horn assembly for increased efficiency.

COMPRESSION RATIO (E)   The numerical ratio of the decibel increase in input level of a compressor (above the threshold) that produces a one decibel increase in output level. Example: If the increase in input level is 5 dB for every 1 dB increase in output, the compression ratio is 5:1.

COMPRESSOR (E)   A signal-processing device consisting of an amplifier

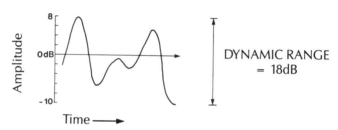

INPUT SIGNAL

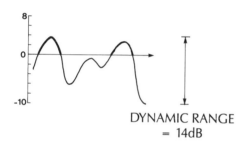

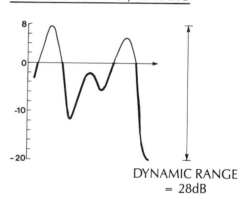

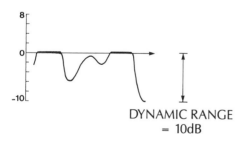

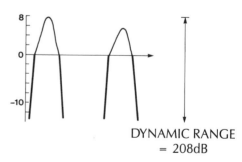

COMPRESSION RATIO. Given that the threshold in all the above illustrations is at 0dB, the thickened lines show the affected portions of each waveform.

(A) = Advertising • (B) = Business & Law • (C) = Computers • (D) = Digital • (E) = Engineering & Scientific •
(F) = Film • (G) = Music & General • (I) = Interlock & Sync • (J) = Jokes & Jargon • (P) = Music Publishing •
(R) = Record Industry • (S) = Synthesizers • (U) = Unions • (V) = Video

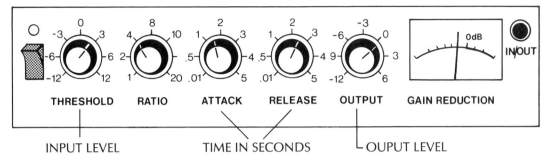

THRESHOLD — INPUT LEVEL

ATTACK / RELEASE — TIME IN SECONDS

OUTPUT — OUPUT LEVEL

COMPRESSOR.

(E)

whose gain decreases automatically as the input signal level increases above a specified threshold. Some models use their own output signal to control gain reduction. The result is a decrease in the dynamic range of the signal from input to output, primarily by reduction of the level of transients or peaks in the signal. This can prevent overload on steep transients and, when the gain prior to compression is greater than unity, provide a boost for very-low-level signals. (*See* GAIN REDUCTION; LIMITER.) VOICE-OVER COMPRESSOR. A compressor that reduces the level of the ongoing program signal in response to an intermittent voice (or other sound). Used mostly in radio and television broadcasting, where the disc jockey's voice keys a voice-over compressor to reduce the ongoing level of music. (*See* DUCKING.)

COMPULSORY LICENSE   A mechanical license (granted by the publisher) for a new release of a composition that has previously been released in any form. By federal law, the publisher cannot deny such licenses unless he feels that the new version will (a) diminish the composition's future ability to earn money, or (b)

(P,R)

damage the composer's, the composition's, or the publisher's reputation. This might be true, for example, if the new recording mocks the composition itself, or if newly written lyrics might cause some third party to launch a libel suit, etc. It is quite legal, therefore, for the original publisher to request a copy of the new version before issuing the "compulsory" license.

CONCEPT   In advertising, the "message," slogan, and/or verbal or visual "thoughts" around which an advertisement or entire campaign is designed. Examples: "The Real Thing" and "Coke is it!," for Coca-Cola, or "Oh! What a feeling," for Toyota.

(A)

CONDUCTOR   See LEADER.

CONSIDERATION   In general, any payment one party to a contract or agreement makes to the other party. Consideration can vary from a $1 token payment for creative services essentially donated to a project, to full union scale, retail price, or even some premium rate or amount. Legally, some consideration must be paid in order for a contract to be valid and fulfilled. Only then will legal title to the result of creative services be

(B)

transferred to the client or sponsor of the project.

CONSIGNMENT   A business relationship in which a buyer accepts
(B)   goods with the intent of reselling them on behalf of the supplier, while legal title to the goods remains with the supplier. If the goods are not sold, the buyer may return them to the seller without penalty. Often used for the sale of locally released records through stores, whose owners will only buy releases by known artists. Other terms may be added to consignment sales via written agreement between supplier and buyer. A type of bailment.

CONSOLE AUTOMATION   See AUTOMATION, CONSOLE.

CONSOLE, RECORDING   The set of controls (and the enclosure con-
(E)   taining them) by which the recording engineer selects various input signals (mic, line, or tape playback), adjusts their relative volume, tone, etc., and routes them, either to multi-track tape, mixdown, control room monitors, studio headphones, or other destination. Also called a board or desk.

CONTACT MICROPHONE   A mic that is physically attached to the
(E)   body of an instrument or sound source. It is primarily the vibration of the microphone's body itself that is converted into an electrical signal. By comparison, normal microphones contain an internal diaphragm or membrane that vibrates in response to sound carried to it through the air—the body of the mic itself remains motionless.

CONTACT PRINT   A type of answer print or release print made by run-
(F)   ning the camera original through the printer with its emulsion in direct contact with the emulsion of the print stock. Light passing through the original creates the image on the print.

CONTINGENCY   A percentage of the total proposed budget for a film,
(B)   TV, or music production, added to cover unpredictable costs for reshooting, extra editing time or overdubs, or any reasonable increase in one or more budget categories. A 10–20% contingency is common in film, TV, and advertising productions. For in-house album projects, many record companies prefer to budget each line item amply, rather than adding an overall line item for a contingency.

CONTINGENT SCALE   Monies payable by record companies to
(U,R)   AFTRA singers, over and above their original scale wages and benefits, for performances on records whose sales exceed specified minimum numbers of units. These sales plateaus are defined in the AFTRA Code of Fair Practice for Phonograph Records. (*See* COVERED.)

CONTINUITY   In a motion picture or video shoot, the process of keep-
(F,V)   ing track of everything that appears on-screen and the positions of all actors during the individual shots. The continuity person notes the location of every prop, what every actor wears, and, if possible, their positions and facial expressions at the beginning and end of each shot. Done to insure that the

various shots of a scene will edit together without any jarring visual inconsistencies.

CONTRACT   An agreement made be-
(B) tween two parties that outlines rights, responsibilities, and rewards of the parties involved. When signed by all parties, contracts are legally binding and can only be modified by separate written and signed agreement. Any two people or companies may write and sign a contract. However, there are many federal, state, and local laws that govern the entertainment industry. In addition, practices and payments in the industry change rapidly. Thus, both parties to a contract should consult an entertainment lawyer *before* signing any significant contract. To be valid, a contract must contain an offer, an acceptance, and must specify a consideration. (*See* CAPACITY; COMPETENT.)

CONTRACTOR   1. In AFM recording
(U) sessions, when more than twelve musicians are called for any session, the producer or client must make an additional scale payment to a "contractor." This union member is responsible for hiring all the other musicians; informing them of the date, time, place, purpose, and booked length of the session; and telling them which instruments and accessories to bring. The contractor may be one of the musicians performing at the session, in which case he is paid scale for each of his two roles. However, AFM rules prohibit the contractor being paid a third scale wage for acting as "leader." The contractor also fills out and submits forms to ensure

that all musicians receive proper payment, and monitors working conditions during the session. AFTRA also requires a contractor be paid on sessions with three or more singers. Rates depend on the
(B) type of session. **2.** Strictly speaking, the party to a contract who is hiring or employing the other party to deliver a product or a service. The contractor generally writes the contract himself, or has it written on his behalf. The deal is therefore likely to be written in his or his company's favor. Opposite of contractee. The law also regards an independent contractor as the person or company who signs a contract to provide goods or services to another party. Be sure to clarify the context in which you use this term.

CONTROL TRACK   In videotape
(V) recording, an analog track recorded near one edge of the videotape, and containing a frame-synchronizing signal recorded at the same time as the picture. The signal—a series of pulses generated at the beginning of each video frame—ensures proper scanning alignment of this tape with any other video source used during editing or broadcast. In 1″ and 3/4″ formats, SMPTE information is sent to a separate "address track," which leads to some confusion about the names of both these tracks. (*See* ADDRESS TRACK; FORMAT, **5** (illustration).)

CONTROL UNIT   The section of a
CPU that regulates the flow of
(C) data and the sequencing of operations to be performed. Also guides

data flow to and from auxiliary storage and peripherals.

CONTROL VOLTAGE (or CONTROL SIGNAL)   A voltage generated by a controller, used to vary one or more operational parameters of a signal generating or processing device. (*See* SIDE CHAIN; KEY CODE.)
(E,S)

CONTROLLED COMPOSITION   In recording contracts, any song or composition the artist wrote or co-wrote, or any song in which he owns a share of the publishing. (Both words are capitalized.)
(R,P)

CONTROLLER   An electronic circuit or device whose output voltage is used to control the operation of another circuit or device. (*See* ENVELOPE FOLLOWER.)
(E,S)

CO-OP ADVERTISING   Advertising whose cost is paid for jointly by a group of persons or companies who might profit from sale of the product or service, including the manufacturer, distributors, retail outlets, and/or chains. In the record industry, for example, the record company, a local record store, the artist's agent, and the promoter of a scheduled concert might co-op a full page ad in the local paper. Or a TV spot for designer jeans might be aired at the joint expense of the manufacturer and a local department store, usually with that store's ID appearing at the end. This ID is known as a "dealer tag".
(A,R)

COPY   The words planned for inclusion in an advertisement—i.e., the text that may later be typeset, read by a narrator, or read by an actor for a TV spot.
(A)

COPYEDITING   The process of re-recording or copying selected extracts from original recordings (sound or video) and rearranging their order as they are copied, so that the copy will have all the desired segments in the correct order. This copy is called an assembly, and will generally need fine editing in order to meet timing requirements or establish an acceptable dramatic pace. (*See* ASSEMBLY-EDIT.)
(V,A,E)

COPYIST   A person who produces the individual musical charts to be used by each sideman or singer in a recording session. The copyist copies each part from the conductor's chart onto separate sheets of paper.
(G,U)

COPYRIGHT NOTICE   The familiar © symbol, which signifies that the composition or performance is protected by copyright registration. This symbol should be accompanied by the year of registration and the name of the copyright holder—e.g., ©1986 W. Wadhams.
(R,P)

COPYRIGHT REGISTRATION   1. The process by which a composer or author establishes the date of composition of a work, and by which he secures all customary composer's, writer's, and/or publisher's rights to the work. The most important of these rights is to collect royalties and fees for use of the work in live performance, audio recordings, or in film or television performances. Copyright can be secured by filing the appropriate form directly with the Registrar of Copyright at the Library of Congress, or by licensing the work to a publishing com-
(P,B)

---

pany, which does this in the composer's name. For any compositions copyrighted after 1976, protection is guaranteed until 75 years after the death of the last living composer or writer. After that the composition goes into the public domain and can be recorded or performed without paying a royalty or fee. (*See* COMMON LAW COPYRIGHT; (R) PUBLIC DOMAIN.) **2.** Sound recordings can also be copyrighted. Since the performances embodied in the recording of music are as intangible as the composition itself, these performances can be registered with the Library of Congress using Form SR. If a record company fails to place the usual copyright notice on the record label or jacket, the performances can be construed as being in the public domain. On the other hand, since the record, compact disc, etc. itself is a tangible product with a definited configuration of grooves, pits and ridges, etc., it must also be patented. (*See* PATENT NOTICE; NOTICE.)

COPYRIGHT ROYALTY TRIBUNAL (CRT) A five-member com-
(P,R) mittee appointed by the President of the United States to establish the payment rates that will "afford the copyright owner a fair return for his creative work and the copyright user a fair income under existing economic conditions." The tribunal sets payment rates for small rights, with input from AS-CAP, BMI, NMPA, and other organizations.

COPYWRITER The ad agency em-
(A) ployee who writes copy. He is often responsible for coming up with new concepts, and is fre-

quently involved in music production for commercials whose lyrics he has written.

CORPORATION A business entity whose purpose, participants, and
(B) services or products are registered with the state where it is formed. The state in turn licenses the corporation to conduct business (which may be intended to make a profit or *not* to, a fact that must be stated in its bylaws), monitors its financial procedures on a regular basis, and collects taxes (as do the federal and sometimes local governments) from those profit-making corporations that actually make a profit. Since the corporation itself is a legal entity, it protects its shareholders and officers from almost all personal liability suits or other losses resulting from actions taken on its behalf.

CORPORATION FOR PUBLIC BROAD-CASTING See CPB.

COST PER THOUSAND (C.P.T.) In any print or broadcast medium, the amount a client must spend to have his print ads or spots seen or heard by each thousand viewers or listeners.

COUNTRY MUSIC The trade journal that promotes the interests of
(R) country music internationally.

COUNTRY MUSIC ASSOCIATION (C.M.A.) The Nashville-based
(R) organization whose membership includes publishers, artists, producers, record companies, and other professionals involved in making and promoting country music. The C.M.A. also gives annual awards at a ceremony no less

---

grand than the Grammies themselves.

COUNTS *(F,V)*   A slang term for footage numbers or cues for specific events in a film or videotape. Also called footage counts.

COUPLING *(E)*   The process of or means by which energy is transferred from one system or medium to another. A good example is the coupling of acoustic energy from a loudspeaker to the surrounding air. (*See* HORN; ACOUSTIC LABYRINTH.)

COVER *(R)*   1. (noun). The cardboard jacket in which records are packaged, usually printed with information, graphics, or photos. **2.** (verb). To re-record another version of a popular song, either to revive its popularity (if the song is an oldie) or to stylize the song differently for a different market.

COVER ART *(R)*   Strictly speaking, the original artwork or photograph(s) commissioned for the front cover of a record's jacket. The record's cover art is the most important graphic image by which records will be sold. It attracts attention to the record, forming a first impression in the potential buyer's mind. Thus it should reflect the sound, feel, style, or theme of the music itself, and generate interest in the record even if the buyer has not yet heard it.

COVER RECORD *(R,P)*   1. Another recorded version of a previously released song, generally a former hit. Publishers try to get many artists to cover a song, which of course

generates more mechanical and broadcast royalties, etc. **2.** A recording produced to sound identical with an earlier version of a song, usually the original hit version. Covers are made for oldies albums, inclusion in film or TV soundtracks, or any use in which it would be impossible or too expensive to license the original hit.

COVERED *(U,R)*   As defined in the AFTRA Code of Fair Practice for Phonograph Records, an album, single, or Side for sales of which contingent scale payments must be made by the record company. A covered artist is one to whom such payments are due. (*See* CONTINGENT SCALE.)

CPB *(V,R)*   Corporation for Public Broadcasting. The American non-profit corporation that funds the production and acquisition (from foreign sources) of educational and cultural programming for radio and television. Its products are broadcast on PBS television, National Public Radio, and their many affiliate stations.

CPS *(E)*   Cycles Per Second. The old name for hertz, abbreviated Hz.

CPU *(C)* *(V)*   1. Central Processing Unit. The integrated circuit chip in a computer that actually performs most operations on data. (*See* ALU.) **2.** Another name for the edit programmer or edit controller that performs an auto-assembly or runs the on-line editing session.

CRAB *(F,V)*   To move the camera sideways, generally using a dolly mounted on wheels or rails.

CRI
(F)
Color Reversal Intermediate. A type of reversal print stock designed for making duplicates of camera negatives. With very low contrast and high resolution, the resulting CRI print is almost a verbatim copy, and made without the two steps of optical degradation (negative to interpositive to internegative) that would otherwise be necessary.

CRIA
(R)
Canadian Recording Industry Association. The Canadian organization analagous to the RIAA in the United States. CRIA awards gold records to singles selling 75,000 units and albums selling 50,000 units, respectively, and platinum records to singles selling 150,000 units and albums selling 100,000 units.

CRCC   See CYCLIC REDUNDANCY CHECKING CODE.

CROSS INTERLEAVING REED-SOLOMON CODE   See CIRC.

CRITICAL DISTANCE   In acoustical measurements, the specific distance from sound source to ear or microphone at which the levels of the direct and indirect sound (i.e., the total reverberant sound) are exactly equal. Usually measured broadband, even though the frequency spectrum of direct and indirect sounds will doubtless be quite different.
(E)

CROSS COLLATERALIZATION   In the computation of profits or royalties, the accounting practice of deducting the losses suffered by one project from the profits accumulated by another. A royalty
(R,B)

artist's contract, for instance, may permit the record company to cross-collateralize the deficit of a flop album against the profits from a hit. The record company will, of course, want the right to do so.

CROSSCUT   To intercut shots of a scene taken alternately from the perspective of two characters, especially when the dramatic tension is mounting.
(F,V)

CROSS FADE   A gradual audio "dissolve" from one sound source or group of sources to another, accomplished by fading out one source or group while fading in the other.
(E)

CROSSOVER FREQUENCY   Loosely, the frequency above and below which an audio signal is divided into two bands, each of which is directed to a separate destination. Strictly speaking, the frequency at which each of these two bands is attenuated 3 dB by the crossover network. (*See* FILTER, BANDPASS; TURNOVER FREQUENCY.)
(E)

CROSSOVER NETWORK   A circuit or device that divides a broadband audio signal into two or more separate bands, each of which can be sent to separate amplifiers, processors, etc. Used most often in speaker systems to divide the amplifier's output into two or more bands, directing only the proper frequency bands to each type of driver. (*See* BI-AMPLIFICATION.)
(E)

CROSSOVER RECORD   A record originally made to sell in one market (country music, for example) that later becomes a hit in
(R)

one or more additional markets, achieving high chart positions in all of them. A record company's dream!

CROSSTALK (E)   Any unwanted leakage of one audio signal into another, usually caused by proximity of signal lines or, in tape recorders, adjacency of tracks. Also known as bleeding. (*See* SEPARATION; FRINGING EFFECT.)

CRT (E,V) (P,R)   **1.** Cathode Ray Tube. Either black and white or color. Although there are all shapes and sizes of CRTs, the most familiar is the picture tube of every television. (*See* MONITOR.) **2.** Copyright Royalty Tribunal.

CRTC (R,V)   Canadian Radio and Telecommunications Commission. The Canadian government agency that regulates all broadcasters on AM and FM radio, broadcast and cable television, etc. Analagous to the FCC in the United States.

CRYSTAL SYNC (F,V)   A system for generating a sync signal that will ensure proper synchronization of film footage and its corresponding sync sound without using any sync reference, such as the 60 Hz line frequency of AC power in the United States. Two piezo-electric crystals, each tuned to the same high frequency, are installed in the camera and recorder. The crystal in the camera precisely controls the motor speed during shooting. The crystal in the recorder produces a sync tone that is recorded on tape in the same way which the camera motor speed would be recorded through the conventional sync cable. Because the two crys-

tals are tuned identically, the dailies, when synched with the magnetic film copy of the original sound takes, will maintain perfect sync once the clapstick marks are aligned as usual. Crystal sync generators are also installed in portable video cameras and VTRs. Since picture and sound are recorded on the same tape, these crystal generators simply ensure that the frame rate of footage shot on location will be exactly identical with that of studio footage.

C-SECTION   See BRIDGE.

CU (F,V)   Close-up. A shot including only the head and shoulders of one actor or person.

CUE (F,V)   **1.** The time, footage, or event that signals that another event must begin on-screen or in the sound track. For example, when a door slams on-screen, this may be the cue for music to begin. **2.** Any single segment of music written to go with a specific scene of film or videotape. An hour show may require an opening and closing theme, and perhaps five to fifty individual cues during the body of the program. (*See* SPOT.)

CUE (or HEADPHONE) BOX (E)   A wall-mounted or movable box that receives one or more headphone or cue mixes from the recording console, and that has jacks to plug in several sets of headphones that can be used by singers or instrumentalists in overdubbing, by a narrator, or other talent in the studio.

CUE LINE (F)   A line drawn on the workprint, meant to be seen during projection in post-dubbing or scoring, and that will give the actor or conductor a visual cue to begin.

CUE MIX (E)   The blend of live inputs and/or previously recorded tracks sent by the engineer to the headphones of performers playing or singing in the studio. Also called the headphone mix.

CUE MODE (E)   A tape machine operating mode in which the tape lifters are defeated while the playback electronics remain operative. Used most often during editing, thus also called edit mode.

CUE SEND (E)   The section of the recording console that controls the source and volume of the signal to be sent to the cue box. There are normally cue send volume controls at each module, all of which are mixed and fed via the cue bus(es) to a master cue send volume control located in the monitor or master control module.

CUE SHEET (F,V)   A list of the footages and frames, starting from 0:00 in the head leader, at which various specific shots or scenes begin and end, or certain events occur on-screen. The cue sheet will have a separate column for each reel of film and magnetic film. The footage and frame numbers are used by the dubbing, mixing, or re-recording engineer, who must know what sounds or music are about to be played as the mix proceeds. Another type of cue sheet goes with the Workprint and A and B ROLLS to the film lab, specifying the length and position of each shot in the film, and giving instructions about

exposure, color balance, and any effects that must be performed. (*See* EDIT DECISION LIST.) (Illustration next page.)

CUE SYSTEM (E)   The entire electronic circuitry contained within the recording console that allows the engineer to adjustably feed sound from any input module to the cue, then out to the musicians' or singers' headphones via cue amp and cue boxes.

CUE-UP (E)   To locate a desired point (at which a desired sound event happens) on a reel of tape, and to position that point just ahead of the playback head on a tape recorder. When playback begins, the desired sound will be heard immediately. (*See* CART.)

CURE (B)   In legal parlance, to repair or mend the breach of an agreement. To effect a legal remedy.

CURRENT (E)   The rate at which electricity flows through a circuit, measured in amps.

CURSOR (C)   The indicator or marker that tells the computer operator or programmer the screen location at which he is currently positioned—i.e., where he may input or delete a letter, number, or other symbol. Each screen position corresponds to a single location in memory.

CUT (F,V)   1. (noun). The point at which one shot or scene abruptly ends and the next one begins. 2. (verb). To edit film or videotape—e.g., "I rough-cut the commercial." 3. A particular edited version of a film or videotape program—e.g., "His cut was too long."

52

CLIENT: HBT&O
JOB. NO.: 0114
TITLE: NIGHTBEAT

DIRECTOR: ADAMS
REEL NO.: 4
DATE: 1/15/88

SCENE/ACTION	DIALOG 1	DIALOG 2	FX 1	FX 2	MUSIC	LOOP
00:00:00 Street/Night Sc. 17	Sync	00:09:19 Joey	02:04:08 Car Horn	Traffic		Rain
01:19:20 Cafe/Interior	fade under / 01:24:20 Sync	01:03:12 Mel / 01:33:11 waitress	00:32:16 Car Door / 01:19:20 fade in cafe tone	fade under	01:09:18 Cafe Theme	fade
02:06:22 Kitchen	fade		02:51:05 pot-crash & clatter	02:06:22 kitchen tone	Linda Th.	grill / crickets
03:12:04 Country- same night			03:52:05			

CUE SHEET. Cue sheet for the final mix of a film. This would usually be handwritten.

CUT AND PASTE   In word processing, a command that allows the
(C)   user to identify a section of text or data, remove it from its original position in a longer document, and edit it into another position, perhaps even into another document.

CUT-AWAY   A film or videotape shot showing a person or thing outside
(F,V)   the central action of a scene—e.g., a close-up of someone watching the main action, or a shot of an important prop.

CUT-IN   An agreement between the composer or copyright holder of a
(P)   composition and another person or company, giving that party a portion of the royalties or fees that that composition will earn from specific, limited uses. A producer, for example, may receive a cut-in on a composition that he produces for release on a record—a portion of the mechanical royalties earned by the composition from that recording. The terms and limitations of cut-ins must be specified exactly, since there are no statutory regulations to protect either party to a cut-in agreement. (*See* SPLIT COPYRIGHT.)

CUT-OFF FREQUENCY   In any band-pass filter, a frequency at
(E)   which the output level is attenuated by 3 dB. If the filter is a low-pass or high-pass filter, the rate of attenuation may be very steep beyond the cut-off frequency, typically 12 dB or 18 dB per octave. More precisely called turnover or crossover frequency. (*See* BAND-WIDTH.)

CUT-OUT   A record that has been
(R)   dropped from the current sales catalog of a company, and that is then sold at a reduced cost to distributors or stores, usually on a no-return basis. Royalties are usually not paid to artist or producer for records sold as cut-outs.

CUT-SWITCH   A switch or button that
(E)   mutes an audio signal in a console.

CUTTER   Slang for an editor. One may be a picture cutter, sound cut-
(F)   ter, effects cutter, etc.

CYC   Short for cyclorama. A large, curved backdrop used in sound
(F,V)   stages. The cyc is generally curved forward as it meets the stage floor to eliminate a corner or "seam," and is normally painted flat white in order that it can be (a) "washed" with colored light to represent distant sky or a neutral background, or (b) used as a screen on which transparencies of sets or outdoor locations are projected.

CYCLES PER SECOND   See HERTZ; CPS.

CYCLIC REDUNDANCY CHECKING CODE (CRCC)   An error detec-
(D)   tion scheme in which the numerical value of the audio data is repetitively divided by a constant. The integer portion of the quotient is discarded, and the decimal portion stored to tape along with the audio data itself. During playback, the division is once again performed, and the decimal portion of the new quotient is compared with that read off tape. If they match, the audio data is presumed to be correct, and is sent on for D-A conversion. If not, the audio data is discarded and another error correction process instituted.

(A) = Advertising • (B) = Business & Law • (C) = Computers • (D) = Digital • (E) = Engineering & Scientific •
(F) = Film • (G) = Music & General • (I) = Interlock & Sync • (J) = Jokes & Jargon • (P) = Music Publishing •
(R) = Record Industry • (S) = Synthesizers • (U) = Unions • (V) = Video

- D -

D-A CONVERTER Read "D to A."
(E) (See DIGITAL-TO-ANALOG CONVERTER; DIGITAL RECORDING.)

DAILIES The first print from the laboratory of the film shot on the previous day, usually with the synchronous sound transferred to magnetic film and "synched up" for double-system projection. Also called rushes or rush prints.
(F)

DAMPING Opposition to or inhibition of movement or energy transfer in a mechanical, acoustical, or electrical system. For example, the volume of air inside an acoustic suspension speaker system is calculated to damp the motion of the woofer cone at its natural resonant frequencies.
(E)

DAMPING FACTOR In power amplifiers, the measure (defined by a complex equation) of an amplifier's ability to accurately control the cone of the loudspeaker, preventing spurious excursions due to speaker or baffle resonances, mechanical overshoot, etc. Tube amps have low damping factors, gen-
(E)
erally less than 10. Transistor amps can have damping factors over 100.

DASH Digital Audio Stationary Head. The format adopted by three manufacturers of professional stationary-head digital recording equipment (Studer, Sony, and Matsushita Corporations) for (a) the packaging of audio samples, location data, and error bits into complete 16-bit words for storage on tape, and (b) the actual track format by which this data is then recorded on the tape itself. Without such standardization of formats, it will be impossible to record digitally on one brand of machine and playback on another. DASH equipment is made for 2-track and multitrack recording. All DASH formats can be razor-blade-edited, a great advantage over digital systems, which employ videotape for storage.
(D)

DAT Digital Audio Tape. Also known as DCAC.
(R,E)

DATA BASE Any large body of information through which the com-
(C)

puter can sort to find subsets of data whose members share one or more user-specified characteristics.

DATA BYTES   In MIDI messages, the bytes that follow status bytes, actually telling the slave device what sounds to create, etc.
(S)

DATA STREAM   See BIT STREAM.

DATABLOCK   See BLOCK.

dB   See DECIBEL.

DBX (dbx)   The name of the manufacturer of, among other things, an electronic noise reduction system that partially eliminates noise within the recording or audio system itself. (It does not reduce noise contained in the incoming signal.) The dbx is a broadband compander that compresses incoming signals by a 2:1 ratio prior to recording, then expands the signal by 1:2 during reproduction. The tape noise itself is reduced according to the same 1:2 expansion ratio. The dbx is also used to reduce noise in some optical motion picture soundtracks, many magnetic soundtracks, and even radio or television broadcast sound.
(E)

DCAC   Digital Compact Audio Cassette. Also called DAT. (See R-DAT.)
(R,E)

DDL   Short for Digital Delay. (See DELAY, DIGITAL.)
(E)

DEAD   1. In acoustics, devoid of any reverberant or reflective sound content. A room is considered "dead" when its interior surfaces absorb most or all of the sound that strikes them. 2. Refering to a
(E)

circuit or device, not functioning, or delivering no perceptible signal. If an engineer feeds signals into the cue system, but no sound comes out of the headphones, the system is dead.

DEAL BREAKER   A request or demand made by one party to a potential contract, to which the other party cannot or will not agree. Thus, no deal will be consummated. (See BARGAINING CHIP)
(B)

DEAL MEMO   A memorandum made by one of the parties to a verbal agreement (generally a by-phone agreement), outlining the main points and terms discussed, any specific agreed numbers, percentages, prices, dates, etc. The deal memo is generally written by the person seeking a deal, (a) to remind the other party of everything that should be written into the contract, and (b) to push the other party to speedy action or follow-through. A copy of the deal memo, signed by both parties, can serve as a contract in time-sensitive transactions, enabling services or production to commence.
(B)

DEALER TAG   In co-op radio or television advertising, a short audio and/or visual notice at the end of a spot, showing or telling the listener or viewer the name and location of the local dealer who sells the product or service being advertised. For example, a local car dealership can insert its dealer tag in the last seconds of a spot provided by the car manufacturer.
(A)

DECAY   1. Used both for acoustical and electronic sound sources. The characteristic fall-off in output
(E)

---

amplitude or volume a sound-producing source emits when the force creating the vibrations (or the current powering the oscillator in a synthesizer, for instance) is removed. This term is often confused with release, the fourth section of a sound's envelope. **2.** The second of four sections of a sound or signal's envelope. In order, they are attack, decay, sustain, release. (*See* ENVELOPE (illustration).)

(E,S)

DECAY RATE   The number of decibels per second by which echoes or reverberation of a sound diminish once the sound has stopped. Depending on the sound source and environment, the decay rate may be linear (e.g., a steady number of dB per second), or it may begin to decay slowly and then fall off rapidly, or the reverse. In addition, various frequencies in the sound may decay at different rates.

(E)

DECAY TIME   The length of time it takes for echoes or reverberation of a sound to diminish 60 dB below its original level, effectively to inaudibility. More precisely known as reverberation time or T-60.

(E)

DECIBEL (dB)   **1.** A unit of level used to designate power ratios in acoustic and electric measurements, adapted separately for various power and voltage scales as follows (subscript *b* indicates the initial power (P) or voltage (V), subscript *a* indicates the final P or V):

(E)

   For power level comparisons, N dB = 10log (P_{out}/P_{in}) or 10log (P_a/P_b). Thus, if the power of a signal increases from 10 watts to 500 watts, the corresponding increase in decibels is 10log (500/10) = 10log 50 = 10(1.7) = 17 dB.

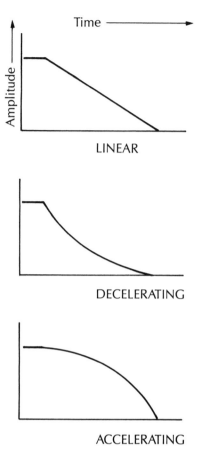

LINEAR

DECELERATING

ACCELERATING

DECAY RATE.

   For voltage comparisons, N dB = 20log(V_{out}/V_{in}) or 20log(Va/Vb). For example, the dB difference in the level of two signals of 1 Vand 0.002V = 20log(1.0/0.002) = 20log 500 = 20 (2.7) = 54 dB. P_b and V_b may be specified as standard reference power or voltage levels, in which case the units of dB field measurements are designated by three letters, as follows:

   dBA A decibel level referenced to the A weighting scale, whose frequency response curve approximates the human ear's response at 40 phons.

   dBB A decibel level referenced to the B weighting scale, whose response curve approximates the human ear's response at 70 phons.

dbC A decibel level referenced to the C weighting scale, whose response curve approximates the human ear's response at 100 phons.

dBm A decibel power level referenced to a standard P_b that results when 1 milliwatt is disipated through a 600-ohm line. To be meaningful, P_a must also be measured in a 600-ohm line.

dBV A decibel voltage level referenced to a V_b of 1.0 volt.

dBVU Same as dBVU, where $V_b = 0.775$ volts. This standard level is used (in the U.S.) to define 100% modulation in VU meters. (*See* WEIGHTING; WEIGHTING

(E) NETWORK.) **2.** Loosely, the smallest increment in perceived volume that the average human ear can detect. In early experiments with sound, it was noted that 1/10 bel is very close to this increment; thus, precise measurements of volume are standardized in decibels. (*See* BEL.)

DECK PLATE   In a tape recorder transport, the heavy metal plate on (E) which the headstack, rollers, and other related parts are mounted.

DECODING   **1.** In signal processing, restoring a signal to its original or (E) normal state by applying electronic processing exactly the opposite of that used during earlier encoding. Example: A noise reduction system's reexpansion of the signal dur-

(D) ing playback. **2.** In digital recording, the entire process converting the encoded data stream back into an analog signal, including the application of error correction

procedures—i.e., digital-to-analog conversion. (*See* ENCODE.)

DEDICATED   Referring to a piece of audio equipment, computer or (E,C) program, designed for and allocated to a single specific use.

DE-ESSER   A fast-attack, fast-release compressor or limiter whose con- (E) trol channel is shelf-equalized to preemphasize very high frequencies, usually by at least 15 dB at 10 kHz. When the threshold is set properly, high-frequency signals will be compressed more than low-frequency signals of the same incoming level. Thus, the unit reduces vocal sibilants or takes "esses" out; hence its name. Developed originally to prevent high-frequency overload in optical motion picture soundtracks. Now used in many recording and broadcast applications.

DEFAULT (or DEFAULT VALUE)   An option (or numerical value) the (C) computer employs if the user does not specify another option. In word processing, for example, single-spacing may be the default value for the line-spacing option if the user does not specify double-, triple-, or other spacing.

DEFERRED COSTS (or PAYMENTS) Expenses in any kind of production (B) that are not to be paid until some later date, or the occurence of some later event(s)—e.g., the date when a master tape is signed to a record company for release; or when the producer has received a recoupment advance; or when the production has broken even. For example, a musician who charges more than union scale may agree to defer his premium charges until the producer receives a recoupment advance.

DEFINITION   A qualitative term that denotes the clarity or distinguishability of a sound. A sound without definition may, like some woodwinds in their middle ranges, be easily mistaken for another similar sound. In recording, the apparent definiton of a sound can be increased by boosting those frequencies characteristic of the specific sound or instrument, and reducing frequencies it has in common with other sounds in the same audio program.

(E)

DEFINITIONS   In many entertainment contracts, the subject of the first complete paragraph or numbered section. This paragraph defines words and phrases in current use in the sector of the industry in which the contract applies. Although the exact meaning of technical, manufacturing, and marketing terminology changes regularly, the terms defined in a contract are fixed, influencing the rights, responsibilities, and rewards of both parties as long as the contract remains in force, especially if a disagreement arises.

(B)

DEGAUSSER   1. A hand-held device—essentially an electromagnet—that can be brought into contact with the heads and metal parts of a tape recorder in order to demagnetize them, or remove any residual magnetism that may have accumulated in these parts. 2. See BULK ERASER.

(E)

DELAY   The time interval between the initial occurence of a sound or signal and its repeat or echo.

(E)

ACOUSTIC DELAY: A delay line in which a speaker and microphone are separated by an extended path length, such as by placing them at opposite ends of a long tube. The delay itself is derived from the time it takes the sound to travel through the air in the tube.

DIGITAL DELAY (DDL). An electronic delay line in which the time delay is created by translating the analog input signal into digital information, which is stored for a determined or adjustable length of time, then reconverted back to an analog signal and sent to the output. Many DDLs allow adjustable regeneration or feedback, causing multiple repeats, and other effects such as flanging or chorusing of the input signal. (Illustration opposite.)

TAPE DELAY. A delay produced by recording and playing back a sound or signal simultaneously on the same recorder, taking advantage of the time it takes the tape to travel from the record to the playback head. Also, the tape and recorder with which this is done. Tape delay was used long before digital and other systems were developed. Because the heads are stationary, the only way to adjust the delay time is by changing the tape speed itself. Sometimes called a slapback. (*See* DEPTH; RATE.)

DELAY LINE   Any device—acoustic or electronic—that intentionally introduces a time delay between its input and output signals.

(E)

DELTA MODULATION (DM)   A sampling system that employs an extremely high sampling rate—so high that any possible change in the incoming analog signal requires

(D)

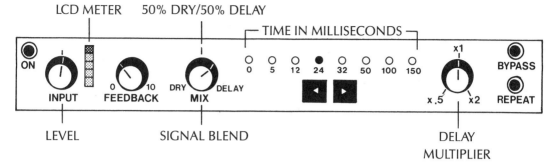

DIGITAL DELAY.

no more than 1 bit to represent each subsequent sample. That bit will simply note whether the next sample is higher or lower than the last. DM is thus a type of differential PCM system, each sample recording the change in signal level rather than its absolute value. Used by dbx and some other manufacturers of PCM systems, but not yet accepted as an industry standard.

DEMAGNETIZATION   1. The neu-
(E)   tralization by an electromagnet of any residual magnetism in the tape heads, rollers, or other parts of the tape deck or transport. Accomplished with a degausser. **2.** (rarely). The erasure of the magnetic signal recorded on tape. (*See* BULK ERASER.)

DEMO   A sample or demonstration
(R)   recording of a song, arrangement, or performance, made either to solicit a recording artist to use one's material, or to solicit a recording contract for the performer(s) on the demo tape itself. Demos are also made by artists already under recording contract, as a sort of working "sketch" of the planned master tape. Fills, riffs, horn, and string parts can be tried inexpensively when working on a 8-track demo by using synthesizers. This

can later save time when employing union musicians in making the master tape.

DEMOGRAPHICS   The description of
(A)   a target market in terms of age, sex, income, education, and other specific known characteristics. For example, the target market may be single women, college graduates, age 22–35, with incomes of $15,000 to $25,000. Ethnic background, religious, and other considerations may also be specified, but are sometimes separately designated as ethnographics or sociographics.

DE-MULTIPLEXER   A device that
(C)   converts serial to parallel data. (*See* MULTIPLEXER.)

DEPTH   In a digital delay or flanger, a
(E)   control and circuit that cyclicly (and adjustably) modulate the length of the delay around the specified delay time. Because this happens in real-time, the pitch of the incoming signal is varied, causing the output signal to have an apparent vibrato. The speed of this vibrato is set by the rate control. (*See* DELAY, DIGITAL (illustration).)

DEPTH PERCEPTION   A listener's
(F)   ability to perceive the relative dis-

tance that separates him from the various instruments present in a live performance or recording.

DERIVATIVE RIGHTS   See SUB-SIDIARY RIGHTS.

DERIVATIVE WORK   Loosely, a musical composition (with or without lyrics) based on one or more pre-existing compositions. It can be a published arrangement of an already-copyrighted work, a sound recording, a translation, a condensation, a dramatic production based on the original work, etc.
(P)

DES   Acronym for Dolby-Encoded Stereo, the noise reduction system employed for reproduction of stereo optical tracks in movie theaters.
(F)

DETECTOR   See LEVEL-SENSING CIRCUIT.

DGA   See DIRECTORS GUILD OF AMERICA.

D.I.   Direct Input. (*See* DIRECT BOX.)
(E)

DIALOGUE TRACK   1. The edited track of magnetic film that contains the dialogue portions of a film's sound. In some cases, there may be a separate dialogue track for each actor appearing in a specific scene. 2. In a 35mm three-track mix, the recorded track that contains all dialogue re-recorded from one or more dialogue tracks as defined in 1.
(F,V)

DIAPHRAGM   The part of a microphone (the membrane) or loudspeaker (the cone) that moves in response to sound waves or an incoming signal, respectively. A part of the
(E)

mic's capsule. (*See* MICROPHONE, by design and functions (illustration).)

DIFFRACTION   In acoustics, the bending of sound waves around corners or any obstacles they encounter. The exact angle of diffraction is a function of the wavelength of the sound and the radius of curvature of the edge past which the sound travels. In general, low frequencies are diffracted much more strongly than high frequencies. Often confused with refraction. *See* DISPERSION.
(E)

DIGIT, BINARY   In binary numbering, either a "1" or a "0", by use of which (in various sequences) all decimal numbers can be represented. (*See* BIT.)
(C)

HEXADECIMAL DIGIT: In the hexadecimal numbering system, any of the sixteen symbols (the arabic numerals 0 through 9 and the capital letters A through F) used to express the numbers 0 through 15.

DIGITAL AUDIO   The consumer and trade journal that tracks developments in the digital audio field. Includes thorough reviews of new consumer equipment, new CD releases, research and technological developments that may lead to future products, etc.
(D,G)

DIGITAL AUDIO TAPE   See R-DAT and DCAC.

DIGITAL DELAY   See DELAY, DIGITAL.

DIGITAL COMPACT AUDIO CASSETTE (DCAC).   A consumer product that allows recording and playback of digital audio. Capable
(R,E)

---

of almost the same sound quality as CDs, but less flexible because of the linear nature of tape, which prevents random access to any point in the program, a big plus with compact discs. (*See* DAT; R-DAT.)

DIGITAL RECORDING   Conceptually, any recording process in which the voltage of the original analog sig-
(E,D)

nal is repeatedly sampled and stored as numerical data during the recording, then reconverted back to an analog waveform during playback.

DIGITAL REVERBERATION SYSTEM
An electronic device used in the studio to generate artificial reverb, entirely without any mechanical components or acoustical trans-
(E)

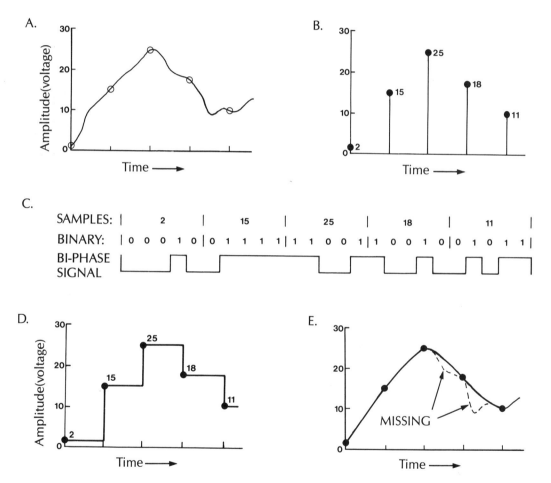

A-E: INCORRECT SAMPLING RATE

(*Continued next page*)

DIGITAL RECORDING. The original analog waveform (A) is sampled, yielding a voltage value for each sample (B). These values are converted to binary numbers which are encoded on tape as a biphase signal. (C). Upon playback, the voltage values are reconstructed (D), then filtered and smoothed (E). Sampling at a rate less than the nyquist frequency results in an incorrect replica (E) of the original waveform (A). Sampling at or above the nyquist frequency results in a duplicate (F-I) of original waveform (A).

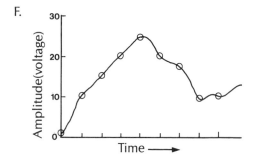
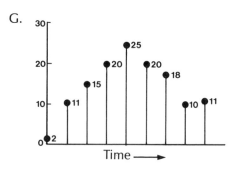
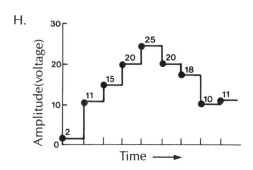
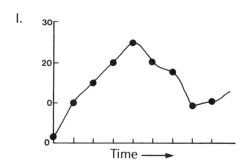

Digital Recording *(Cont.)*

F-I: CORRECT SAMPLING RATE OR NYQUIST FREQUENCY

ducers. The device employs one or more internal, factory-written computer programs that mathematically mimic the parameters of various sources of reverberation (hall, room, chamber, plate, spring, etc.) by generating and blending complex sequences of delays of the incoming signal. Audio signals sent to the device are digitally sampled, and each sample is used as input data for the program in use. The sum of the digital reverb data is then reconverted to analog and output.

DIGITAL SEQUENCER   A sequencer in which signals to be stored and later replayed are entered and output in digital form, either from

(S)

a synthesizer or directly as binary data from another source.

DIGITAL-TO-ANALOG CONVERTER (D-A)   A group of electronic circuits that reads and decodes sequential numerical voltage samples, then recreates a stepped waveform that approximates the analog waveform existing before initial encoding. The voltage samples may come from any storage medium, tape, RAM, a buffer memory, etc. (*See* DIGITAL RECORDING; SAMPLING RATE; SAMPLE AND HOLD CIRCUIT.)

(D,E)

DIRECT BOX   A device containing an impedance-matching transformer (and sometimes a pre-amplifying

(E)

circuit) that allows the output of an electric instrument to feed the input module of a recording console directly. Also called a D.I. (direct input).

DIRECTIONAL CHARACTERISTICS

(E) The polar response of a microphone, speaker, or other transducer. (*See* MICROPHONE, POLAR PATTERN: RADIATION PATTERN.)

DIRECT READ AFTER WRITE   See DRAW, 2.

DIRECT MAIL   Advertising sent out

(A) by mail instead of being placed in the media. Often called "junk mail" by its recipients. It is in fact a very sophisticated type of marketing, and there are many companies specializing in such campaigns, carefully developing mailing lists of persons who are able and most likely to purchase specific products or services.

DIRECT METAL MASTERING   A

(R,E) system for cutting a metal mother on a record mastering lathe, eliminating the lacquer master and metal master steps. Release pressings made from a stamper are thus only two steps from the DM master, and thus have less surface noise and distortion than made by the older five step process. Developed by Teldec Corporation, the DMM process is also used in CD mastering.

DIRECTOR   The person who controls

(F,V) the action seen by the film or video camera. He instructs the actors on their movements, recitations, etc., instructs the cameraman on techni-

cal requirements for each shot, and is responsible for translating the story and mood of the script into the most effective (and commercial) visual terms. He usually decides what sounds are necessary on the soundtrack, including music and effects.

DIRECTOR OF PHOTOGRAPHY (D.P.)

(F,V) The union technician in a motion picture or television production who is in charge of all the technical crews who affect the way actors and objects look when on camera. Working within the goals defined by the production designer, and taking specific instructions from the director on what must be seen in each shot and how it should look, the D.P. selects the kind and quantity of lighting, lenses, camera mounts and accessories, etc. that are necessary, instructing each crew member how to deploy or use them.

DIRECTORS GUILD OF AMERICA (DGA)   The professional or-

(F,V) ganization that represents directors of motion picture and video productions in negotiations with the major film studios, networks, and independent production companies.

DIRECTORY   See CATALOG.

DIRECT OUTPUT   A recording con-

(E) sole output taken directly after the input module and main channel fader, but before the pan pot and output bus assignment switches. This output mode is sometimes used to avoid crosstalk that may be introduced if the signal is allowed to flow through the remainder of its normal module path.

DIRECT PICKUP   1. In the recording of non-acoustic instruments, patching the instrument's output directly into the console without the use of amplifier(s) or microphone(s), but often employing a direct box. **2.** Used loosely to refer to a contact microphone employed in the recording of an acoustic instrument.

(E)

DIRECT SOUND   1. The component of sound that reaches the listener's ear via a straight line path from the sound source. It contains no reverberation or echoes. (*See* CRITICAL DISTANCE.) **2.** The sound received at the recording console from an electronic instrument when using a direct box. Direct and amplified sound are often blended to achieve a certain overall effect for the sound of an instrument.

(E)

**DIRECT-TO-DISC   A method of making records in which no magnetic tape is used. The outputs of the recording console go directly to the disc-cutting lathe, and the master lacquer (and perhaps many duplicate lacquers on separate lathes) are made at the time of the performance in the studio. This process requires perfection from the performers and engineers, since the music has to be performed (for an album) in complete 20- or-more minute segments, and mixed perfectly for a complete side of the record. No correcting of mistakes or remixing is possible.

(R,E)

**DIRECT-TO-TWO-TRACK   A method of recording in which the instruments and vocals are mixed and recorded directly onto a stereo half-track or digital tape. No future changes or remixing are pos-

(E)

sible. The fidelity, editability, and relatively low cost of direct-to-two-track digital recording has revived the popularity of this medium for making master tapes, especially those intended for release on compact discs.

**DIRTY DUPE   A slop print.

(F)

**DISK JOCKEY   See DJ.

**DISCHARGE   To void or terminate an agreement or contract, usually by completing all commitments that were made in that contract, including any final payment.

(B)

**DISK DRIVE   Short for Floppy Disk Drive. The record/play device that writes data onto and reads it off floppy disks. Sometimes built into microcomputers, but also available as a peripheral. A separate drive is necessary for each size disk. (*See* HARD DISK; TAPELESS RECORDING STUDIO.)

(C,V,E)

DISPERSION   1. In acoustics, the dissemination of sound through some horizontal or vertical angle. **2.** Another term for refraction, the splitting up of a complex sound wave into separate frequency bands as the original wave passes from one elastic medium into another—e.g., from air into water. Similarly, a prism disperses white light into the familiar rainbow of colors, bending the shorter wavelengths (violet or blue) least, the longer wavelengths (red) more. (*See* DIFFRACTION.)

(E)

**DISPLACEMENT   The distance between some measured position of a moving object—e.g. a speaker

(E)

cone—and its rest or other original position. Also applies to the position of air molecules in a sound wave. (*See* COMPRESSION, AIR; RAREFACTION.)

DISSOLVE (F,V)   An optical effect in which two film or video shots are superimposed over each other, one fading out as the other is fading in. The result is that the image fading out seems to "melt" or "dissolve" into the image fading in. The length of dissolves is specified on the cue sheet in frames or seconds.

DISTANT MIKING (E)   In recording only, the placement of one or more microphones quite far from the sound source. The opposite of close or tight miking, distant miking picks up a substantial portion of reflected or reverberant sound, and is therefore used to make most classical or orchestral recordings to capture the audience's point of view. In the studio, close and distant mics on any instrument may be blended in the console to aurally define the space in which the instrument is playing, or for some special effect. (*See* CRITICAL DISTANCE.)

DISTORTION (E)   Any change in the waveshape of a signal that occurs between the input and the output of an audio device. Strictly speaking, equalization and compression are types of distortion, even though they are used to "enhance" sound or make it more usable. Specific distortion ratings are expressed in percentages, representing the amount of distortion present in the total amplitude of the output waveform.

HARMONIC DISTORTION: The unwanted addition (by an acoustic environment or electronic device) of harmonics of a pure tone when that tone is propagated in the environment or input to the device.

INTERMODULATION DISTORTION: The unwanted addition (by an acoustic environment or electronic device) of frequencies that represent various arithmetic sums and differences of the frequencies of two or more tones simultaneously propagated in the environment or sent to the input of the device.

THIRD HARMONIC DISTORTION: That part of harmonic distortion representing only the third harmonic (three times the frequency) of a pure tone input to an electronic device. The third harmonic of any tone is musically an octave and a fifth above the original tone, and is easily noticeable in the output. For this reason, maximum usable output level of analog tape recorders, for example, is often specified as that level at which third harmonic distortion reaches 3%.

TRANSIENT DISTORTION: A type of distortion introduced by many electronic circuits, occuring during any large, instantaneous change in signal level. The circuit may reduce the level of transients (as is intentionally done by limiters and compressors), or may expand or overshoot proper transient level.

DISTRIBUTOR, RECORD (R)   A company that purchases records (or cassettes, compact discs, etc.) at wholesale price from several labels, then sells them at a profit to individual stores or chains. Or, the

---

(A) = Advertising • (B) = Business & Law • (C) = Computers • (D) = Digital • (E) = Engineering & Scientific •
(F) = Film • (G) = Music & General • (I) = Interlock & Sync • (J) = Jokes & Jargon • (P) = Music Publishing •
(R) = Record Industry • (S) = Synthesizers • (U) = Unions • (V) = Video

regional office of a major label that warehouses and sells that label's products to other dealers in that region, both wholesalers and retailers. (*See* ONE STOP; RACK JOBBER.)

DITHER
(D)
In digital playback or reproduction, a low-level analog noise—actually white noise—that is added to the reproduced analog waveform, effectively eliminating quantization noise, an unavoidable side-effect of all digital reproduction.

DJ
(R)
Disc Jockey. The announcer of a radio program, who usually selects what records will be played. Similarly, the person who selects the records played at a discotheque and actually blends them together for the dance floor. Both types can be very helpful in promoting records.

DMM
See DIRECT METAL MASTERING.

DOLBY
(E)
A brand name of noise reduction system that compresses one or more bands of the entire audio spectrum during record, then expands them during playback. Noise in each processed band is reduced by about 10 dB. Named after Raymond Dolby, who patented the original circuit. The Dolby A system, used professionally in studios, divides the audio spectrum into four bands, companding each. The Dolby B and C systems, which compand one and two bands in the high and midrange frequencies, respectively, are used primarily in home systems. The Dolby SR (Spectral Recording) system is replacing the A-type for studio recording. It offers over 20 dB of noise reduction, and is widely considered equal or superior in overall sound quality to professional digital systems. The processing technique and circuitry is proprietary. (*See* COMPANDER; COMPLEMENTARY SIGNAL PROCESSING.)

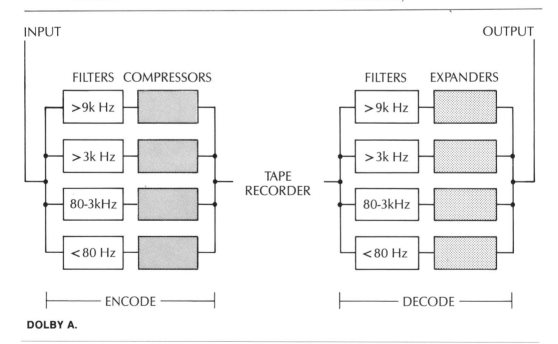

DOLBY A.

DOLBY-ENCODED STEREO.   See DES.

DOLBY TONE   A reference tone, usu-
(E)   ally recorded at the head of a
Dolby A encoded tape, by which
the threshold levels of the Dolby
system are adjusted for proper encoding and decoding of the noise-
reduced signal.

DOLLY   A wheeled platform on which
the camera (and sometimes a
(F,V)   tripod) can be mounted and moved
in order to achieve smooth tracking shots. Also used instead of a
tripod for stationary shots, simply
because it can be moved quickly.
(See TRACK; ZOOM.)

DOMAIN   In magnetic recording tape,
the smallest ferric oxide particle
(E)   that can be considered a separate
"magnet." Defined as 10^{18} molecules
of ferric oxide, which is less than
one billionth of a gram!

DONUT   A radio or TV musical spot
in which the client's theme (musi-
(A)   cal and/or verbal) is stated at the
beginning, and again at the end,
leaving a "hole in the middle" during which music continues, allowing a narrator to announce weekly
specials, specific times of an event,
or other detailed information. Since
the musicians and vocalists are
generally the most expensive in-
gredients in the ad, the donut format allows a client to reuse its
theme regularly, spending only a
small percent of the original
production budget for the addition of weekly specials, for instance. Sometimes donut is used to
refer to the space left for the narrator's specific message—i.e., the

"hole" as defined above. (See WIN-
DOW.)

DOPPLER EFFECT   The apparent
change in frequency of sound
(E)   heard as the sound source moves
toward or away from the listener.
As the source approaches, the
frequency will appear higher
than it actually is. As the source
moves away, the frequency will
sound lower than if heard while
stationary.

DOS   Disk Operating System (pronounced "doss"). A suffix used by
(C)   software and hardware manufacturers to describe the way their
products organize data and package
it for storage. Each manufacturer
has its own operating system, although the acronym DOS is often
mistakenly taken to imply that
there is one universal system.

DOUBLE DENSITY   A data-writing
format that allows twice the nor-
(C)   mal amount of data to be written
onto and read from floppy disks.

DOUBLE-SYSTEM   The normal system by which picture and sound
(F)   for a film are recorded on two
separate strips of material—namely,
film and magnetic tape. Each strip
contains information (sprocket
holes and/or synchronization tones
and pulses) by which it can later
be reproduced in proper sync.
Also, any type of projection in
which picture and sound are
reproduced in sync from separate
sources. For example, any flatbed
editing machine runs film via
double-system projection.

DOUBLING   1. In AFM recording ses-
(U)   sions, the playing by any musician

of a second instrument from the same family (i.e., keyboards, mallet instruments, etc.) as the instrument already played and recorded. The musician must be paid an additional 20% of all wages for the first double and 15% more for each double thereafter. Check the appropriate union contracts for details and payment variables. **2.** Sometimes mistakenly used to mean tracking, the recording on multitrack tape of a second performance of an instrumental or vocal part already recorded once (played or sung by the same performers), usually done to achieve a fuller sound. (*See* TRACKING; ADT.) **3.** Loosely, creating the aural impression of more players and/or singers than were originally recorded by mixing a slightly delayed duplicate of their track(s) in with the direct signal. **4.** A type of harmonic distortion present in some speaker systems that do not reproduce deep bass well. Low notes may be reproduced as one or two octaves above their actual pitch, thus doubling the frequency in the original signal.

DOWNBEAT   The major international trade journal for jazz music, including interviews, reviews of new record releases, technical articles on new instrument developments and recording, etc.
(R)

DOWNLOAD   To receive or print data transmitted by a remote or separate computer. (*See* UPLOAD.)
(C)

DRAW   **1.** An advance paid by an employer to an employee, usually deducted from his earnings in commissions, sales, fees, etc. The exact terms are negotiated on an in-
(B)

dividual basis, especially when the employee's actual earnings may come out less than the draw already paid. **2.** DIRECT READ AFTER WRITE. A compact disc system that allows optical recording of the disc by the user, as well as playback.
(E)

DRIFT   In tape recording, any extended deviation from the nominal tape speed. Can be due to excessive take-up tension, improper capstan motor control, etc.
(E)

DRIVER   Any single loudspeaker—e.g., a woofer, midrange speaker or tweeter.
(E)

DRIVE TIME   To radio as "Prime Time" is to television. The hours of the day when the largest audience is tuned in, and consequently the hours during which the station can charge the most money for air time. It coincides with morning and evening rush hours, when commuters are listening to radio.
(A)

DROP-FRAME   In SMPTE time code devices, an electronic procedure by which 108 frame numbers per hour are discarded from the continuous code of a monochrome program. Since the monochrome frame rate is 30.00 frames per second (fps), while the color rate is 29.97 fps, drop-frame mode correctly adapts the running time of monochrome shows for taping or broadcast on color systems.
(V,I)

DROP-FRAME FLAG   In SMPTE time code, the presence of a "1" in the tenth code bit, which instructs synchronizing or VTR playback equipment to operate in the drop-frame mode.
(V,I)

DROPOUT   In playback of recorded audio or video tape or in an optical storage medium, a sudden loss of sound level or quality due to a local imperfection in the oxide coating or other storage medium. (*See* BURST ERROR.)

(E,V)

DROP SHADOW   A technique used to highlight written titles or make them legible against distracting backgrounds, accomplished with an optical printer or character generator. A second image of the lettering is produced, slightly dislocated from its original position (usually beneath and to the right). By giving the lettering and its "shadow" different colors, a three-dimensional effect is created.

(F,V)

DROP SHADOW.

DRUM BOOTH   An isolation booth or small room primarily intended as an enclosure for drums, traps, or other percussion instruments and their players. Acoustically sealed off from the main studio, and having built-in bass traps that absorb low frequencies, the booth prevents the loud percussive transients from being heard through microphones used to record much softer sounds in the studio, such as acoustic instruments or voices. Some drum booths are not fully enclosed. Obviously, this type does not provide complete isolation, but it does avoid the problems of small-room acoustics (i.e., standing waves and lower midrange resonances) that

(E)

can give enclosed booths an unnatural, "closety" sound.

DRUMSLAVE   A MIDI circuit that converts trigger pulses generated by up to twelve Simmons or other drum pads into MIDI data.

(S)

DRY SOUND   The sound of an instrument or voice, reproduced through a console or from tape, without reverberation or echo. Thus, the direct sound of the instrument or track. Opposite of wet sound.

(E)

DUB   **1.** To make a taped copy of any program source—e.g., a record, compact disc, or another tape. Also, to make a mechanical copy such as an acetate. Also, the copy itself. **2.** To mix together onto a single track all the separate edited sound tracks of a film or television production. **3.** To substitute a foreign language or other replacement for the original dialogue track in a film or television production. Usually done by substituting the new language on the dialogue track of the 35mm three-track mix.

(E,R)

(F,V)

DUBBER   A playback-only machine for sprocketed magnetic film, reproducing one or more tracks of sound. Some dubbers, equipped with dual sets of sprockets, can reproduce more than one size of magnetic film—e.g., 16mm/35mm dubbers.

(F)

DUBBING FEES   In AFM and AFTRA payment schedules for radio and television commercial performances, payments that must be made by the advertiser when a recording originally made for a single spot or campaign is dubbed or copied for use in another spot

(U,A)

or campaign to be aired in the *same* medium. If these spots are made for a different medium, new use fees must be paid, not dubbing fees. (*See* NEW USE.)

DUBBING THEATER   Three facilities in one, all of which work together
(F,V) to produce the final, mixed soundtrack of a film. The machine room houses dubbers and projectors, isolating their mechanical noise from a recording studio or booth in which dialogue, narration, sound effects, or music can be recorded in sync with film projected on a screen visible through a plate glass window. The screen hangs in a theater equipped with a mixing console controlling the sounds played back by all the dubbers, other prerecorded sources, and the sounds made in the recording studio. The theater itself is designed to approximate the acoustics of a cinema in which the film may eventually be shown when released for distribution. Also called mixing studio, re-recording studio, or simply theater.

DUBNER   The brand name of a video
(V) graphics and animation device, digitally based, which allows the drawing, via light-pen and other sources, of two and three dimensional objects on the video screen, and then enables the animator to rotate these in space, zoom in or out of them, and otherwise animate their movement on the video screen. (*See* also PAINTBOX; BOSCH.)

DUCKING   See COMPRESSOR, VOICE-OVER.

DUMMY LOAD   See LOAD RESISTOR.

DUMP EDIT   See EDIT SWITCH.

DUTY CYCLE   1. The percentage of
(S) each complete cycle of a wave during which it is in its positive phase. 2. For any piece of equipment, the maximum recommended time of operation before it needs a rest.

DYNAMIC RANGE   1. The number of
(E) decibels between the levels of the loudest and softest sounds that can be made by an instrument, or between the loudest and softest passages in a live or recorded piece.
(E) 2. In a tape recorder, or with respect to a specific type of recording tape, the decibel level difference between its inherent noise level and the signal level at which 3% total harmonic or third harmonic distortion is present at the output or on tape.

DYNAMIC SIGNAL PROCESSOR   Any
(E) electronic device whose type or degree of operation changes in

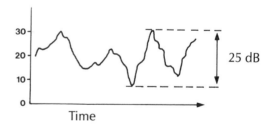

DYNAMIC RANGE (definition 1)

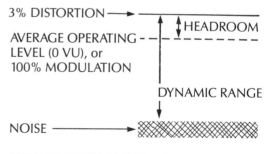

DYNAMIC RANGE (definition 2).

response to level or other characteristic of the input signal—e.g., compressors, noise reduction systems, flangers, etc.

DYNAMICS   The range of volume levels, or their rate of change, within (G)   a piece of music.

DYNE   A standard unit of mechanical force or pressure. The human ear (E)   is sensitive to sounds from 0.0002 dynes/cm^2 (the threshold of hearing) up to about 2 billion dynes/cm^2 (the threshold of pain). The ratio of these extremes, about 10^{14}, corresponds to the 140 decibels between the two thresholds.

- E -

EBU European Broadcast Union. The organization that sets broadcast and videotape standards for most European countries. Analagous to the N.T.S.C. in the United States.
(V)

ECHO One or a few discrete acoustic or electronic repetitions of a sound or audio signal, respectively. Often confused with reverberation.
(E)

ECHO CHAMBER A hard-surfaced room built especially to generate reverberation or echo effects to be recorded on tape, generally in a mixdown. One or more loudspeakers play back sound to be reverbed, and one or more microphones pick up the reverb, channelling it back into the console.
(E)

ECHO PLATE See PLATE REVERBERATION SYSTEM.

ECHO, PRE- or POST- Routing of a signal to an echo-send bus either before (PRE) or after (POST) that signal has passed through the input fader of a console. Also, the echo-send select switch or button by which each of these options is selected.
(E)

ECU Extreme Close-Up. A shot in which an actor's face, or perhaps just the eyes, fill the screen.
(F,V)

EDB Error-Detection Bits. (*See* ERROR BITS.)
(D)

EDGE CUT The border between a foreground being chroma-keyed or overlayed on a background scene. Some combinations of foreground and background image contrasts, backlit foreground objects, bright-over-dark images, etc. unpredicatably cause objectionable edge cuts. (*See* BETACAM.)
(V)

EDGE NUMBERS A set of numbers and letters printed (usually at intervals of one foot) along the edge of most motion picture film stock. Printed in during manufacture, these numbers generally print through from the camera original to the workprint, which facilitates the conforming or matching of the original with the edited workprint. Also called key number or footage number.
(F)

EDGE TRACK 1. In multi-track recording, either of the recorded
(E)

(F)   tracks located along the edge of the tape. **2.** The U.S. standard position of the recorded track on 16mm magnetic film—i.e., along the edge opposite the sprocket holes.

EDIT DECISION LIST (EDL)   The list of SMPTE codes corresponding to all the segments of footage the editor of a videotape production has decided to use in the fine cut. The SMPTE numbers include footage for fades, dissolves, and instructions on other special effects. The EDL, sometimes stored on a computer floppy disk, provides data by which the edit programmer controls an on-line or auto-assembly editing session. (*See* CUE SHEET.) (Illustration next page.)

(V)

EDIT DROID   A computer-based motion picture editing system manufactured by a division of Lucasfilm Corporation. The system allows the editor to deal mostly with picture and sync sound information, electronically marking the exact points in each shot at which he wishes to cut, fade, dissolve, etc. Internally, however, the system keeps accurate logs of the SMPTE time codes of all these edit decisions. It then allows electronic assembly of the sequences for preview. The droid thus offers the speed of CMX editing, while limiting the amount of numerical data with which the user must deal. (*See* SOUND DROID.)

(F)

EDIT PROGRAMMER   A computer used to perform on-line edits and auto-assemblies. The video editor enters the edit decision list, a sequence of SMPTE codes corresponding to the shots and specific frames to be connected. (This list

(V)

may already be written as data on a floppy disk generated during off-line or CMX editing.) The edit programmer then controls the video playback and re-recording decks to produce the edited video master tape according to the editor's instructions. Depending on the sophistication of the specific unit used, the editor may have to perform some special effects manually, on prompts given by the edit programmer. Also called CPU or edit controller.

EDIT SWITCH   On a tape recorder, a switch that engages the play mode but not the take-up motor. Tape is driven past the playback head and reproduced, but then spills off the machine and may be edited out. This process is called a dump edit. On some machines the edit switch merely defeats the tape lifters, allowing hand winding of the tape past the playback head in either direction. The operator can thus find exact editing points along the tape.

(E)

EDITING   The process of cutting and splicing magnetic tape (or motion picture film, magnetic film, etc.) to remove or rearrange certain sections. Also, the process of assembling one continuous take of a recording by cutting together portions from several takes. Generally, the process of reorganizing any sound and/or visual materials for final presentation, even if that process (like videotape editing) requires that the original material be copied onto a second-generation copy.

(E)

ELECTRONIC EDITING: The process of making the audio or video master tape by copying

(V,D)

74

TITLE: NATURAL WONDERS, R. 03
FC MODE: NON-DROP FRAME

1	2	3	4	5	6	7	8	9
028	BL	AA/V	C		00:00:00:00	00:00:00:00	00:59:00:00	00:59:00:00
028	004	AA/V	D	010	16:32:21:13	16:38:24:28	00:59:00:00	00:59:03:15
019	004	V	C		16:30:44:22	16:30:48:22	00:59:03:15	00:59:07:15
005	071	A	C		00:10:12:26	00:10:15:00	00:59:03:15	00:59:10:24
006	071	A	C		00:10:15:04	00:10:19:07	00:59:10:22	00:59:14:25
018	098	A2/V	C		00:07:57:26	00:08:01:18	00:59:07:15	00:59:12:17
020	098	V	C		00:07:58:16	00:07:58:16	00:59:09:04	00:59:09:04
020	004	V	D	030	16:23:33:19	16:23:37:02	00:59:09:04	00:59:12:17
007	071	A2	C		00:10:19:11	00:10:20:24	00:59:14:21	00:59:16:04
021	004	V	C	015	16:23:36:03	16:23:36:03	00:59:11:18	00:59:11:18
021	098	V	D	015	00:03:12:01	00:03:16:01	00:59:11:18	00:59:15:18
008	071	A	C		00:10:20:26	00:10:22:19	00:59:16:04	00:59:17:27

EDIT DECISION LIST. The numbered columns of data represent: 1). Shot-, cut-, or event-number of its type, e.g., audio-only cuts, etc.; 2). Source or reel-number of the original footage, video and/or audio; 3). The track(s) onto which the new material will be recorded; (A) = audio 1, (A2) = audio 2, (V) = video, etc.; 4). The playback machine on which the shot should be located; 5). The length of an effect in video frames: fade, dissolve, etc.; 6,7). SMPTE code locations of the beginning and end of the source shot to be copied onto the edited video master. Called source-in and source-out points; 8,9). SMPTE code locations on the master at which recording will begin and end. Called record-in and record-out points.

segments from various takes of the original tapes or footage onto a second generation copy. Start and end points of these segments are designated by the corresponding SMPTE code numbers. The assembly can be done manually or automatically, depending on the equipment available. (*See* ASSEMBLY-EDIT; ON-LINE/OFF-LINE EDITING; EDIT PROGRAMMER.)

(E,F)   RAZOR BLADE EDITING: The process of physically cutting pieces of magnetic tape or motion picture film with a razor blade (or other precision cutting device such as a guillotine splicer for film), and splicing these segments together with splicing tape.

EDITING BLOCK   A cast metal block with a channel that holds magnetic
(E,F)   tape firmly and in a straight line. Diagonal slits through this channel allow a razor blade to make precisely angled cuts in pieces of tape, so that two separate pieces aligned in the channel may be spliced together. The resulting splice, if properly made, will be inaudible as it passes over the playback head of the recorder.

EDITOR   The person who assembles film or video shots into sequence,
(F,V)   following the director's and the script's recommendations, but often changing the specified order, intercutting, and adjusting the length of each shot to achieve the best possible dramatic effect.

EDITORIAL SYNC   Alignment of picture and sound tracks such that
(F)   their start marks are equal numbers of frames prior to the first frames of picture and sound,

respectively. (*See* PROJECTION SYNC.)

EDL   See EDIT DECISION LIST.

EFFECT SEND, POST   A signal routing by which a signal is sent to an
(E)   auxiliary mixing bus after it has passed through the main fader of the input module. Thus, the signal sent is subject to all the volume changes made at the fader.

EFFECT SEND, PRE   A signal routing by which a signal is sent to an
(E)   auxiliary mixing bus before it has passed through the main fader of the console module. Thus, the signal goes to the auxiliary bus at full level, without level changes introduced by the fader.

EFFECTIVE RATING POINTS   See ERP.

EFFECTS RETURN   The signal path and associated controls that affect a signal returned to the console from outboard processing equipment.

EFFECTS TRACK   1. An edited track of magnetic film containing sounds
(F,V)   other than dialogue or music. There can be many effects tracks prepared for a film mix. In videotape productions whose sound is assembled on a multi-track tape, the track or tracks on which sound effects are recorded. (*See* EFX.) **2.** In the 35mm three-track mix of a motion picture, the recorded track that contains sounds mixed from all the effects tracks as defined in **1.**

EFFICIENCY   The numerical ratio of output power to input power in an
(E)   audio device, particularly a speaker.

A 20% efficiency rating indicates, for example, that 100 electric watts input to a speaker will produce 20 watts of acoustic power. The remaining 80 watts of electric power is dissipated as heat in the voice coil and nearby parts. The overall efficiency of a speaker system depends on the drivers selected and the design of crossover network and the enclosure or baffle. Most ratings are between range 2% (for some acoustic suspension systems) and 25% for a few horn loaded systems.

EFM   EIGHT TO FOURTEEN BIT
(D)   MODULATION. A data-formatting process used on compact discs. Groups of eight data bits are regrouped into fourteen bit blocks by an EFM modulator during cutting of the CD master, permitting about 25% greater data density to be laser-inscribed on the disc and allowing easier error recognition. An EFM demodulator in the CD player reconverts the data to its original format.

EFX   Short for Effects Track or Ef-
(F,V)   fects.

ELECTRET   A principle in electronics
(E)   by which the plate and diaphragm of some condenser microphones are permanently charged during manufacture, producing a capacitance between them that varies as sound waves cause the diaphragm to vibrate. Electret capsules are generally used in lavalier and other microphones that must be very small or concealed. (*See* MICROPHONE, by mode of operation.)

**ELECTRONIC INDUSTRIES ASSOCIA-
(B)   TION, CONSUMER DIVI-
SION**   The association that

represents major manufacturers of consumer electronics, proposes and establishes technical standards (sometimes in cooperation with the AES and other associations), deals with legislators on issues of foreign competition and trade, and monitors the health of the consumer electronics industry as a whole.

**ELECTRONIC NEWS GATHER-
ING**   See ENG.

ELECTRONIC PUBLISHING   Liter-
(P,B)   ally, publishing without paper. Providing and/or selling information (books, magazines, newspapers, etc.) via any of the computer-based media. Loosely, this includes the sale of floppy disks, CD-ROM and CD-I formats (with digitally encoded music, words, and real-time video images on a single compact disc), or access to any data base the user may receive by computer modem (telephone lines), satellite-to-dish broadcast, ROM-chip, etc.

**EMPLOYEE PENSION AND WEL-
FARE FUND**   See EPW.

EMULSION   The light-sensitive coat-
(F)   ing on unexposed motion picture film, or the same coating after processing, with the negative or reversal (positive) image clearly visible.

ENCODE   1. The whole process of
(D)   converting the already sampled, numerical voltage of the analog input into binary numbers and assembling these with any location and error-related data generated elsewhere into complete digital
(E)   words, usually of 16 bits. **2.** The application of any type of processing to a signal before recording,

which will later be removed by application of precisely opposite processing during playback. Most noise reduction systems, which compand the signal, are good examples of the encoding and decoding process. (*See* DECODE; COMPLEMENTARY PROCESSING.)

END OF FILE   See EOF.

END OF TRANSMISSION   See EOT.

ENERGY CONVERSION   Transformation of one type of energy into another—e.g., electric to acoustic, mechanical to electric, etc. The essential function of all transducers.
(E)

ENERGY DISTRIBUTION CURVE   A graph of energy with respect to another variable, generally frequency. Such curves are often plotted for specific sound sources—e.g., a human voice, piano, drum, etc. Similar to an RTA plot, but measuring the acoustic power present in each range rather than the voltage present in that range within a complex signal. (*See* REAL-TIME ANALYSIS.)
(E)

ENERGY TRANSFER   The passage of energy from a source to a transducer or load, in which the energy is used and/or converted to another form.
(E)

ENG   Electronic News Gathering. Videotaping of events on location. Also, the type of equipment normally used for such news gathering, generally 3/4″ U-matic or Betacam (not home Betamax) formats. Portable 1″ equipment is too expensive for most ENG work.
(V)

ENGINEER   The studio technician responsible for evaluation and
(E)

proper use of the recording environment and making the musicians comfortable in it. He selects and operates the recording equipment, executes the final mix, and prepares the tape for disc-mastering or other types of reproduction.

ENTER   To provide or input data to any computer-controlled device. One may enter SMPTE codes into an edit programmer, prices into a spreadsheet, or simply enter one's name or user number for computer access.
(C,V,G)

ENVELOPE   If the amplitude vs. time graph of a musical sound is plotted, the envelope of the sound is the overall shape of this graph. More exactly, the curve and its reflection that enclose the waveforms comprising a sound. A sound's envelope includes its attack, decay, sustain, and release. (*See* ADSR.) (Illustration next page.)
(S,E)

ENVELOPE FOLLOWER   A device that generates a DC output voltage proportional to the contours of the envelope of an audio input signal. (*See* CONTROL VOLTAGE.)
(S)

ENVELOPE GENERATOR   A device that produces a control voltage that varies with time according to the user's specifications. This voltage, applied to each note played on a synthesizer, gives notes the desired envelope. Also called a contour generator. (*See* CONTROLLER.)
(S)

EOF   End Of File. A computer prompt indicating that there is no more data in the program or data file that has been in use.
(C)

EOT   End Of Transmission. A computer prompt indicating that the computer has finished transmitting
(C)

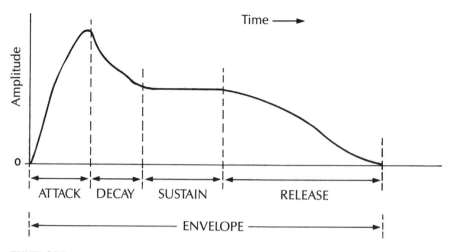

Time ⟶

Amplitude

0

ATTACK   DECAY   SUSTAIN   RELEASE

ENVELOPE

ENVELOPE.

the file or data as previously instructed.

EP

(R)

(R,F,V)

1. Extended Play. A type of 7″ phonograph record, usually played at 33 1/3 rpm, allowing two songs to be cut on each side (for a total time of up to 7 minutes). Also, a 10″ or standard 12″ album with between three and seven songs on it—i.e., less than a full album of songs. EPs are intended to sell at less than album prices, and are a way of establishing new artists without requiring record buyers to pay full LP prices. **2.** Executive Producer.

EPW

(U)

Employee Pension and Welfare Fund. A retirement fund maintained by the AFM for its members. All employers of union musicians are required to contribute to the fund, the percentage or amount varying according to the type and length of employment. In recording sessions for phono record master tapes, for instance, the mandatory EPW payment equals 10% of all wages, including doubling, overtime, etc.

AFTRA maintains a similar EPW fund.

EQUALIZATION ("EQ")

(E)

The process by which one electronically modifies the frequency response of an audio system, and thereby the relative frequency content or energy distribution curve of an audio signal passing through it.

(E)

COMPOSITE EQUALIZATION: The overall frequency response modification produced when a signal passes through more than one equalizing circuit in the same device, or through several equalizers in series.

(E)

RECORD- or PLAYBACK-EQUALIZATION: In tape recording, the internal and complimentary alteration of the frequency response of input signals prior to recording and output signals after playback. By boosting highs prior to record and reducing them after playback, some tape noise is eliminated. In addition, the equalization curve can compensate for nonlinear response of the specific type of recording tape in use. The NAB, C.C.I.R., and I.E.S. established standard record/playback curves used in the United States, Europe and elsewhere.

(E)   ROOM EQUALIZATION: The alteration of the frequency response of signals that will be sent to speakers or monitors, done in order to compensate for resonances or other response problems inherent in the room itself. These problems are generally identified by sending pink noise to the speakers, then adjusting the frequency response of the resulting sound that arrives at the listening position. Real-time analysis and other lab tests are often tempered by human judgment in setting room EQs.

EQUALIZER   Any signal processing device used to change the frequency response, relative frequency content, or spectrum of signals passing through it. Equalizers are sometimes mistakenly called filters. Filters may be used in equalizer circuits, but only the passive equalizer can properly be called a filter, since it can only detract from the input signal.

(E)   ACTIVE EQUALIZER: An equalizer that employs active electronic components such as transistors or ICs in its processing circuit(s). A pre-amplifying circuit generally follows each stage of actual equalization, boosting the signal level to restore unity gain. If the unit allows overall adjustment of output level, the engineer can A-B the flat and equalized signal.

(E)   GRAPHIC EQUALIZER: An equalizer whose controls are a set of sliding pots, usually arranged in a row, and each of which adjusts the amount of boost or cut in a specified band of the input signal's overall frequency content. The positions of all the controls gives a "graphic" representation of the frequency response curve that is applied to any input signal.

(E)   PARAMETRIC EQUALIZER: An equalizer in which the center of the frequency band that each boost/cut control affects can be continuously varied over a wide range. The amount of boost or cut for each band is separately adjustable. Sometimes the bandwidth that each boost/cut control affects can also be varied by a second control. The bandwidth parameter is often erroneously called Q. (Illustration next page.)

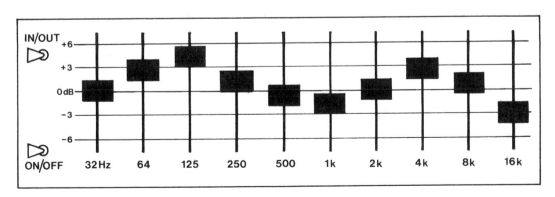

GRAPHIC EQUALIZER (10 band).

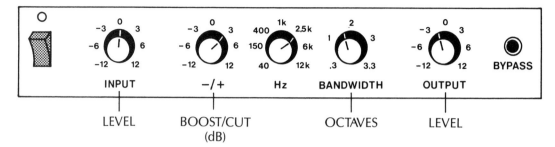

PARAMETRIC EQUALIZER (single band).

(E)   PASSIVE EQUALIZER: An equalizer that employs only passive electronic components—i.e., resistors, capacitors, and/or inductors. Since these components consume some of the signal internally, passive equalizers can only cut each operating band. The output signal is thus lower in level than the input.

(E)   SHELVING EQUALIZER: An equalizer that raises or lowers frequencies beyond its turnover frequency by a fixed and continuous amount. A shelf boost of 6 dB above 5 kHz will thus increase all frequencies in the signal above 5 kHz by dB.

EQUAL LOUDNESS CONTOURS   A
(E)   set of superimposed graphs plotting the human ear's sensitivity to sound vs. frequency, each graph representing this phenomenon at a different loudness level. Also called the Fletcher-Munson curves, after the scientists who derived them. A new version, the Robinson-Dadson curves, is gaining favor.

EQUITY   Properly, Actors Equity As-
(U)   sociation. 1. The professional association that represents the interests of actors and directors in theat-
(B)   rical production. 2. Ownership, partial or total, in a company, busi-

ness venture, or any piece of real or intangible property—e.g., a house or a song's copyright.

ERASE OSCILLATOR   A very high
(E)   frequency oscillator built into a tape recorder to supply current to the erase head. In most machines, the same oscillator supplies the bias and erase frequency. Erase frequencies range from 150 kHz to 300 kHz.

ERPS   Effective Rating Points. A
(A)   numerical system used for measuring the effectiveness that repeated broadcasts of spots have in causing listeners or viewers to buy products. In general, spots with music require fewer broadcasts to achieve higher point values. A certain minimum number of erps will achieve "audience awareness breakthrough" for the product: continued broadcast will eventually cause "audience saturation," which negates the values of the entire campaign. The proper media budget should insure high awareness but avoid saturation.

**ERROR BITS (EBs) (or ERROR-DETEC-
TION BITS, EDBs)**   Any data
(D)   added to the audio samples prior to recording them on tape, and whose purpose is to allow the

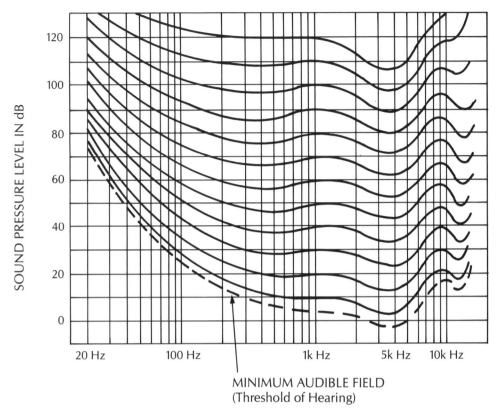

EQUAL LOUDNESS CONTOURS (Robinson Dadson).

detection (and subsequent concealment or correction) of errors during playback. CCRC remainders,
the repetitive writing of samples
via interleaving, and parity bits are
all examples of EBs or EDBs. (*See*
ERROR DETECTION (illustration).)

ERROR CONCEALMENT   In digital
(D)   playback, the short-term masking
of portions of the audio output for
which data is missing or incorrectly
read from the tape. Data from adjacent blocks is used to construct
decoded analog output which, in
effect, performs a crossfade between the last valid data before the
defect and the next valid data immediately following it. (*See* ER-

ROR CORRECTION; INTER-
POLATION.)

ERROR CORRECTION   In digital
playback: 1. The reconstruction of
(D)   valid data to replace missing or
damaged samples or data blocks,
drawing upon redundant data located elsewhere on the tape. Since
it takes a small but finite amount
of time to detect and correct errors, the process mandates the introduction of a buffer memory
between the playback head and
the D-A converter. 2. Loosely used
to designate error concealment.
(*See* INTERPOLATION.)

ERROR DETECTION   In digital
(D)   playback, the use of error bits and

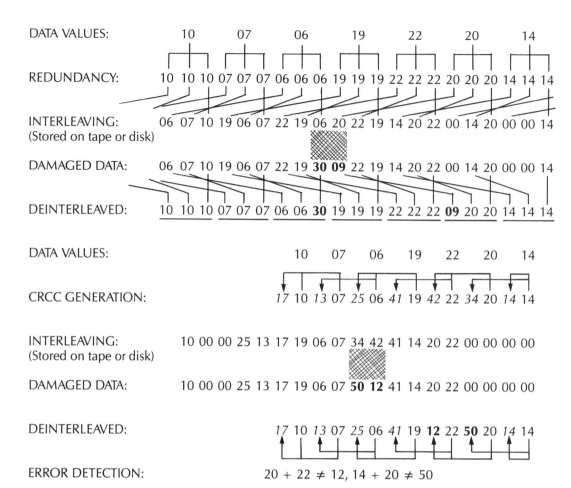

ERROR DETECTION. (A) Redundancy: The data values of each sample are made redundant by repetition. Since data tends to be lost, or damaged, in bursts, the duplicate values are *interleaved* according to a pre-determined scheme before storage. If damage occurs, it is unlikely to destroy all duplicates of the sample value. Upon de-interleaving, errors become apparent and can be corrected by throwing out the values which do not match within the group of duplicates; (B) Cyclic redundancy check code (CRCC): Here, additional values (cyclic redundancy check words) are generated by adding together each pair of sample values. Errors are detected on retrieval when the sums do not match. Because each sample value contributed to two CRC words, it is possible to derive the proper values, correcting the errors.

data derived from the audio samples to check the completeness and accuracy of the audio data before passing it on for D-A conversion. (*See* PARITY CHECKING; CYCLIC REDUNDANCY CHECKING CODE; INTERLEAVING.)

ERROR MESSAGE   A message that tells a computer user he has done something wrong in formatting or
(C)

writing a command, or in submitting data.

ERROR PROTECTION   All the circuits and data handling procedures that together accomplish error detection, concealment, and/or correction functions in any digital recording and playback format.
(D)

ERROR SIGNAL   A voltage applied to a circuit in order to restore its operation to some desired standard
(E,I)

or condition. For example, a BTX or Q-LOCK synchronizing device, upon detecting a difference in time codes between master and slave, applies an error signal to the slave, the voltage of which is proportional to the amount of correction needed to restore proper sync.

ESTABLISHING SHOT   A wide-angle shot showing the entire location in which a scene will occur, so that the viewer will understand where the respective characters are located in upcoming close-ups, etc.
(F,V)

ETHNOGRAPHICS   Characteristics of a target market having to do with family nationality and other ethnic considerations. (*See* DEMOGRAPHICS.)
(A)

EUROPEAN BROADCAST UNION See EBU.

EXCITER   Short for Aphex Aural Exciter.
(E)

EXECUTIVE PRODUCER (EP)   The financial backer of a production, or the person who secures backing from investors, by the pre-sale of rights, or from any other source. The EP is ultimately the boss. He literally employs all other participants in the production, including the producer and the director.
(R,F,V)

EXECUTORY PROVISION   In a contract, an obligation or requirement that extends beyond the termination of the contract itself. For example, a record company must continue to calculate and pay royalties for an album to the artist, even after that artist's contract has expired and he has signed with another label.
(B)

EXPANDER   An amplifier whose gain (a) is unity for signals below a specified threshold, then increases for higher input signal levels, or (b) is unity for signals above a designated threshold, then decreases for input signals below that threshold. Most professional units employ the second design. Noise gates are good examples of the b-type expander.
(E)

EXPANSION RATIO   The absolute value of the ratio of decibels by which the output level of an expander changes in response to a 1 dB change in input level beyond the threshold. In many units this ratio can be adjusted by the engineer. For example in EXPANDER(b), if the threshold is set at −2 dBm and the expansion ratio is 2:1, an incoming signal at −6 dBm would be output at −10 dBm. For every dB in signal level below the threshold, the output will be reduced by 2 dB.
(E)

EXPANSION, PEAK   The adjustment of an expander's threshold so that most program material passes through unaffected, but peaks or transients are heavily expanded. Used to restore peaks to program material that has been overly compressed. (See EXPANDER (a).)
(E)

EXPERT SYSTEM   A complex software package able to analyze situations and make recommendations by applying the tricks of the trade, rules of thumb, and some of the intuitive judgments made by experts in the field for which it is designed.
(C)

EXPLOITATION OF SONGS   The process of making money from songs by having them used in
(P)

royalty-earning or fee-earning situations. Widespread exploitation is the primary goal of publishers, and in larger companies is the professional manager's job.

EXPONENT   A letter or numerical superscript written above and to the right of a number, designating the power to which that number is raised. For example, 4^3 designates the third power of 4, which equals $4 \times 4 \times 4$, which in turn equals 64.

(E)

Similarly, 12^n designates the n'th power of 12.

EXTENDED PLAY   See EP.

EXTINCTION FREQUENCY   In magnetic recording, the high frequency beyond which significant cancellation occurs because its wavelength on tape (at the specified tape speed) approaches the width of the head gap.

(E)

EXTREME CLOSE-UP.   See ECU.

- F -

FABRICATION The process of gluing the printed album cover, or slick, onto a large sheet of cardboard, then folding and gluing the cardboard into the finished album jacket. This is generally done at the record pressing plant, not by the printer who makes the slick itself.
(R)

FADE 1. Short for FADE OUT or FADE IN. Optical effects in which a shot (film or video) is printed with exposure increasing from (FADE IN) or decreasing to (FADE OUT) blackness. (*See* DISSOLVE.) 2. In an audio program or signal, the increase in level from (FADE IN) or decrease of level to (FADE OUT) total silence. Fade outs are used to end many album cuts and singles when the arrangement itself has no definite ending.
(F,V)
(E)

FADER An adjustable level or "volume" control, usually linear in design and operation. Sometimes called a mixer, especially in England and Europe. Functionally, a potentiometer.
(E)

MASTER FADER: A single fader that controls the level of all the tracks being recorded or mixed.
(E)

FAIRLIGHT A brand of highly sophisticated synthesizer that allows creation and manipulation of waveshapes by direct interaction with a video monitor display, in addition to other standard digital synthesis techniques. Fairlights can be purchased with a complete tapeless recording system using hard disks for mass storage.
(E,D)

FAIR USE (or FAIR REPRODUCTION) Any type of duplication or reproduction of a copyrighted composition or recording that, in the eyes of the courts. Is not an infringement of the rights held by the copyright owner, and for which the user is not required to pay the copyright owner royalties or fees. "Fairness" is decided based on the nature of the work and the specific use or reproduction, the amount or percentage of the whole work used, and the effect the use may have on the future earning power
(P,R)

of the original work. Private users, educational institutions, libraries, etc. have separate limits placed on their fair use rights.

FEATURED   1. One of the four performance categories used to determine the amount of broadcast royalties or the fee due to the copyright holder of a song or recorded performance. A featured use earns the highest payment, since the song or recording will be the main attraction of that portion of the show—played at full volume, with no announcer or dialogue over it. (*See* USE WEIGHT.) **2.** One of the performance categories that determines broadcast royalties and residuals payable to AFTRA singers.

(P,R)

(A,U)

FEATURE MULTIPLIER   One of the factors used by ASCAP in determining how many performance credits are ascribed to a specific broadcast performance of a composition. The multiplier, always more than 1.0, gives extra credit for people hearing the song in places that are not surveyed, such as restaurants, stores, etc. All this translates into the amount that will be paid to the composer and publisher for that performance. (*See* PERFORMANCE CREDIT.)

(P,A)

FEDERAL I.D. NUMBER   A number assigned by the I.R.S. to a business or corporation. It is used like a social security number, to identify the business in all tax and regulatory transactions. If the business is a sole proprietorship or general partnership, the social security number is used as a federal I.D. number.

(B)

FEDERAL TRADE COMMISSION (F.T.C.)   The government organization that regulates trade within the United States. For the music industry, the F.T.C.'s most important functions are in monitoring, regulating, and arbitrating differences among unions such as the AFM, AFTRA, AGMA, SAG, etc. The F.T.C. also oversees fair collections and distributions of royalties by the performing rights societies such as ASCAP and BMI, and of mechanical and synchronization royalties by Harry Fox Agency, etc. Lately, the F.T.C. has also acted with the F.B.I. on the ever-growing problem of tape and record piracy—i.e., illegally made copies of popular albums, tapes, and videos.

(B)

FEED   In signal routing, an output from one device that is sent or "fed" into another.

(E)

FEEDBACK   1. The return of part of the output signal of a system into its own input. This may happen acoustically, where the amplified sound in a room returns into a microphone that is the source of the amplified sound itself, or electronically by feeding some of the output signal of a device back into the input. In a digital delay, feedback is used to create repeating delays. Also called regeneration. (*See* FEEDBACK, ACOUSTIC.) **2.** Information supplied by disc jockeys and their record pools to the record labels that supply them with promotional copies of records (and music videos). Each "jock" in a pool will rate new releases via standard feedback forms, giving personal and audience

(E)

(R)

reactions, and commenting on the quality of the mix, pressing, etc.

(E)   ACOUSTIC FEEDBACK: An annoying howl or squeal produced when feedback occurs between a speaker and a microphone whose output is being amplified through that speaker. The howl is caused when certain frequencies are re-amplified over and over, the specific frequencies depending on the acoustics of the room, the placement of the mic and speakers, and other acoustic factors. Feedback can also occur at lower frequencies, producing a loud rumbling or single bass tones. Because the feedback increases in volume each time it passes through the system, it can eventually damage the amplifier or speakers if not controlled.

FEET/FRAMES   Footage numbers, written with a colon between them. (F,V)   For example, 120:15 indicates a point in the film 120 feet and 15 frames after the starting point of 0:00. There are 16 frames per foot of 35mm film, and 40 frames per foot of 16mm film. (*See* FOOTAGE COUNTER; FRAME RATE.)

FERRIC OXIDE   Actually gamma ferric oxide, the chemical name for (E)   the magnetic material that is the "active" ingredient in recording tape. There are many types of iron oxide. Gamma ferric oxide takes magnetic charges smoothly, is easily processed into the microscopic powder that becomes the domains on tape, and behaves well when mixed with the binders that will ultimately affix it to the base. (*See* MAGNETIC RECORDING TAPE (illustration).)

FIDUCIARY   1. A person or company to whom another party has en-(B)   trusted the management of some assets, resources, or things of value. The fiduciary is responsible for the well-being of anything entrusted to him. Stock brokers, bankers, and trustees are fiduciaries. **2.** Describing the situation in which a professional person acts instead of or on behalf of another person whom he represents. Lawyers and agents have fiduciary relationships with their clients.

FIELD   In NTSC television broadcast and videotape recording, a sub-(V)   group of visual data consisting of either the odd- or even-numbered lines of any frame. Each field is displayed separately for 1/60 second within the total frame duration of 1/30 second. For each frame, field number one contains lines #1, 3, 5,...525; field number two contains lines #2, 4, 6,...524. PAL television broadcasts use an analogous scheme, but applied to a different frame rate and number of lines per frame.

FILE   A collection of data given a "name" by the user so that it can (C)   easily be stored or recalled. In console automation, for instance, the data for each trial mix is stored as a separate file on floppy disk or other medium.

FILE TYPE   A suffix following a file name that tells the computer what (C)   sort of data that file contains. Generally separated from the file name by a period. Examples: FILE.DOC means the file is a text document, FILE.BAS means the file is a program written in the BASIC lan-

---

guage, FILE.COM means the file is a program containing commands. This type is known as a BINARY FILE, since it is written internally in machine language, not as the text the user sees on-screen.

FILM CHAIN   A device consisting of a motion picture projector and video camera, used to copy films onto videotape or to broadcast them directly. To adapt the 24 frames per second U.S. motion picture frame-rate to the 30 frames per second NTSC video frame-rate, some film chains use a projector with a five-bladed shutter, which shows each frame of film five times onto the vidicon tube of the video camera. The resulting 120 film images per second are regrouped four-at-a-time into 30 video images per second.
(F,V)

FILM STOCK   Unexposed motion picture film as supplied by the manufacturer. Also called STOCK or RAW STOCK. (*See* NEGATIVE; REVERSAL FILM.)
(F)

FILTER   An equalizer that attenuates designated frequencies or bands. These bands may be very narrow or quite wide.
(E)

BANDPASS FILTER: An equalizer that attenuates frequencies above and below a designated band. A low-pass filter thus allows low frequencies but not high frequencies to pass through.

COMB FILTER: A filter that, through phasing cancellation, notches out a series of different frequencies in an incoming signal. This is the principle by which flanging is achieved.

CUT-OFF FILTER: An equalizer that sharply attenuates all frequencies that are above or below a designated limit.

DYNAMIC FILTER: An equalizer whose operating bandwidth changes automatically in response to changes in program level, frequency content, or some other parameter.

LOW-FREQUENCY (or HIGH-FREQUENCY) SHELVING: An equalizer that attenuates frequencies uniformly below or above the designated turnover frequency, respectively.

NOTCH FILTER: A filter that severely attenuates a very narrow band of frequencies. Often used to eliminate steep resonances in an instruments' response, or to get rid of motor hums, feedback, room resonances, and other unwanted sounds that may have been present when a signal was recorded.

PROXIMITY EFFECT FILTER: A passive filter built into some cardioid microphones to roll-off low frequencies that are abnormally accentuated when the microphone is used very close to the singer or instrument.

SCRAPE-FLUTTER FILTER: In tape transports, a smooth or low-friction non-magnetic, low-mass flywheel installed in the tape path in order to minimize the pressure with which the tape meets guides, rollers, or other potential sources of scrape-flutter.

TELEPHONE FILTER: A band pass equalizer used to simulate sound as heard through a telephone. Only frequencies between 200 Hz and 2.5 kHz are allowed to pass through.

FINAL CUT   The right to approve the completed editing done to a motion picture or videotape produc-
(F,V)

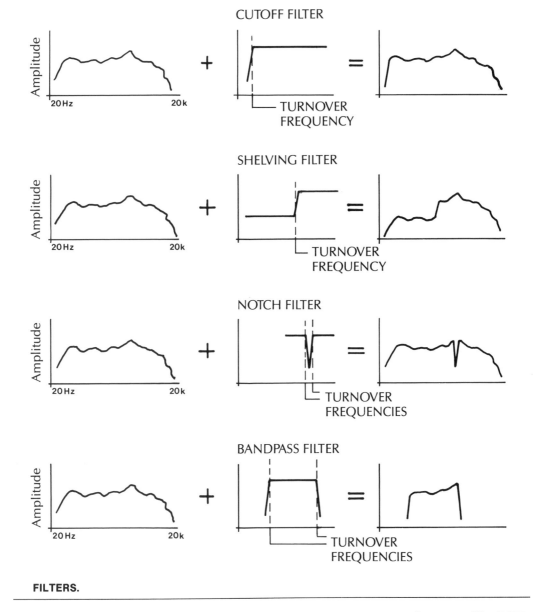

CUTOFF FILTER

SHELVING FILTER

NOTCH FILTER

BANDPASS FILTER

FILTERS.

tion. If the executive director has "final cut," he can approve the editing or order it to be reworked, even hiring new editors if he feels that the original editors cannot improve on the present version.

FINANCING   The means by which
(B)   money is acquired in order to undertake a specific project, or to set up an ongoing business. (*See* BORROWING MONEY.)

FINDING   The legal opinion handed
(B)   down by a judge or court of law, or the verdict of a jury.

FINE CUT   A stage in the editing of a
(F,V)   film or video production at which the workprint (or EDL) is com-

pleted, denoting that the production is ready for final cut approval by the producer, director, or backer. (*See* ROUGH CUT; ASSEMBLY.)

FIRST-CALL MUSICIAN (or SINGER)
(U)   The performer whom a contractor prefers to hire to play a specific instrument or sing a specific part (soprano, alto, tenor, bass, etc) when a producer calls for such a performance.

FISHPOLE   A lightweight pole on
(F,V)   which a microphone can be suspended over the action being filmed or videotaped. Often used in confined spaces or whenever a standard boom would be inconvenient.

FIXED COPY   With reference to a
(P,R)   copyrighted work, a relatively permanent copy or recording that may be read, performed, or reproduced in such a way as to uniquely specify the nature and contents of the copyrighted material.

FIXED COSTS   In a business, those
(B)   expense categories that remain basically the same regardless of how few or how many products are sold. For example, rent, heat, phones, utilities, salaries. However, it takes more electricity to run record presses longer, so there is no sharp line dividing fixed and semi-variable costs. (*See* VARIABLE COSTS.)

FLANGE   The round metal sides of a
(E)   tape reel that keep the tape aligned as it winds onto the hub.

FLANGING   The characteristic sound
(E)   created by mixing a direct signal with the same signal, slightly delayed by a continuously varying amount of time. As the delay time varies, certain frequencies in the signal are reinforced or completely phased out. These frequencies travel up or down throughout the entire spectrum as the delay time varies, "combing" the spectrum. Originally discovered when playing two copies of the same tape synchronized on separate decks, then manually applying drag to the flanges of one tape reel or the other so that a small delay is introduced between the two identical programs. Flanging is one of a number of effects called "comb filters." (*See* DELAY, DIGITAL; DEPTH.)

FLAT   1. Unequalized, uncompressed,
(E)   and otherwise unprocessed, describing a signal from any source, mic, instrument, or tape playback. (*See* FREQUENCY RESPONSE; COL-
(F,V)   ORATION.) 2. A piece of scenery made for a film or video set, representing a three-dimensional object such as a building by a two-dimensional or "flat" look-alike—e.g., a painting.

FLATBED EDITING MACHINE   A
(F)   type of film editing machine on which the spools of workprint and magnetic film lie horizontally on flanges, usually just wound on cores. The film feeds left to right, passing through projection and playback heads, then winding onto take-up cores mounted on other flanges. Flatbed machines are quieter and quicker to work on than the conventional vertical Movieola. In addition, because flatbed machines use a prism rather than an intermittent movement for

projection, flatbed machines are much gentler on workprint.

FLAT WIND   (E)   To employ a slower-than-normal fast forward or rewind mode on a tape transport in order to wind the tape smoothly and evenly onto the reel or hub, usually for storage. Flat winding prevents edge curling and other types of deformation damage.

FLETCHER-MUNSON CURVES   (E)   Equal loudness contours, which show the volume (or SPL in decibels) of a sound the ear perceives as being of equal loudness as the frequency of the sound increases for 20 Hz to 20 kHz. Since the ear is most sensitive at around 3 kHz, it takes a much higher volume of tones at low and high frequencies before the ear perceives them as being "equal" in volume to a 3 kHz tone. (*See* EQUAL LOUDNESS CONTOURS (illustration); ROBINSON-DADSON CURVES.)

FLOATER   (B,G)   A kind of insurance policy issued to cover loss of or damage to purchased or rented equipment, etc. Floaters are usually added to a producer's blanket policy at his request to protect him against such disasters on a single production or shoot, or for a limited period of time. One might secure a two-month, $20,000 camera floater.

FLOOR   (E)   In a noise gate, the amount of attenuation applied to an input signal whenever it is below the threshold level. For example, in a gate whose threshold is set to −10 dBm and whose floor is set to −30 dB, 30 dB of attenuation is applied whenever the incoming signal drops below −10 dBm.

FLOPPY DISK   (C)   A thin, flexible disk coated with magnetic oxide, and used as a permanent storage medium for data and/or programs. Various computers require different sized floppies—either 8″, 5 1/4″, or 3 1/2″ in diameter. Of these, the 5 1/4″ floppy is the current favorite. Newer disk drives are capable of writing double-density data on both sides of the floppy, quadrupling its original capacity.

FLOW CHART   (E)   In recording consoles, a functional "roadmap" of all the signal paths that are either factory-wired or that can be selected by the engineer via switches, channel-send matrices, and the like, or by rerouting in the patch bay.

FLUTTER   (E)   In tape recorders, a rapid fluctuation (or "warbling") in musical pitch caused by fluctuations in tape speed. These in turn are caused by dirt or oxide deposited on the capstan or guides, a flattened or deformed capstan idler, or any irregularity in the tape path. Flutter can actually appear as a part of the program on tape if the recorder had mechanical problems during record, or heard only in the playback. If the tape sounds all right on a second machine, the first playback machine needs maintenance, but the tape itself is flutter-free. Measured and specified in average percentage variation from nominal tape speed, flutter should never exceed 0.05% in professional applications. (See WOW.)
(E)   SCRAPE-FLUTTER: Any flutter caused by mechanical drag or other friction between recording tape and guides, rollers, or tape heads. Residue from splicing tape,

---

oxide build-up, and misalignment of guides are among the major scrape-flutter sources.

FLUX   Lines of force surrounding a
(E)   magnet.

FLUX DENSITY   In measuring the
(E)   strength of a magnetic field at a particular location, the number of lines of force per unit area in a plane perpendicular to the direction of the lines. The standard unit in tape recording is the nanoweber per meter, which equals one billionth of a weber.

FLUXIVITY   The numerical measure of maximum flux density a specific
(E)   type of recording tape can hold. Usually specified in nanowebers per unit of track width.

(E)   REFERENCE FLUXIVITY: A standardized amount of flux, specified in nanowebers per meter, which is laboratory-recorded on a test tape at various frequencies. Such tapes are used to calibrate tape recorder 0 dBVU playback levels. (*See* TEST TAPE.)

FLYER   Usually a single-page, small poster-like announcement circu-
(R)   lated by hand to promote a live appearance or perhaps a locally released record.

FLY IN   1. To mix sounds from a non-
(A,V,E)   sync source into the live sound for a television show, or into the mix for a videotape production or spot. One may fly in a narrator, footsteps, etc. 2. To record sections from one or more tracks of a multi-track tape onto a second recorder (generally a two-track), then copy them back onto the multi-track in another section of the performance.

One might take the background vocals from the second chorus of a song and "fly them into" the first chorus, where none was recorded originally. Short fly-ins can be done without SMPTE sync, although it usually takes a few trys to get the timing correct between the machines.

FM   Frequency Modulation.
(E,S)

FM SYNTHESIS   A process of signal production in which the frequency
(S)   of a carrier wave is modulated by the amplitude of an audio signal, in turn generated in response to control voltages from a keyboard, etc.

FOCUS GROUP EXPOSURE   Previewing a radio or TV spot for a small
(A)   segment of the intended audience or target market, to test the spot's effectiveness and to ensure that nothing in it will inadvertently alienate or insult that audience.

FOCUS PULL   The act of changing the distance at which the lens is
(F,V)   focused during a shot. Done either to keep a moving object in focus as it approaches or departs from the camera, or to make the entire scene lose focus, usually to dissolve into another shot.

FOLDBACK SYSTEM   A cue system. This term is used mostly in England
(E)   and Europe.

FOLDOVER FREQUENCY   Any spurious frequency created by aliasing
(D)   in an A-D circuit. If the sampling rate is 44 kHz and we attempt to sample a 36 kHz tone, we will get

an 8 kHz foldover frequency in the output. (*See* ALIASING.)

FOLEY STAGE (F,V)   A recording studio equipped with various types of surfaces and devices used to create footsteps and other sound effects needed in film or video sound tracks. The foley artist will generally preview each scene of the film, select the devices needed, arrange them in order of their use, and perform the effects in real-time for the entire sequence or scene.

FOOTAGE COUNTER/FRAME COUNTER (F)   A device for measuring the length of a reel of film, counting feet and frames of film from a starting point. In 35mm there are 16 frames per foot of film, and film runs through the camera or projector at 90 feet per minute when being shot or shown at 24 frames per second. In 16mm there are 40 frames per foot, and film runs through the camera or projector at 36 feet per minute, again at 24 fps. The counter can be attached to a synchronizer, flatbed or vertical editing machine, or installed in the camera or projector.

FOOTAGE NUMBERS   See EDGE NUMBERS.

FORCE MAJEURE (B,R)   French for "a greater force." Any industry-wide or world event that would hinder or preclude the execution of the terms of an agreement. A *force majeure* clause in a contract dictates how each party will make accommodation for such an event— e.g., a shortage of recording tape, a strike by musicians or technicians, etc. Not an act of God.

FOREIGN SALES (R)   In record contracts, foreign sales are generally covered by a completely different set of clauses, constraints, and royalty rates than domestic sales. Under certain circumstances, particularly when first releases of an album will be foreign, Foreign sales clauses can be read as applying to later domestic release, so be careful in reading these clauses of a contract.

FORMAT (R)   1. In records, the size of the disc and its rpm rating. These two constraints determine how much music can be put on each side of the record. Examples: 7" 45 rpm (the familiar "single"), 12" 33 1/3 rpm (the standard LP), 7" or 10" 33 1/3 rpm (usually called "E.P."), 12" 45 rpm (a disco single, or simply "12 inch," originally introduced to get high volume, low noise discs out to discotheques, but (C) now sold in stores. 2. In computers, to choose all the parameters by which a text will be printed on paper—i.e., page length, line length, character and line spacing, justification (left and/or right). (*See* WORD PROCESSOR.) 3. To designate the parameters that control how and where a computer stores data on a floppy disk or other so-called hard memory. Formatting parameters include the types of data, data density on the disk, size of any matrices, how data is grouped for easy retrieval, etc. Compatibility among computers often depends on their formatting, rather than internal operation. 4. The physical specifications (F) of a specific film or print. Format includes the film's width (Super 8mm, 16mm, 35mm, or 70mm), the type of sound track (optical or

SUPER 8mm

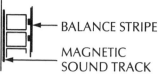

BALANCE STRIPE

MAGNETIC
SOUND TRACK

16mm

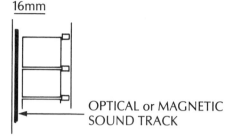

OPTICAL or MAGNETIC
SOUND TRACK

35mm
(Academy)

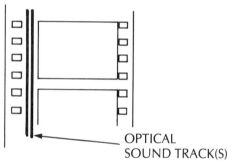

OPTICAL
SOUND TRACK(S)

70mm

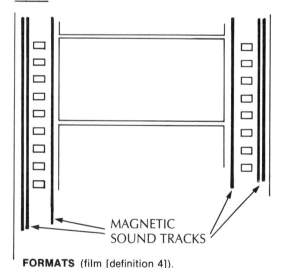

MAGNETIC
SOUND TRACKS

FORMATS (film [definition 4]).

magnetic, mono, or stereo, with or without noise reduction), and whether it is color or black and white. If the print is made using an anamorphic process such as Cinemascope, that may be noted too.

(V) **5.** The width of a videotape, and the designation of the electronic system by which it is recorded—e.g., the 1/2″ VHS, 1″-C, 3/4″ U-matic formats. (*See* VHS; BETAMAX; BETACAM; U-MATIC; C-FORMAT; B-FORMAT; QUAD-

(R,V) RUPLEX RECORDER.) **6.** In radio and television, the type of programming featured by any specific station—e.g., AOR, "Top 40," music, videos, all-news.

(E)   TRACK FORMAT For any tape recorder or recorded tape, the number of tracks, their width and position with respect to the tape, and the overall width of the tape itself. Tape speed is not always included. In general use, some factors are left out if the remaining factors uniquely specify a particular format. For example, "quarter track" uniquely specifies 1/4″ tape width with two pairs of stereo tracks, each pair recorded in one direction on the tape. Similarly, 8-track 1″ and 24-track uniquely specify two common professional formats.

The common formats for 1/4″ tape are: **Full-Track (mono),** in which a single track is recorded across the entire tape width. **Half-Track (or Two-Track),** in which the tape contains two tracks of information, which can be recorded in separate directions as mono tracks, or simultaneously in the same direction as stereo. The professional standard for stereo master mixes. **Quarter-Track,** as described above, with the pairs of

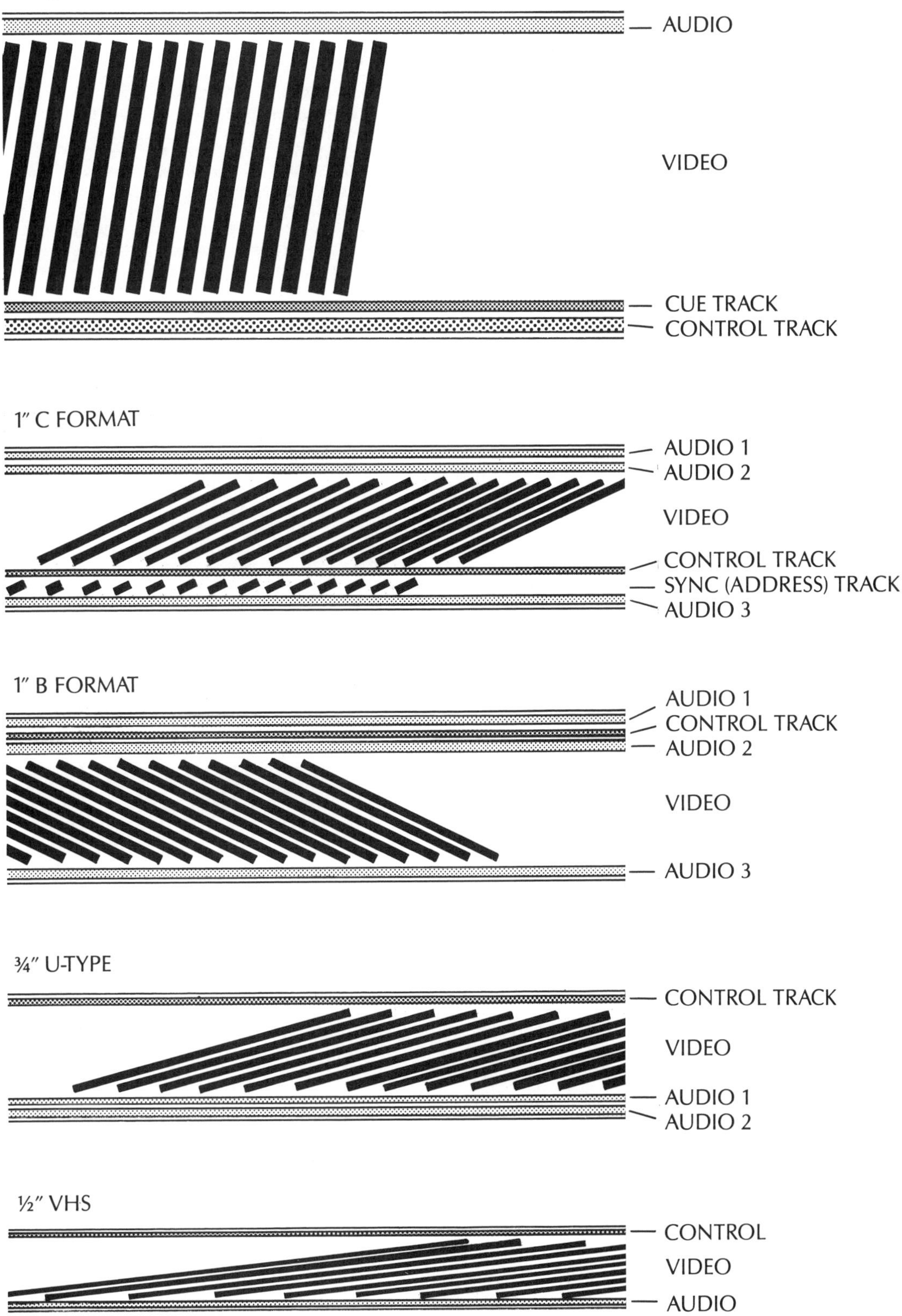

2″ QUADRUPLEX

— AUDIO

VIDEO

— CUE TRACK
— CONTROL TRACK

1″ C FORMAT

— AUDIO 1
— AUDIO 2
VIDEO
— CONTROL TRACK
— SYNC (ADDRESS) TRACK
— AUDIO 3

1″ B FORMAT

— AUDIO 1
— CONTROL TRACK
— AUDIO 2
VIDEO
— AUDIO 3

¾″ U-TYPE

— CONTROL TRACK
VIDEO
— AUDIO 1
— AUDIO 2

½″ VHS

— CONTROL
VIDEO
— AUDIO

FORMAT (video [definition 5]).

(A) = Advertising • (B) = Business & Law • (C) = Computers • (D) = Digital • (E) = Engineering & Scientific • (F) = Film • (G) = Music & General • (I) = Interlock & Sync • (J) = Jokes & Jargon • (P) = Music Publishing • (R) = Record Industry • (S) = Synthesizers • (U) = Unions • (V) = Video

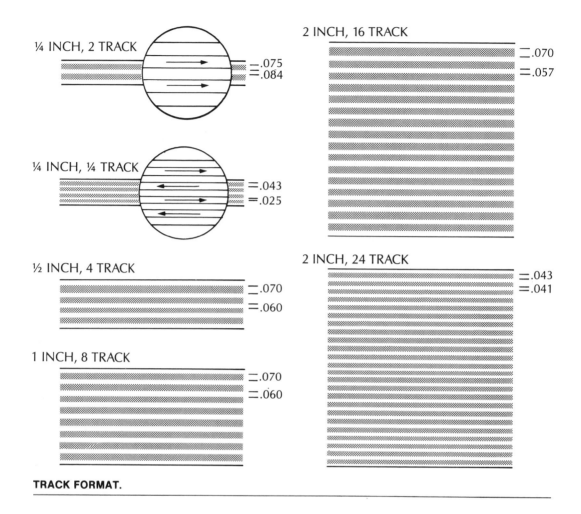

¼ INCH, 2 TRACK
=.075
=.084

¼ INCH, ¼ TRACK
=.043
=.025

½ INCH, 4 TRACK
=.070
=.060

1 INCH, 8 TRACK
=.070
=.060

2 INCH, 16 TRACK
=.070
=.057

2 INCH, 24 TRACK
=.043
=.041

TRACK FORMAT.

stereo tracks (indicated as 1-3 and 2-4 pairs) arranged across the tape in 1-4-3-2 order. Considered a home reel-to-reel format.

FORMAT MUSIC   Syndicated advertising music that complies with one or another of the standard spot formats—e.g., a donut consisting of 5-second vocal front and tag, with a 20-second bed in the middle.

(A)

Common 1/2″ tape formats are: **Two-Track** (sometimes called Full-Track) stereo, with each track nearly 1/4″ wide, used for the highest quality analog stereo master mixes. **Four-Track,** used for

quadraphonic mixdowns and the production of stereo mixes with separate SMPTE or other synchronizing tracks. **Eight- and Sixteen-Track,** considered semi-pro formats, and used mainly in making demos.

The only 1″ pro format is Eight-Track, with Sixteen-Track available on some machines for semipro demo applications.

2″ formats, because of the expense of the tape transport needed to manipulate such wide tape, are all professional. Most machines are Sixteen- or Twenty-Four-Track, athough custom machines of 32-

and 40-Track configurations have been built.

FORTRAN
(C)
(A)
A high-level language developed in the 1950s and still used, mainly for scientific applications. Short for FORmula TRANslation.

FOUR As   A.A.A.A. (American Association of Advertising Agencies). A professional organization whose members are the largest agencies in the United States. Together they set industry-wide policies, decide certain ethical issues concerning advertising, and represent the entire industry in collective bargaining with other unions, in Congressional lobbies, etc.

FOURIER ANALYSIS
(D,E,C)
A mathematical operation (based on the theorem developed by French mathematician Fourier) that allows complex sound waves to be represented as the summation of a constantly changing group of pure sine waves. Used in digital recording to achieve accurate sampling rate conversions. By the application of fourier analysis to a series of audio voltage samples taken at a 50 kHz rate, a computer can predict the value of samples that might have been taken from the same audio wave if the original sampling rate had been 44.1 kHz, for example.

FPS
(F,V)
Frames Per Second. See FRAME RATE.

FRAME
(F,V)
In motion pictures, a single photographic image on the negative or print. In videotape, the picture information that is displayed as a complete screen image of 525 lines in the NTSC system, or 625 lines in the PAL system. One complete screen. (*See* FIELD.)

FRAME RATE
(F,V)
In motion pictures and television, the number of frames of visual information which are photographed or recorded, and subsequently projected or displayed, per second. Expressed as fps. International standard motion picture frame rate is 24 fps. The NTSC, U.S. standard television frame rate is 29.97 fps (although many people say 30 fps for convenience). PAL standard frame rate, used throughout Europe and in some other countries, is 25 fps. For this reason, American films shown in Europe seem faster-paced while European films shown in the U.S. have a slower, more pensive quality.

FRAME SYNC
(I)
In SMPTE synchronization of any two playback machines (video and/or audio), a mode of synchronizer operation that keeps the time code on the slave machine aligned with the master's code to within an accuracy of plus or minus one-half frame. Because the synchronizer makes relatively gradual speed adjustments to the slave in this mode, little flutter is introduced to an audio slave. Thus, frame sync mode is used for post-scoring of video productions. (*See* SUBFRAME; PHASE SYNC.)

FRANCHISED
(B,U)
Describing agents, managers, or other professionals who are licensed to practice their trade by the appropriate artist's trade union or guild.

FRAUD
(B)
An intentional misrepresentation of some material fact, based on which another person suffers a

---

(A) = Advertising • (B) = Business & Law • (C) = Computers • (D) = Digital • (E) = Engineering & Scientific •
(F) = Film • (G) = Music & General • (I) = Interlock & Sync • (J) = Jokes & Jargon • (P) = Music Publishing •
(R) = Record Industry • (S) = Synthesizers • (U) = Unions • (V) = Video

loss. The law is unclear on where innocent misrepresentation ends and fraud begins. In general, however, if one portrays himself as an expert in any field, then gives either uninformed or intentionally false recommendations based on which another person loses money by the first's action *or* inaction, fraud has been committed.

FREE SPACE   In acoustics, any completely reflection-free environment—e.g., an anechoic chamber or open air.

(E)

FREEZE FRAME   1. The operating mode of a video playback unit or film projector which enables the device to stop the continuous motion of film or tape and show a specific frame or image continuously on the screen. 2. A strip of film produced in an optical printer, in which a single frame is printed repeatedly onto print stock. Like a still picture, this optically "freezes" the action when projected continuously at the normal frame rate. 3. Loosely, the "frozen" image itself as it appears on the motion picture or video screen.

(F,V)

FREQUENCY   Concerning any acoustic sound wave or cyclicly varying electric signal, the number of complete vibrations or cycles per unit

(E)

of time, measured in hertz (Hz). Formerly called cycles per second (cps).

FREQUENCY MODULATION (FM)   1. The use of a low-frequency signal to modulate or change the frequency of a higher frequency signal. For example, in FM radio broadcast, the audio signal containing frequencies between 20 Hz and 20,000 Hz modulates the carrier frequency assigned to each station, between 88 MHz and 108 MHz. 2. The method used to generate and modify sounds produced by synthesizers manufactured by Yamaha Corporation—specifically, its DX series.

(E)

(S)

FREQUENCY RESPONSE   1. A graph of the amplitude vs. frequency, either for an acoustic sound or for a signal passing through any piece of audio equipment. (*See* ENERGY DISTRIBUTION CURVE; REAL-TIME ANALYSIS.) 2. The graph that shows an audio device's output amplitude through a wide frequency band, when the amplitude of the input through that band is constant. So-called "flat" response indicates a horizontal, straight line response "curve" (as it is often called), which in turn means that the device passes all frequencies equally well, or without coloration.

(E)

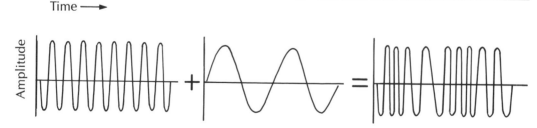

FREQUENCY MODULATION.

FRIDAY MORNING QUARTERBACK
(R) A radio programming guide published weekly, and very influential in FM and AM programming. It reviews new releases and tracks the progress of records on their way up.

FRINGING (or FRINGE) EFFECT
(E) A rise in low-frequency response caused by reproducing a tape track with a playback head that is narrower than the head with which it was recorded. Low frequencies from the recorded areas adjacent to those actually being played back "bleed" into the playback signal.

FRONT
(A) The vocal or instrumental opening of a radio or TV spot. This musical signature or ID may be followed by a bed, and finally by a tag, usually repeating the ID.

FRONT PROJECTION
(F,V) A technique used to project a background or setting on a screen behind foreground action. When the live action and projected image are shot simultaneously, it will (hopefully) appear that the actors were at the location projected behind them.

F.T.C. See FEDERAL TRADE COMMISSION.

FULL COAT
(F) Magnetic film coated with oxide across its entire width, available in 16mm and 35mm sizes

FULLTH
(J) A subjective term applied to a recorded musical program with a lot happening in the lower midrange frequencies—cellos and violas, background vocals, rhythm piano, etc.—giving the production a lush or heavy richness. Called gush by some producers.

FULL-TRACK
(E) A 1/4″ tape format in which a single, mono track is recorded across the entire tape width. Loosely used to refer to wider tape formats in which each of two or four tracks is 1/4″ wide.

FUNDAMENTAL
(E,G) The primary frequency, or lowest frequency, present in a sound source or musical note. Frequencies caused by beating between two notes or sound sources, but that are not inherent in either source, are *not* fundamentals. (*See* HARMONIC; OVERTONE; PARTIALS.)

(A) = Advertising • (B) = Business & Law • (C) = Computers • (D) = Digital • (E) = Engineering & Scientific •
(F) = Film • (G) = Music & General • (I) = Interlock & Sync • (J) = Jokes & Jargon • (P) = Music Publishing •
(R) = Record Industry • (S) = Synthesizers • (U) = Unions • (V) = Video

- G -

GAIN (E)   The ratio of the signal level at the output of an audio device to the signal level at its input. Normally expressed in decibels (dB), but sometimes as a ratio of voltages. Unity gain, for instance, denotes identical input and output levels. A gain of 6 dB indicates that a device amplifies signals by 6 dB, equivalent to a doubling of the signals' voltage. The voltage ratio here is thus 2:1. (*See* DECIBEL.)

GAIN-BEFORE-THRESHOLD (E)   In a compressor or limiter, the decibel gain applied to signals below the threshold level—i.e., before the compression circuit(s).

GAIN CONTROL (E)   The fader that controls the strength of the output signal of an amplifier. This term is a misnomer in many amplifiers, since the gain remains constant while the "gain control" actually adjusts the signal input level. Erroneously called "volume control" on some consumer equipment.

GAIN REDUCTION (E)   In a compressor or limiter, the instantaneous number of decibels by which the signal is reduced from the value it would have without compression in effect. (*See* COMPRESSOR (illustration).)

GAIN RIDING (E)   The process of manually adjusting the gain in a device or circuit in order to decrease a signal's dynamic range. An engineer normally rides gain in recording such sources as vocalists, whose high notes may be much louder than lower notes. This prevents tape overload and ensures that softer passages, boosted by the engineer, will retain the listener's attention.

GALLEY (A)   A proof print made from the typeset copy that the writer, editor, or art director can proofread and check for layout and other design flaws. Galleys will be returned to the printer or typesetter marked with any corrections to be made. Then the final "repro" copy is made.

GANG (F,E)   1. To mechanically or electrically interconnect two or more devices so that they operate in unison. One may gang two pots so that their levels go up and down together. A two-gang sync block has two sprocketed wheels to keep any two film or mag film rolls in perfect sync. **2.** Any of the individual mechanical or electronic parts or systems that are connected together as described in definition 1.

GAP WIDTH   The distance between the pole pieces of a magnetic tape
(E)   head—i.e., the dimension of head gap measured along the tape path. Typically about 90 millionths of an inch for professional playback heads, 150 millionths for a record head, and 400 millionths for an erase head. Sometimes specified in microns.

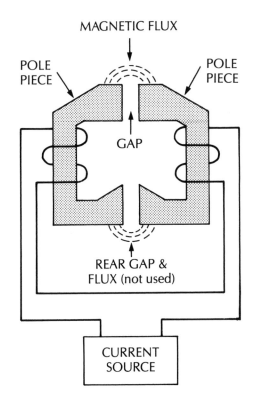

MAGNETIC FLUX

POLE PIECE

POLE PIECE

GAP

REAR GAP & FLUX (not used)

CURRENT SOURCE

RECORD HEAD (top section)

GAP WIDTH.

GATE   **1.** The part of a movie camera
(F)   that has an opening to allow light from the lens to expose the film, and that holds the film steady during that exposure. In a projector, the light source illuminates the frame held steady in the gate. The lens then projects an image of that
(S)   frame onto the screen. **2.** A control voltage generated by any key on a synthesizer keyboard that instructs signal generators and other devices
(E)   to begin operating. **3.** Short for noise gate.

GAUGE   The width of a particular film
(F)   stock, e.g. 8mm, 16mm, 35mm, 65mm or 70mm. (See FORMAT, **4.**)

GAUSS   **1.** The unit of magnetic field
(E)   strength, reflecting maximum flux density—i.e., that present in a cross section through the magnet's polar axis. **2.** The unit of measurement for remanent magnetization on recording tape.

GAVIN REPORT   A radio programming guide published weekly, and
(R)   very influential in FM and AM programming. It reviews new releases, and tracks the performance of records already released, etc.

GENERATION   A descriptive term for the number of times a sound has
(E)   been copied on tape since it was first recorded. The original recording is the first generation, a copy from that the second generation, and so forth. A single tape may contain sounds each of which is a different generation with respect to its original recording.

GHOST   The slight pre-echo heard on
(R)   a record one revolution before the

beginning of a loud band, or just after a loud band stops. The waveform carved by the cutting stylus in the modulated groove deforms the adjacent blank groove, resulting in a faint repeat of whatever the modulated groove contains. Analogous to print-through in recording tape.

GLASS SHOT   A special effect shot in which a piece of glass is placed (F,V) between the camera and the scene. One or more stationary foreground objects, or a distant background, are painted on the glass. With proper lighting of the painted and real-life scenes, both seem to merge when filmed. Used to insert beautiful landscapes, mask unwanted foreground or background objects in real locations, etc.

GLIDE   Same as portamento.   (S)

GOBO   Any kind of sound-absorbing surface or panel used in recording (E) sessions to acoustically separate two or more sound sources. Also called a baffle.

GOLD   A sales level designation awarded to a record release by the (R) RIAA. A "gold single" has achieved sales of 1 million copies or units. An album that has "gone gold" has brought its record company $1 million in wholesale receipts. Gold records are associated with lower sales levels in foreign countries. (*See* PLATINUM; RIAA.)

GOLDEN SECTION   In acoustics, a ratio of room height-to-width-to- (E) length suggested by the ancient Greeks to achieve "good" acoustics. The Greeks were right, and the actual ratio is 1:1.62:2.62.

GRAMMY AWARDS   The awards ceremony sponsored annually by the (R) National Association of Recording Arts and Sciences (NARAS). The ceremony is broadcast internationally, and gives recognition to top artists, producers, writers, and engineers, along with a wide variety of other creative and technical specialists. The award itself is a statuette in the shape of a gramophone.

GRAND RIGHTS   1. Generally, those rights in and to a composition for (P) which payments or fees are *not* designated by federal statute or standardized by industry convention. Opposite of small rights. Strictly, synchronization rights are one of the the grand rights. Fees for any grand right must be negotiated between the publisher (grantor) and potential grantee. **2.** In common parlance, the right to use a composition in a dramatico-musical presentation—e.g., a live Broadway or off-Broadway show.

GRANULATION NOISE   Another (D) name for quantization noise.

GRID   Short for lighting grid. A rectangular network of pipes from (F,V) which permanent or temporary lighting fixtures are hung in a sound stage. A catwalk above the grid generally provides speedy access to these lights, saving much time during shooting.

GROSS RATING POINTS   See GRPS.

GROUND   An electrical pathway or conductor connected to the earth, (E) or a conductive object so large that its potential is considered zero.

GROUND LIFT   1. Generally, a three-prong AC plug adaptor used
(E) without its ground connected in an attempt to eliminate the occurence of a ground loop through the power cord of a piece of equipment. 2. On a D.I. box, the switch that disconnects the common ground between its input and output. Used to help eliminate hums and buzzes in the signal, caused by improper grounding of some instrument pickups, or by the effect of RF fields on magnetic pickups, etc.

GROUND LOOP   An electronic prob-
(E) lem caused if the common return wire of a system has two or more connections to ground. The resulting closed path or "loop" is susceptible to electromagnetic induction from AC fields, resulting in hum or RF pickup by the system.

GROUP   1. Loosely, the background vo-calists singing in a radio or televi-
(A) sion ad. If there is no lead vocalist or soloist, the "Group" is all singers collectively, whether they carry melody or harmony parts in the
(U) score. 2. A payment category of scale wages due to AFTRA singers for all types of recording sessions. Different amounts are due to singers performing in groups of 3 to 5, 6 to 8, 9 to 16, and over 16. The designations for these group sizes are S3, S6, S9, and S17, respectively.

GROUP MASTER   In a console, any single fader that controls the levels
(E) of a designated group of other faders. The master and group "members" can all be standard or VCA-controlled faders, but not a

mixture of these types. Also called a submaster.

GRPS   Gross Rating Points. A measure-ment of the total audience exposure
(A) to radio or TV spots, without regard to how effective each exposure may be. (*See* ERPS.)

GUARD BAND   The area on an audio or video tape between recorded
(E) tracks, or between the edge tracks and the edge of the tape. Also, the actual distance between tracks or between edge tracks and the edge of the tape on the recording or playback head itself. Guard bands reduce crosstalk, fringing, and other types of bleeding from adjacent tracks. Exact dimensions for guard bands are set in the United States by the A.E.S. and SMPTE for audio and videotape formats, respectively. (*See* FORMAT, **5**, FORMAT, TRACK.)

GUILLOTINE SPLICER   A type of splicer for motion picture film and
(F) magnetic film that is generally used to assemble the workprint and edited soundtracks. For picture cutting, it slices along the frame line between images. A second blade can slice magnetic film diagonally to avoid "pops" or "bloops" on playback. While holding the two ends of picture or mag film to be joined in a sprocketed channel, non-stretching tape is applied, completing the splice itself. The editor can undo the splice if he does not like the result, and thus reassemble the pieces in their original or any other order. Sometimes called a tape splicer. (*See* RIVAS SPLICER.) (Illustration next page.)

GUSH   See FULLTH.

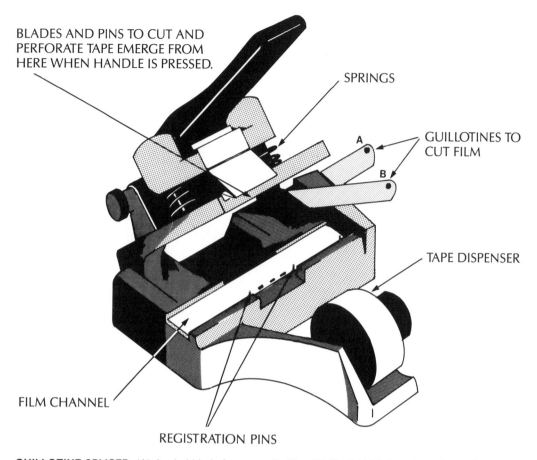

BLADES AND PINS TO CUT AND
PERFORATE TAPE EMERGE FROM
HERE WHEN HANDLE IS PRESSED.

SPRINGS

GUILLOTINES TO
CUT FILM

A

B

TAPE DISPENSER

FILM CHANNEL

REGISTRATION PINS

GUILLOTINE SPLICER. (A) Angled blade for magnetic film; (B) Straight blade cuts on frame line.

-H-

HAAS EFFECT The tendency of the human audio perceptual system to judge the actual position of a sound source by the direction from which an initial stimulus reaches the ears, even if a subsequent repeat of that signal from another direction is much louder. Also called precedence effect.
(E)

HALF TRACK A recording format in which two parallel tracks are recorded in a single pass on 1/4″ tape, each track slightly less than half the tape width. On some machines, a very narrow track with SMPTE or other synchronizing information is recorded and reproduced in the guard band between the audio tracks. In this case the data is FM modulated onto a very high frequency tone in order to minimize crosstalk or bleeding into the audio. (*See* FORMAT, TRACK (illustration).)
(E)

HALFTONE The process by which black and white photographs are broken up into a dot-patterned screen. When viewed at a distance, half tones give the illusion of a full range of tones from black
(A,R)
through gray to white. In three- or four-color printing, each color separation is processed into a halftone whose corresponding printing

HALFTONE.

---

plate deposits only one primary or secondary color of ink onto the final print.

HANDSHAKE AGREEMENT   In the entertainment industry, a verbal (B) agreement or contract, "signed" or confirmed by a handshake. Such an agreement is legally binding as long as the terms are clear and complete. In agreements negotiated by phone, the parties will confirm that a deal has been reached by saying that they have a handshake agreement. Legal paperwork on such agreements normally follows, especially if a substantial amount of money is at stake. (*See* DEAL MEMO.)

HARD COPY   In computers, a printed copy of a program or its results, or (C) of a data base or any other batch of information.

HARD CUT   A normal cut from one (F,V) shot to another, without any effects between them. Same as straight cut.

HARD DISK   A data storage and retrieval device consisting of a disk (C,D) drive and one or more permanently installed, precisely machined rigid disks. The advantage of this system is that a single hard disk drive can hold upward of 40 MEGAbytes of data, compared with less than 1 Mbyte on floppy disks. This enables hard disks to be used for digital sound recording and in "tapeless studio" systems. (*See* FAIRLIGHT.)

HARD-WIRED   In any signal path, a type of connection that cannot be (E) broken in ordinary use by patching, unplugging, etc. A hard-wired connection is permanently soldered or made via terminal strips or other such device.

HARMONIC   A integer multiple of the fundamental frequency of a sound. (E) The first harmonic (also called a "partial") is the fundamental itself, the second harmonic is two times the fundamental, etc. (*See* OVERTONE; PARTIAL.)

HARMONIZER   A signal processing device that allows the pitch of (E) musical notes in the input signal to be raised or lowered. Thus, the output can be adjusted to sound a harmonic interval, such as a third, fifth, or even an octave, with respect to the input signal. "Harmonizer" is a trademarked name of Eventide Corp. Other manufacturers call similar devices pitch transposers, etc.

HARMONY   An accompanying vocal or instrumental part in any score (G) or musical performance—i.e., not the lead vocal part or melody. Also used to denote the actual performance by a singer or musician.

HARRY FOX AGENCY   A company in New York City that collects and (R,P) distributes monies for member publishers (and the composers they represent) from (a) record companies who owe mechanical royalties for copies of compositions sold on records, cassettes, compact discs, musical video tapes, etc., and (b) purchasers of synchronization licenses under which compositions are used in the soundtracks of motion pictures or certain types of television productions. Publishers can grant the agency as

---

(A) = Advertising • (B) = Business & Law • (C) = Computers • (D) = Digital • (E) = Engineering & Scientific •
(F) = Film • (G) = Music & General • (I) = Interlock & Sync • (J) = Jokes & Jargon • (P) = Music Publishing •
(R) = Record Industry • (S) = Synthesizers • (U) = Unions • (V) = Video

much control over their copyrights as they desire. Owned by the N.M.P.A.

HDM
(V)   High-Density Modulation.

HDTV
(V)   High-Definition Television. A term designating any television system using many more than the standard number of lines per frame specified in the NTSC, PAL, or SECAM systems. Experimental HDTV systems have been developed to provide high-resolution computer animation for motion pictures, flight simulators, etc., but they will not be used for broadcast purposes for many years to come unless the selected HDTV system is compatible with today's commercial broadcast standards.

HEAD
(E)   1. On a tape recorder, an electromagnetic transducer that (a) converts electrical energy in the signal into a magnetic field that induces magnetization of the tape, or (b) produces an electrical signal in response to the varying remanent magnetism stored along a passing length of tape. (*See* GAP WIDTH (illustration).) 2. In general, the transducing mechanism used in recording or playing back signals on various media—e.g., the cutting head of a record mastering lathe, the optical head of a motion picture projector, etc.
     ERASE HEAD: The head on a tape recorder that erases magnetic information that may be present on the tape, located just before the record head in the tape path. A high-level, high-frequency (about 200 kHz) tone, fed through the erase head, effectively scrambles the orientation of the tape's

magnetic domains so that the signal to be recorded will have no other magnetic information mixed with it.
     PLAYBACK HEAD: The head on a tape recorder that is used to detect the varying remanent magnetism present on the tape. The output of this head is then amplified and heard as the recorded program.
     RECORD HEAD: The head on a tape recorder that applies a varying magnetic force to the tape so that the audio signal will be recorded on tape for later playback. A very high frequency signal is mixed with the audio program before it reaches the record head. This so-called "bias" signal helps to "linearize" the overall response of the tape itself, thereby reducing distortion. Digital recorders do not require bias since the signal consists only of a datastream of 1's and 0's, regardless of the audio frequency being recorded. (*See* BIAS; BIAS FREQUENCY.)
     SYNC HEAD: 1. The record head of a tape recorder with two or more channels, when used for playback purposes during overdubbing via sel-sync mode.
(F,V)   2. On a recorder used for synchronization of sound with motion pictures or videotape, a separate head that records and plays the synchronizing tone or signal.

HEAD BLOCK   The armature, plate,
(E)   or mounting device on a tape recorder to which the erase, record, and playback heads are attached. Loosely used to designate all the heads and their mounting plate, which together are more correctly called the head stack. (*See* HEAD STACK (illustration).)

HEAD DRUM   The rotating cylindrical drum around which the tape is wrapped (in a helical scan system), and that contains the actual video record and playback heads. (*See* HELICAL SCAN.)

(V)

HEAD LOSSES   Limitations in the frequency response of the signal a tape head can transfer to or read from tape due to its inherent design or construction.

(E)

HEAD SHIELD   A metal shield installed around as much of the playback head as is possible, and that keeps the stray magnetic fields of nearby motors, etc. from being picked up. Usually made of a mu-metal alloy.

(E)

HEAD STACK   The three heads of a multitrack recorder, referred to collectively. Sometimes all three heads are mounted on a removable metal plate called the headblock, allowing quick interchange of different head stacks for various track formats—i.e., 8, 16, or 24-track—on the same tape deck. (*See* FORMAT, TRACK (illustration).)

(E)

HEADPHONE BOX   See CUE BOX.

HEADPHONES   Very small loudspeakers mounted in enclosures no larger than the palm of one's hand, and intended to be worn by the listener (by means of an over-the-head strap or metal mounting clip) for private listening. Used in

(E)

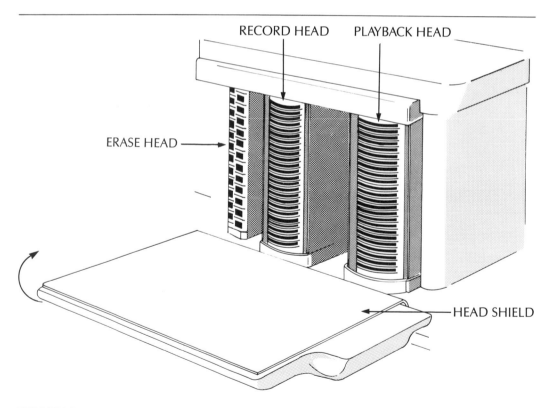

HEADSTACK.

multi-track sessions where musicians or vocalists must play or sing along with a click track, pre-recorded tracks, or other sounds being made in a separate studio or booth. If played through normal loudspeakers, these other sounds would be heard through the live microphones and recorded onto the new tracks.

HEADROOM (E)   1. In an audio device or system, the decibel difference in level between normal operating level (0 VU) and a higher level at which unacceptable distortion sets in. Most professional audio equipment has a minimum of 10 dB headroom, with some consoles achieving well over 25 dB. **2.** In magnetic tape, the decibel difference between the designated operating level (0 VU) and the level at which third harmonic distortion reaches 3%. This figure is different with every tape and—to a lesser extent—with every batch of tape.

HEADS-OUT (E)   A designation for the way a tape is wound on the reel. The head of a tape is its beginning. Thus, if the head is at the outside or beginning of the reel, the tape will be heard correctly when played back, whereas a tails-out tape will be heard backward if played back.

HEIGHT (E)   One parameter in tape head alignment that determines proper positioning of the individual track heads across the width of the tape. (*See* ALIGNMENT, TAPE HEAD (illustration).)

HELICAL SCAN (V)   A type of videotape, data, or audio recorder in which the tape is wrapped around a large rotating drum, on which the actual record and playback heads are mounted. Since the heads rotate quickly and write parallel tracks at a very small angle with respect to the tape path, the signal written on tape is many times the actual length of the tape itself. Thus, helical scan

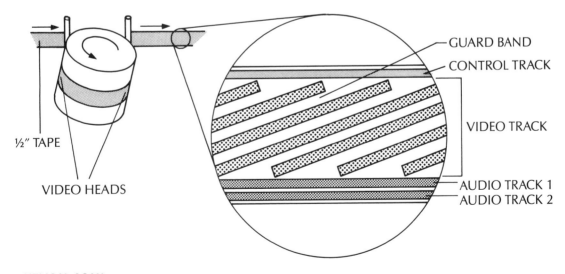

GUARD BAND
CONTROL TRACK
VIDEO TRACK
AUDIO TRACK 1
AUDIO TRACK 2
½" TAPE
VIDEO HEADS

HELICAL SCAN.

recording offers very high resolution at low tape speeds. Almost all consumer and professional videotape formats employ the helical scan principle. (*See* FORMAT, **5.**)

HELMHOLTZ RESONATOR
(E)
In the acoustical design of studios or control rooms, a device that absorbs specific frequencies. The resonator consists of an enclosed volume of air—which by virtue of its size and shape has a desired resonant frequency—connected to the air in the studio or control room by a narrow opening or neck. When studio sound at the desired resonant frequency approaches the neck, the air inside resists compression, effectively cancelling out the fre-

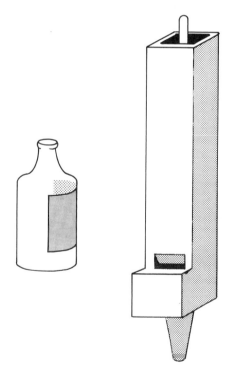

HELMHOLTZ RESONATOR. A bottle is a simple Helmholtz resonator, as is an organ pipe. The handle at the top of the organ pipe moves a stopper or plug. The position of the stopper determines the length or tuning of the pipe.

quency at the juncture of studio and neck.

HERTZ
(E)
Abbreviated Hz. Formerly called cycles per second. The unit by which frequency is measured and specified.

HEXADECIMAL   See DIGIT.

HI-FI VIDEO SOUND
(V)
The result of encoding the stereo soundtracks input to Hi-Fi type VHS or Beta format videotape recorders on an FM modulated carrier wave. This information is recorded along with picture data via the video record heads. Reproduction of Hi-Fi sound affords almost all the benefits (greater dynamic range, low distortion, etc.) of normal digital recording.

HIGH BAND
(V)
A type of video system in which the picture information is encoded on a much higher carrier frequency than early color video systems. The broadcast standard in current use.

HIGH-DEFINITION TELEVISION   See HDTV.

HIGH-DENSITY MODULATION
(D)
(HDM) Any digital recording scheme that, by special organization of the data, allows greater amounts of data to be recorded per unit of tape length. (*See* EFM.)

HIGH-OUTPUT LOW-NOISE TAPE
(E)
(HOLN) A type of recording tape with very high sensitivity to applied magnetic fields, and with very high signal-to-noise ratio. Most tapes used professionally are HOLN.

HIGH-RESOLUTION TV   Also called
(V)   Hi-Res for short. (*See* HDTV.)

HITS   In post-scoring, specific timings,
(A,F,V) frame counts, or SMPTE codes within a TV spot, film, or television production at which the music must do something to coincide with or reinforce the on-screen action. The producer may require musical hits for a door-slam, an actor's sneeze, or for synchronization with a quick camera move, rapid editing within a scene, etc.

HOLN   High-Output, Low-Noise re-
(E)   cording tape.

HOOK   In record production, the part
(R)   of any song that is most memorable. The hook can be the melody or lyrics of the song's chorus, a guitar riff or other repeated musical phrase or, or even a unique, repeated rhythmic motif or passage. That which catches the listener's ear.

HOOK-UP WEIGHT   One of the fac-
(P,A)   tors used by ASCAP in calculating the number of performance credits that a specific TV broadcast or a song will generate for the composer and publisher. It represents the number of network affiliates that carry the program in which the song is heard.

HORN   A type of speaker enclosure
(E)   named for its characteristic shape, with the speaker itself mounted in the narrow end of its tapered interior surface. Because the waves emanating from the speaker itself are internally enlarged before they exit from the larger end of the tapered surface, horn enclosures are highly efficient. Also, any horn-

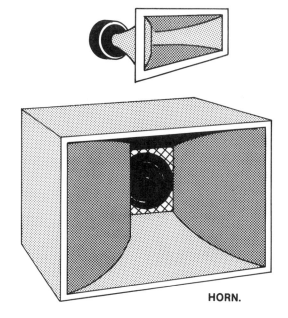

HORN.

shaped device placed in front of a speaker to disperse sound.
(E)   MULTICELLULAR HORN: A cluster of horns that spread the sound from a single speaker over a wide angle of radiation. Used mainly to disperse high frequencies, which tend to travel in narrow beams otherwise.

HORN-LOADED SYSTEM   A speaker
(E)   system whose enclosure is a horn, or that uses a horn to project sound from one or more of the drivers.

HOT SPLICER   A film splicer used to
(F)   make A and B rolls. Film cement joins two pieces of film, the ends of which have been scraped to reduce the final thickness of the splice, as well as to provide a better bond. Heat is applied to the splice point to aid in bonding.

HOUSE AGENCY   An advertising
(A)   department that functions as an ad agency within a single company.

HOUSE PRODUCER   A staff producer on salary with a production company or within a house agency.
(A)

HUB   The cylindrical plastic or metal center of a tape reel to which the tape is attached and around which it is wound.
(E)

HUM   A low-frequency unwanted noise of definite pitch—generally 60 Hz or multiples thereof—that usually imposes itself on a signal through the effect of stray magnetic fields, the proximity of AC lines, or through improper grounding.
(E)

HYSTERESIS LOOP   The graph of applied magnetic force vs. remanent magnetism. Measured both for an applied field as it increases from zero to saturation, and as it declines from saturation to zero. One measure of a specific recording tape's performance. Hysteresis itself encompasses two problems in magnetic transfer: the time delay
(E)

between applied and retained magnetism, and the failure of magnetic tape to retain as much magnetism as may be applied.

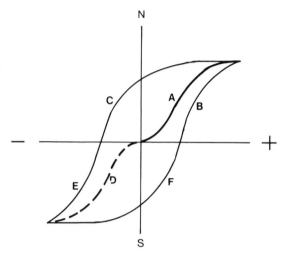

HYSTERESIS LOOP. Applying a north magnetic field (A) results in a north field (B) on tape. As the applied magnetism is reduced to zero, (C) results on tape. An applied south field (D) results in (E) on tape, and it is reduced to zero and then full north applied you get (F).

- I -

IATSE
(U)
International Alliance of Theatrical and Stage Employees. The union originally formed to represent all technicians working in theatrical productions, and that later expanded to include motion picture and television technicians. Like the AFM and AFTRA, IATSE sets pay scales for normal and overtime work, collects and administers employee benefits, and makes sure that producers maintain specified working conditions.

IC   Integrated Circuit.   (C)

ID
(A)
Short for identification. Any sort of logo, icon, or insignia—visual or aural—by which a television or radio station or any company is primarily known. A station ID reminds listeners or viewers what radio or TV station they are tuned in to. (See SIGNATURE.)

ILLUSTRATOR
(A,R)
The person who prepares preliminary sketches, original drawings, or paintings for approval of the art director at an agency, the A&R person at a record company, or other sponsor of the final artwork.

IMAGE SHIFT
(E)
In stereo sound reproduction, a change in the apparent left-to-right position from which a particular instrument or source seems to speak.

IMAGING
(E)
The ability of stereo speakers to give the listener an accurate impression of the left-to-right position of various instruments or voices in the stereo program.

IMPEDANCE
(E)
The measure of an electronic device's opposition to the flow of alternating current. Derived both from simple resistance of the circuit's components and their combined reactance, impedance can vary with the frequency content of the signal. The basic unit is the ohm.

(E)
HIGH IMPEDANCE: By convention, a circuit impedance of more than about 5,000 ohms.

(E)
LOW IMPEDANCE: By convention, a circuit impedance of 600 ohms or less.

INCHES PER SECOND   See IPS.

(A) = Advertising • (B) = Business & Law • (C) = Computers • (D) = Digital • (E) = Engineering & Scientific •
(F) = Film • (G) = Music & General • (I) = Interlock & Sync • (J) = Jokes & Jargon • (P) = Music Publishing •
(R) = Record Industry • (S) = Synthesizers • (U) = Unions • (V) = Video

INCHING   Moving a film or videotape
(F,V)   through a viewer, editing machine,
projector, or VCR frame by frame
for close examination of a shot.

INCOHERENT SIGNALS   Two com-
(E)   plex waveforms that are partially
or completely out of phase most
of the time. (*See* COHERENT
SIGNALS; REINFORCEMENT.)

INDEPENDENT PROMOTION   Re-
(R)   cord promotion paid for by the
record company or the recording
artist, and done by freelance promoters or companies. If commissioned by the record company, it
is generally considered special promotion and is charged to the artist's
royalty account.

INDUCTANCE   The measure of an
(E)   electronic component's or circuit's
opposition to a change in the current flowing through it. The basic
unit is the henry.

INDUCTOR   Any electronic com-
(E)   ponent or circuit that opposes a
change in current flow.

INERTANCE   In acoustics, a sound
(E)   barrier's opposition to the flow of
energy through it. Analogous to the
inductance of an electronic circuit.
Can be measured broadband or
for specific frequencies or bands.
Since a dense, fully reflective barrier exhibits high inertance, the
term is not necessarily related to
the absorption coefficient or sabine
ratings of surface or insulating
materials. (*See* ACOUSTIC BAF-
FLE.)

IN-HOUSE   Work done within a com-
(A,R)   pany, not hired out to another company. (*See* HOUSE AGENCY.)

INITIALIZING   The process of specify-
(V,C)   ing and defining in the computer
video editor or edit programmer
the proper starting parameters for
an editing session.

IN-LINE CONSOLE   A console com-
(E)   prised of complete I/O modules—i.e.,
with all controls for each channel
located on the corresponding
module.

IN-STORE PLAY   Playing a record in
(R)   a record store, which usually
generates a lot of sales. However,
many stores charge record companies for this added sales effort,
generally taking payment in records
rather than cash.

IN THE MUD/IN THE RED   Slang
(E)   terms for a signal level or level on
tape that is (a) too low (hardly
moving the VU meter), and (b)
too high (above 0 dBVU) and thus
likely to produce distortion, respectively.

I/O   Input/Output. A term used to
(E)   describe the modules used in most
in-line consoles. Each module contains two or more inputs (mic, line,
tape, etc.), outputs, and monitor
controls for that channel or signal.

INPUT   1. The connector by which a
(E,G)   signal enters an electronic device,
or the incoming signal itself. 2. An
electronic operating mode in tape
recorders, in which the input signals to various tracks are routed
directly to their outputs.

INSERT   1. A promotional card or
(A,R)   postcard included in a magazine
or record, or an informational or
photographic sheet or booklet such
as those that reproduce lyrics and

---

pictures of the performers in some albums. **2.** Another name for a cutaway.
(F,V)

INSERT EDITING   In videotape or digital audio editing, replacing a shot (or part of a take) located between two specific SMPTE code numbers or addresses. Done by the video edit-programmer or digital audio editing console on instructions from the engineer.
(V,D)

INSERTION   In tape-head alignment, another name for wrap.
(E)

INSERTION GAIN (or LOSS)   The change in signal level caused when an electronic device is placed into the signal path. Measured in dB.
(E)

INSTITUTIONAL SPOT   A radio or television spot designed to promote the image of a company rather than any of its specific products.
(A)

INSURANCE   Producers normally carry a "blanket policy," which provides coverage of a number of possible business losses or disasters, including the accidental erasure of tapes or damage to video or motion picture footage, loss in shipment, postponement of sessions due to illness, etc. A policy can be written to include or exclude any specific type of coverage, so you should list what you need and pay only for that, negotiating with the insurance agent.
(B)

INTEGRATED CIRCUIT (IC)   A complete electronic circuit that has been miniaturized and put on a "chip," its more common name.
(C,E)

INTENSITY, ACOUSTIC   The measure of acoustic power flowing per unit
(E)

area. At the threshold of hearing, the measured value is less than 10^{-16} watt/cm^2. At the threshold of pain, the acoustic intensity is over 10^{-3} watt/cm^2. Note that there are more than 13 powers of 10 separating awareness and pain, each power corresponding to 10 dB in the 130+ dB range between these thresholds.

INTERACTIVE COMPACT DISC   See CD-I.

INTERFACE   The inter-connection of two devices or systems, or a separate device that operates between them to assure their optimum joint performance.
(E,C)

INTERLEAVING   An error-concealment scheme in which data words or samples generated in sequence by the A-D converter are separated into defined subgroups such as odd- and even-numbered words within a longer sequence. Each subgroup is then recorded after its mate, shuffling originally adjacent words to positions somewhat distant on tape. Done to allow the reconstruction of continuous valid data in the event of large-scale drop-outs, burst errors or other extended source of erroneous data retrieval.
(D)

(D)   **CROSS-INTERLEAVING:** A further error-concealment scheme in which already-interleaved data is again shuffled into smaller subgroups, each of which is recorded one after the other, often at great distances from the position each word would occupy if recorded in its original sequence. The CIRC system, used in compact disc reproduction, combines cross interleaving with the Reed-Solomon error-correction process. (*See* ERROR DETECTION (illustration).)

INTERLOCK   **1.** The projection of film footage and its corresponding sync sound—either the magnetic film transferred from the original sync tapes, or the completed final mix—in synchronization. **2.** The system by which the projector and sound playback are synchronized during projection. **3.** The operating condition of synchronization between any two or more audio and/or video recorders and/or motion picture equipment. All such machines are running in interlock.
(F)
(F,V,E)

INTERFERENCE MICROPHONE   See MICROPHONE, SHOTGUN: ACOUSTIC LABYRINTH.
(E)

INTERNATIONAL MUSICIAN   A major trade journal for professional musicians, published monthly by the AFM and sent to all active members.
(B,G)

INTERNATIONAL ALLIANCE OF THEATRICAL AND STAGE EMPLOYEES   See IATSE.

INTERNATIONAL CONFERENCE OF SOCIETIES OF AUTHORS AND COMPOSERS   See CISAC.

INTERNATIONAL STANDARD BOOK NUMBERING SYSTEM   See ISBN SYSTEM.

INTERNEGATIVE   A composite negative made from an interpositive. Release prints are made from the internegative. (*See* CRI.)
(F)

INTERPOLATION   The process used to fill in "probable" data for missing samples in digital playback.
(D,E)

The error-correction circuitry reads the last valid data and searches for the next valid data. It then averages these to create a single missing sample, or creates a series of samples that smoothly connect the values of the last and next valid data. A mathematical averaging process at heart. The extent of interpolation is not the same in every machine. In sampling-rate conversion, once fourier analysis "redefines" the original waveshape in computer memory, interpolation is used to calculate samples at the new rate. (*See* PARITY CODE; CRCC; INTERLEAVING; ERROR DETECTION (illustration).)

INTERPOSITIVE   A type of film stock (or a print made on it) used as an intermediate stage in the normal negative/positive print process. A low-contrast, high-resolution print stock. (*See* CRI; INTERNEGATIVE.)
(F)

INVERSION   See PHASE REVERSAL.

INVESTORS   The persons who buy stock or shares in a business or specific project. Their funds are used to complete the project or set up the company. As in the stock market, the investors receive proportional parts of any profit made by the venture. (*See* LIMITED PARTNERSHIP; CORPORATION.)
(B,G)

IPS   Inches Per Second. The standard measure used for various analog tape speeds in the United States. Professional speeds and their European equivalents are: 3.75 ips = 9.5 cm/sec; 7.50 ips = 19.0 cm/sec; 15.00 ips = 38.0 cm/sec;
(E)

30.00 ips = 76.0 cm/sec. Open-reel digital and video recorders use still other tape speeds.

ISBN SYSTEM
(G)
International Standard Book Numbering System. The classification system used for assigning unique letter and number identifications to each work printed and published for distribution to the public, including scores, songbooks, etc. Used by the Library of Congress and all major libraries.

ISOLATION
(E,G)
The separation of one sound or signal from another, achieved either acoustically or electronically. (*See* INERTANCE; ABSORPTION COEFFICIENT; SABINE.)

ISOLATION BOOTH   See DRUM BOOTH; VOCAL BOOTH.

ISOLOOP
(E)
The 3M Company trade name for its closed-loop tape path.

- J -

JACK
(E)
An electrical receptacle or socket. When the jack is wired to the input of an audio device, one can patch or plug a signal into that input via the jack. Conversely, when the jack is wired to the output of a device, one can patch that output to another destination via the jack.

JACK FIELD (or JACK BAY)
(E)
Other names for patch bay.

JAM SYNC
(V,I)
In video synchronization, transferring a time code and user bits from an external reference source to a SMPTE time code generator, either *once* (called one-time jam sync), which will align the two codes at one frame only, allowing each to proceed at its own internal rate from that moment on), or *continuously* (which will force the generator to mimic the code numbers of the reference source continuously).

JINGLE
(A)
The original term for any music written and/or recorded for use in a radio or television commercial. Now used to refer to ad music featuring a catchy foreground melody with or without lyrics, intended to become synonymous with the product. A musical signature.

JOCK
(R)
Short for Disk Jockey or Video Jockey.

JOINT
(E)
In tape editing, the point of connection between two pieces of tape spliced together.

JOINT VENTURE
(B)
A partnership with a very short term (for instance, to produce one record) or limited purpose. Any combination of individuals, companies, or corporations may participate.

JOYSTICK
(E,V)
A multi-gang potentiometer whose user control resembles an automobile's stick shift—i.e., a vertical handle protruding from a slot or socket. In video applications, joysticks in the SEG allow the engineer to transition between two shots via a selected type of wipe, dissolve, or other effect. In audio applications, joysticks function as quadraphonic panpots. In its center position, the joystick sends one input signal equally to four dis-

---

crete output channels. Moving it outward toward its circular limit directs the signal to one or two channels whose monitor speakers correspond to the same direction in the control room. For example, pushing the stick full forward (toward 12:00 on an imaginary clock around it) will direct the signal to the left and right front speakers; pushing it toward 7:30 on the imaginary clock will send the signal only to the left rear speaker.

JUMP CUT **(F,V)**   The jarring effect created by removing frames from the continuous action of a single shot. More generally, any jarring juxtoposition of two shots in the editing of a film or videotape.

-K-

K
(C)
(F,V)
1. Capital letter used as a suffix in specifying quantities of memory space. For example, a program may occupy 8K (or 8,000 bytes) of a 64K memory space, leaving another 56K available for other information. Although it harkens back to "kilo", 1 K equals exactly 1,024 (or 2^{10}) bytes. **2.** The designation of temperature measured by the Kelvin scale. Kelvin temperatures are used to designate the effective "color temperature" of various film and TV lighting sources. Tungsten-halogen lamps are rated at 3,200 degrees K, the noonday sun at 5,400 K. Most color film stocks are chemically balanced to give proper color reproduction at one or the other of these two K ratings. Thus, indoor film is commonly referred to as "32 K" stock, etc. (*See* COLOR TEMPERATURE.)

k
(E)
Lower case letter standing for "kilo"—1,000. For example, 20 kHz means 20,000 Hz.

KEPEX
(E)
KEyable Program EXpander. A noise gate with variable parameters for threshold, attack time, release time, etc. A trade name of Allison Research Co.

KEY
(E,S)
(V)
1. In signal processing, to change the amount or type of processing a device performs on the program signal by using a separate control signal to dictate its operation. **2.** In signal generators such as a synthesizer, to use an external control signal to dictate the amount and/or type of sound produced. **3.** A video effect in which the engineer inserts one image into another, the new image replacing a portion of the original image completely. The engineer can select a certain area of the original shot where he will key-in the new image. Or he may replace any area of the original frame that is a certain color. In this case, the new image would "show through" any point on the screen that was originally that color. This effect is called chroma-keying.

KEY CODE (or KEYBOARD CV)
(S)
The Control Voltage parameter that tells the signal generating circuit exactly which key has been depressed.

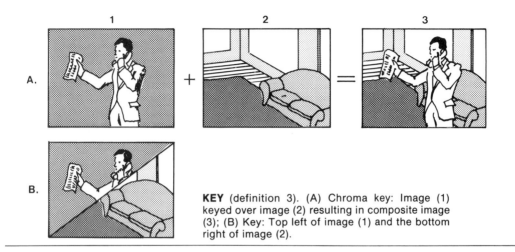

KEY (definition 3). (A) Chroma key: Image (1) keyed over image (2) resulting in composite image (3); (B) Key: Top left of image (1) and the bottom right of image (2).

KEYING INPUT   In a signal processing or generating device, an input for a control signal that determines the type and amount of processing applied to the audio signal, or of sound produced, respectively.
(E,S)

KEY NUMBERS   See EDGE NUMBERS.

KEYING SIGNAL   The signal sent to the keying input of a signal-producing or signal-processing device, which then activates the device.

KEY MAN CLAUSE   In a recording contract or any agreement whose success depends on the continued input or help from specific creative or business persons, a clause that allows one party to invalidate the contract if such a "key man" leaves the company or group named as the other party. For ex-
(R,B)
ample, a record label may exercise its option to cancel a group's contract if the lead singer quits. Conversely, the group may request a key man clause that allows them to leave the label if their designated A&R person quits or is fired.

KEYSTONING   An optical distortion of a projected image that results when the center of the projector beam is not oriented exactly perpendicular to the screen surface. The image is wider on the part of the screen farthest from the projection lens.
(F,V)

KILO   A prefix used in the metric system, designating one thousand times the unit of measure that follows. Thus, kilograms are units each containing one thousand grams. Designated by lower case k.
(E)

(A) = Advertising • (B) = Business & Law • (C) = Computers • (D) = Digital • (E) = Engineering & Scientific •
(F) = Film • (G) = Music & General • (I) = Interlock & Sync • (J) = Jokes & Jargon • (P) = Music Publishing •
(R) = Record Industry • (S) = Synthesizers • (U) = Unions • (V) = Video

- L -

LAB
(F)
Short for motion picture or film laboratory. The facility at which the camera original is developed and printed, and that generally makes the optical track, opticals, internegatives, CRIs, etc.

LABEL
(R)
A record company, usually identified by the design of its label. Colloquially, the term has come to mean the company itself, even if, like CBS, RCA, or any of the "majors," it has many different label designs for various divisions.

LABOR CONTRACT (or LABOR AGREE-MENT)
(B)
(U)
1. An individual verbal or written contract under which an independent composer, arranger, or other creative source person agrees to work for the producer of an advertisement or campaign. **2.** The generic contract agreed upon by the AFM, AFTRA, or other union and their signatories. The signatory ad agencies and producers are bound to pay all AFM, AFTRA, or other union members whom they employ according to the appropriate, specified pay scales, and treat them according to all other terms of the contract.

LABOR UNIONS
(B,U)
Organizations run by officers elected from among the ranks of groups of people working in any specific profession—e.g., musicians, singers, etc. Union officers bargain collectively with the major employers of the union members, setting uniform wage and working condition standards. These employers, who then become signatories to the resulting labor contracts, include major record labels, concert promoters, orchestras, television producers and broadcasters, motion picture studios, etc.

LACQUER
(R)
Short for LACQUER MASTER. The master disc made on a record-cutting lathe. The disc itself is made of sheet aluminum (called the substrate) covered with a thin, evenly distributed coating of soft acetate lacquer, through which a stylus cuts very easily. Since the lacquer cannot be played because it is so fragile, an identical lacquer, called a reference (or test)

---

lacquer or acetate, is cut so that the producer can hear what the final record will sound like without damaging the lacquer master. The test lacquer or acetate is equally fragile, however, and starts to deteriorate in sound quality after a few plays. Thus, it should be saved for comparison with the test pressing. The primary ingredient of the lacquer coating is nitrocellulose acetate, a violent explosive used in Civil War weapons. (*See* PREVIEW HEAD; LAND; ACETATE; MATRIX NUMBER.)

LAMINATION
(R)
The application of a thin plastic coating to the printed surface of the slick (or record jacket), both for protection from stains and fingerprints, and to make it more attractive. Done at the time of printing, not during fabrication.

LAND
(R)
1. The flat area of vinyl between the grooves of a record. Ideally, the grooves should be made as close as possible to each other, which allows the longest possible program to be cut onto each side of the disc. If length of program is not a major consideration, minimizing land will keep the grooves from extending in too far toward the center of the disk, where groove distortion increases. Land is wasted space on the record, and should be minimized whenever
(D) possible. 2. The flat area between the laser-carved pits of a CD, CD-ROM, etc.

LANGUAGE
(C)
A set of words and symbols by which the user can communicate with or program the computer, or use any software that has been prepared to expedite specific tasks. Not the software itself. Thus,

BASIC, COBOL, LISP, and FORTRAN are computer languages. A spreadsheet or word-processing program is not.

LARGE-SCALE INTEGRATION   See LSI.

LASERDISC   See OPTICAL DISC.

LAVALIER MICROPHONE   See MICROPHONE (3).

LAWYER
(B,G)
A professional whose part-time services are absolutely necessary in setting up a record company, publishing company, limited partnership, or any other type of music-industry business. Lawyers will write and sometimes help negotiate contracts, give advice on the legality of various fund raising tactics, secure licenses and rights, etc. Entertainment law is a real specialty. The field changes as rapidly as public taste. Thus, it is important to employ a lawyer whose primary business is entertainment, rather than corporate law or wills and estates.

LAYBACK RECORDER
(V)
A videotape recorder, usually 1″ format, on which a mixed sound track with all dialogue, music, and effects can be re-recorded in sync with the edited video master. Because of its special purpose, a layback machine should have less flutter and higher quality audio heads and electronics than on standard 1″ video decks. Some layback machines designed especially for that task have no video repro capability at all. They merely read time code and do an exquisite job of recording audio—nothing else. The layback process is also called re-laying.

LAY-OUT   See CAMERA-READY.

LCD   Liquid Crystal Display. A type
of flat-screen device used for com-
(C,E) puter and other display screens.
Although the LCD has lower resolution and no color, it uses compara-
tively little power, and is therefore
perfect for portable computers.

LCRS   Left, Center, Right, Surround.
The four channels of audio
(F) reproduction used in 35mm stereo
motion pictures. Also, quad encoding of the stereo tracks on current
pre-recorded videotape releases,
which allows the four LCRS channels to be reproduced on home
equipment. In theaters, the L, C,
and R speakers are located behind
the screen. The S channel, which
may be mono or encoded stereo,
plays through speakers located
above and around the audience.
(*See* FORMAT (illustration).)

LEAD SHEET   The melody, lyrics,
chords, and rhythm of a song, writ-
(G) ten on music paper, usually with
two staves for melody and bass or
chords, respectively.

LEADER   1. In AFM recording sessions, the union member who leads
(U) or conducts the others present. If
the leader also plays an instrument,
he is paid separately and equally
for each role. (*See* CONDUC-
(F) TOR.) 2. Blank (unexposed) motion picture film attached to the
beginning (head) or end (tail) of a
reel of film, usually used for thread-
ing the projector, editing machine,
or magnetic film dubber. Opaque
leader is used in A and B rolls, and
in editing workprints and
soundtracks, generally to fill spaces
between the specific sound effects

or musical segments, or to fill in
for picture or sound segments to
be added later.

LEADER TAPE   Non-magnetic tape,
usually white plastic or paper,
(E) spliced in between sections or
bands of a reel of tape or any
recording. Paper leader tape gives
a visual indication of the beginning and end of each section, and
since it is non-magnetic, produces
no tape hiss or noise. Plastic leader
can pick up a static charge and
produce pops or clicks on adjacent
layers or recorded tape. It is not
recommended for use in master
tapes.

LEAKAGE   Unwanted sound picked
up by a microphone. For example,
(E) the sound of instruments other than
the one the mic is in front of.
    HEADPHONE LEAKAGE:
The unwanted transmission of
sound from a player's or singer's
headphones to a live microphone
in the studio.

LEARNING CURVE   Generally, a
graph that shows improving per-
(E,C) formance vs. the amount one has
learned about a subject. In mechanical systems controlled by computers, the computer's ability to
learn the particulars of a situation
and use this information to improve its control of the mechanism.
For example, in a multi-track tape
transport under the control of a
computerized auto-locator, the
computer has to sense the relative
size and weight of feed and take-
up reels in order to handle them
most efficiently and gently. The
engineer can give it this information by winding once through the
entire reel in both directions.

LEAST SIGNIFICANT BIT   See LSB.

LED   Light Emitting Diode. An electronic component that allows current to flow in only one direction through itself, and emits light whenever current is flowing.

(E)

LED DISPLAY   One or more LEDs used to indicate the operational status of a piece of electronic equipment, or the varying level of a signal being processed, or simply peak or VU levels. The series of LEDs must be driven by a circuit that senses these levels or conditions, turning on only the appropriate LEDs at each moment.

(E)

LEDGER   See BOOKS.

LEFT, CENTER, RIGHT, SURROUND   See LCRS.

LEVEL   Generally, the SPL or "volume" of sound in the listening environment; or the amplitude of the audio signal present on tape, passing through a console or other device, etc. Expressed in decibels according to the various scales that apply to electronic signals or acoustic sound pressure. A potentially misleading term unless the context of its usage is well defined.

(E)

LEVEL-SENSING CIRCUIT   An electronic circuit that generates a control voltage in proportion to signal level. This control voltage can then be used to affect the amount or type of signal processing done by a separate device. Also called a detector.

(E)

LIGHT-EMITTING DIODE   See LED.

LFO   Low-Frequency Oscillator. A circuit whose output is generally used to control some parameter of another signal-generating or signal-processing device. LFO output, when applied to audio signal level, produces a tremolo. When used to modulate delay time, an LFO produces flanging, etc.

(S)

LIABILITY   1. In general, anything real or intangible that can directly cause or indirectly contribute to a business loss or physical harm. 2. Legal responsibility for payment of a bill for goods and/or services, accepted in writing by the buyer. The signature on a charge slip, a client's initialed approval of a session report, etc. establish legal liability for payment. 3. A type of insurance that protects one party from loss in the event that a second party is hurt while on the premises or in the employ of the first party. Businesses should carry enough liability to fend off lawsuits if, for instance, a studio lighting fixture falls and hits a client, or if someone is electrocuted by improperly grounded mics, etc.

(B)

LIBRARY, MUSIC   A large collection of various musical passages, all pre-recorded, sold to producers, studios, and production companies on disc or tape, and available on a per-use basis as background music for commercials, soundtracks, etc. Each time part or all of one of the selections from the library is used, the producer pays a "needle-drop" fee.

(G)

LIBRARY OF CONGRESS   The central library of the United States government, which assigns standardized identifying (ISBN) numbers to all

(B,P)

---

books, records, and tapes released commercially. These numbers enable consistent identification and easy ordering by local and other libraries. A major division of the library is the Registrar of Copyrights, whose office receives and stores manuscripts of books, songs, and shows, plus record releases, etc., and issues protective copyrights.

LICENSOR/LICENSEE (P,R,B)   The person or company who grants a license, and the person or company who purchases or obtains the license, respectively. The publishing company that grants a mechanical license is the licensor; the record company securing it is the licensee. (*See* MASTER LICENSE AGREEMENT.)

LIFT (A)   A section of a longer piece of music, which may be edited out and used independently. For example, in a 60-second radio jingle, the last 7 seconds may be "lifted" for use as the closing of an otherwise nonmusical radio spot for the same client.

LIFT FEE (A)   A payment due to AFTRA singers if a previously produced vocal jingle is later used in another spot. A type of dubbing fee.

LIFTERS, TAPE (E)   In tape transports, one or more devices that lift the tape away from contact with the heads whenever the transport is put in a fast-wind mode. Tape lifters spare the heads the excessive wear caused by high-speed tape abrasion, and prevent overload of the playback preamps, console, amplifiers, speakers, and engineer's ears, which recorded signals can cause when reproduced full-level

at many times the original tape speed. (*See* CUE MODE.)

LIGHTING GRID   See GRID.

LIGHT METRONOME (E)   A device that beats time silently by flashing a light on and off at some designated number of times per second or minute.

LIGHT VALVE (F)   The mechanism which controls the intensity of light or the area on which light falls in the making of an optical soundtrack from the finished mix. For variable-density tracks, it consists of a narrow slit whose width is varied by the waveform reproduced from the mix, and which in turn modulates the width a beam of light that is focused on a continuously moving strip of photographic film.

LIMITED PARTNERSHIP (B)   A type of business and fund-raising vehicle authorized by the federal government in an effort to stimulate the investment of venture capital in highly speculative, one-time projects. Those who propose the project and will actually produce it are called the general partners. Those who invest in the venture, purchasing a portion of the profits from the product, are called limited partners, since their loss is limited to the amount they invest. Law protects the limited partners from additional losses due to mismanagement or cost overruns by the general partners, and from legal judgment against the general partners or the partnership itself. The unique advantage to the general partners is that, until almost all the money needed is raised, no legal entity exists that

---

(like all corporations) must report all transactions to the government, file withholding and other tax forms, and get bogged down in paperwork before the project begins. If the total amount (called the capitalization) is not raised by a pre-selected deadline, investors' funds already received and held in escrow are simply returned without penalty, and all partners move on without further entanglement. Much simpler to start and end than a corporation.

LIMITER Technically, a compressor whose ratio is infinite—i.e., its out-
(E) put level will never exceed a specified value no matter how much the input level increases over the threshold. Practically, any compressor whose ratio is greater than 10:1.

LINE 1. A signal path or actual cable
(E) through which a signal passes. **2.**
(V) One horizontal scan of the raster in NTSC, PAL, or SECAM video signals. For example, there are 525 lines per frame in NTSC images and 625 lines per frame in PAL images. (*See* FIELD; FRAME.)

LINE ART In the process of printing,
(A,R) the part of the artwork that is essentially lines—e.g., type or lettering, borders and rules, and black and white drawings (without shading).

LINE ITEM In a proposed budget,
(B) any single expense or group of expenses that is separately estimated on one line of the budget. The producer's fee may be one line item; the sum of all the stars' salaries may be another. A whole phase of production, such as edit-

LINE ART.

ing, will contain many line items. Has nothing to do with the "line" in above- and below-the-line budgets.

LINE LEVEL A signal whose average
(E) level is about +4 dBm, a level corresponding to 0 dBVU in most professional audio equipment. Home stereo equipment operates about 10–12 dB below this, and microphones or magnetic instrument pickups between 40 dB and 60 dB below line level.

LINE, 600 OHM An audio line or sig-
(E) nal path with an impedance of 600 ohms. This is the professional standard for interconnection of audio devices.

LINE PAD A passive attenuation net-
(E) work that can be inserted in a line.

LINE PRODUCER If a producer can-
(F,V) not be present at the shooting or recording of a project, a line producer is his stand-in or agent-in-fact. The line producer has func-

tional control over the entire production, but cannot change any of the overall budgetary decisions made by the producer.

LINE-MATCHING TRANSFORMER
(E) An electronic component that matches the output impedance of one device with the input impedance of the next device in a signal path. When these impedances are matched, energy transfer will be most efficient and the frequency content of the signal best preserved in the transfer.

LIP SYNC Synchronization of picture and sound that is accurate enough
(F,V) so that actors' lip movements and the sound of their corresponding words seems simultaneous to the viewer. An error of more than one frame will cause a noticeable error in lip synchronization.

LIQUID CRYSTAL DISPLAY See LCD.

LIST In computers, a printout (on screen or paper) of the codes or
(C) commands contained in a program. Often confused with a menu or catalog.

LIVE Acoustically, a room with a large amount of reverberation. Opposite
(E,G) of dead.

LIVE (or LOCATION) RECORDING
A recording made at a concert or
(E) other performance, but not in a recording studio. Also used to describe any recording in which all parts were played simultaneously—i.e., without overdubbing.

LIVE-TO-TWO-TRACK A live record-
(G) ing in which all instruments and

vocalists are mixed straight onto two-track tape, rather than multi-track. No remixing or other alterations to the original tape are possible later on, except editing. Also called direct-to-two-track.

LOAD 1. Any component or device that consumes power produced by
(E) a separate source. Or, to connect a load as defined above to a power source. (*See* RESISTANCE; IMPEDANCE; POWER, ELECTRIC.)
(C) 2. To copy the contents of a file, data base, or program from disk or other storage medium into a computer's working memory. Opposite of SAVE.

LOADING Placing a resistive load across a line, and generally one
(E) that is of lower impedance than the line or device to which it is connected. This draws additional current from the preceding device, and can strain its capacity.

LOAD RESISTOR 1. A simple resistor placed across a transmission
(E) line in order to decrease the impedance, generally for impedance-matching purposes. 2. A resistor wired across the outputs of a power amplifier, simulating the impedance of a speaker. In this case, a test or "dummy" load.

LOBES In a microphone's polar pattern, the expanding curves, the
(E) maximum value for each of which designates one of the directions of highest sensitivity. A bi-directional polar diagram shows two equal lobes; a cardioid diagram, one large frontal lobe and one or more smaller rear lobes. (*See* POLAR PATTERN (illustration).)

LOCAL/REMOTE SWITCH (or CONTROL)   The switch on a synthesizer that selects whether tones will be generated in response to its own keyboard, or from a remote keyboard via MIDI codes.

(S)

LOCATION RECORDING   See LIVE RECORDING.

LOCKOUT   See BLOCK BOOKING.

LOGARITHM (base #10)   For any number, the mathematical power to which 10 must be raised to equal the specified number. Thus, since $1,000 = 10$ raised to the 3rd power—i.e., $10 \times 10 \times 10$—the log of $1,000 = 3$. Fractional logarithms correspond to numbers less than 10. For example, 10 raised to the 1/2 power equals the square root of 10, or 3.16. Negative logarithms designate fractions, or 1 divided by 10 raised to the numerical power. Examples: $10^{-1} = 1/10$. $10^{-3} = 1/1,000$ or .001. Abbreviation, LOG.

(E)

LOGICAL OPERATION   A CPU function that compares two values or the results of two computations, selecting (according to user-defined parameters) which one to use in subsequent arithmetic or logical operations.

(C)

LOGO   An identifying visual symbol, word, phrase, sound, or short musical idea used as a distinctive identification in advertising for a specific company or product. In music, the logo is often called a signature. Examples are CBS's initials superimposed on their famous eye; the block letters "COKE" printed over a wavy line on Coca-Cola soda cans and trucks; Merrill

(A)

Lynch's line drawing of their bull, etc. Also called an ID.

LONG PLAYING   See LP.

LONG SHOT   See LS.

LOOP   **1.** In general, any repeating process or sequence of events. **2.** In recording, a length of recording tape or magnetic film spliced end-to-beginning. If threaded into the deck or dubber in such a way as to maintain proper tension, one can record continuously onto the loop. Loops can be used in this fashion to create tape delays, especially where the effect must be available for longer than the running time of a continuous reel of tape. If used for playback, a loop will contain sound that has been pre-recorded. The loop will then be reproduced endlessly as long as the deck remains in playback mode. The length of the loop and the tape speed determine the time between each repeat. Sound effects such as room tone or crickets are often made into loops. In this way they can be run continuously during a mix, the engineer fading them in whenever needed. Often called a tape loop. **3.** In tape recorders equipped with auto-locators, a transport operating mode in which the engineer has designated a starting and ending point (in tape time or SMPTE code) and instructed the locator and machine to play the enclosed tape segment repeatedly, rewinding to the starting point each time the end point is reached. Most video interlock devices can be programmed to cause both video and any synchronized audio decks to repeatedly reproduce a loop of

(G)

(E,F)

(E,V,I)

(A) = Advertising • (B) = Business & Law • (C) = Computers • (D) = Digital • (E) = Engineering & Scientific •
(F) = Film • (G) = Music & General • (I) = Interlock & Sync • (J) = Jokes & Jargon • (P) = Music Publishing •
(R) = Record Industry • (S) = Synthesizers • (U) = Unions • (V) = Video

picture and its corresponding sound. The engineer may place the audio or video deck into record mode during a portion of each repeat of the loop, either to replace dialogue or other sync sound, or to perform insert edits. (*See* LOOPING; MARK-IN/MARK-OUT
(F) POINTS.) **4.** In cameras and projectors, a slack section of film located just before and after the gate (where one frame at a time is held stationary during exposure or projection). The loop prevents tearing of the film as it passes from continuously turning sprockets to the intermittent movement, and
(C) back again. **5.** In a computer program, a series of commands the last of which instructs the machine to "go to" or return to the beginning of the series. The resulting repeating process can be used to recalculate a value with new input data on each pass, to achieve ever-closer approximations of a desired
(D,S) result, etc. **6.** In digital signal sampling, the process of editing a sampled sound to connect its endpoint to its beginning. An electronic version of the traditional tape loop.
(E)   FEEDBACK LOOP: An electronic signal path in which the output of a device is directly or indirectly routed back to its input. If the gain in the loop is unity or greater at any frequency, oscillation will result. (*See* FEEDBACK.)

LOOPING Recording of dialogue for
(F,V) a scene after it has been shot, usually to replace location sound that is unusable because of background noise, camera noise, etc. The workprint and sync magnetic film transfer for the scene are spliced into continuous loops and

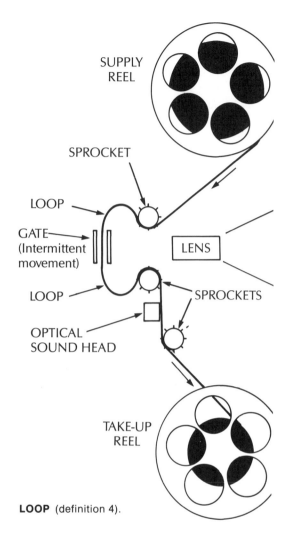

LOOP (definition 4).

projected in a sound studio so that the actors can recreate the phrasing and feeling they had on the set or location. New "takes" are recorded on a separate mag film loop and/or other synchronous tape until an acceptable performance is obtained.

LOUDNESS The apparent intensity of
(E) sound as judged by the listener.

LOUDNESS (CONTROL) On con-
(E) sumer sound reproduction systems,

a circuit and control that progressively adds more bass and treble to audio signals when they are played at lower and lower levels. In theory the loudness circuit applies equal loudness curves to the music, giving the impression of "flat" frequency response even at low volumes.

LOUDSPEAKER (E)   Any transducer that converts the electrical energy of an audio signal into acoustical energy or sound.

DYNAMIC LOUDSPEAKER: **1.** A loudspeaker in which the diaphragm or cone is attached to a coil of wire that moves through a magnetic field in response to the electromagnetic field created when an audio program signal flows through the coil. Also called moving coil loudspeakers. **2.** A loudspeaker whose diaphragm is a ribbon, generally mounted between the poles of a large "U" magnet.

ELECTROSTATIC LOUDSPEAKER: A loudspeaker in which a rigid plate is charged by a DC voltage with one electric polarity and a thin metallic membrane charged oppositely. Variations in this steady voltage potential difference are caused by an audio signal mixed with it, in turn causing a variation in the capacitance between the plate and membrane. This moves the membrane toward and away from the plate, creating sound waves that propagate into the surround-ing air. Also called capacitor (or condensor) loudspeaker.

MOVING COIL LOUDSPEAKER: A dynamic loudspeaker.

LOUDSPEAKER CONE (E)   The vibrating diaphragm of a dynamic or moving coil loudspeaker, usually made of paper and shaped roughly like a cone.

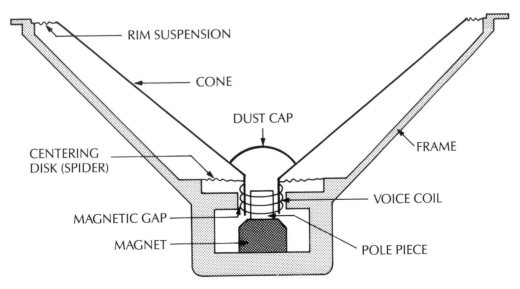

LOUDSPEAKER.

(A) = Advertising • (B) = Business & Law • (C) = Computers • (D) = Digital • (E) = Engineering & Scientific •
(F) = Film • (G) = Music & General • (I) = Interlock & Sync • (J) = Jokes & Jargon • (P) = Music Publishing •
(R) = Record Industry • (S) = Synthesizers • (U) = Unions • (V) = Video

LOW-FREQUENCY OSCILLATOR   See LFO.

LP
(R)
Short for Long Playing record. The familiar 33 1/3 rpm "album" format developed by CBS in the early 1950s.

LS
(F,V)
Long Shot. A composition that shows the entire location or set in which a scene is taking place. Opposite of close-up.

LSB
(D)
Least Significant Bit. The specific bit of audio data in a sample that, if written or read incorrectly, will cause the smallest error in the output signal. Usually the last bit in any sample. Whenever an input signal happens to fall midway between two quantizing increments, the data written will be off by one-half an increment. Thus, the limit of error resolution of a digital system is one half the LSB value used by the sampling circuit.

LSI
(C)
LARGE-SCALE INTEGRATION. The method by which large numbers of ICs are fit onto a single chip, facilitating massive data handling and computational applications. VLSI (Very Large Scale Integration) is the current step in CPU design for ultrapowerful computers.

LYRIC SHEET
(G)
The lyrics or words of a song, printed without music on a page. These are sometimes included with albums. Most often they are supplied by publishers along with demo tapes, so that artists can preview new songs without having to read music or play them from a lead sheet.

– M –

MAGNASYNC/MAGNATECH Two brands of sprocketed tape recorders or playback machines. They can be used to transfer 1/4″ sync tapes or any other sound source onto magnetic film. These brand names are also used generically to indicate a sprocketed tape recorder or playback unit. (*See* DUBBER.)
(F,I)

MAGNETIC FIELD The magnetic flux (or lines of force) surrounding a magnet or any magnetic material, such as recording tape.
(E)

MAGNETIC FILM Recording tape manufactured using a base of the same physical dimensions as various film stocks—i.e., Super 8mm, 16mm, etc. Most magnetic film is 5 mils thick, so that the same length of film and magnetic film will be of equal diameters when wound on reels or cores. Full-coat magnetic film has magnetic oxide applied across its entire width. Striped magnetic film can have one or more thin stripes of oxide applied longitudinally on the film base.
(F)

MAGNETIC RECORDING TAPE A medium capable of recording the changes in an electrical signal in the form of varying intensities of magnetism encoded along its length. Magnetic particles, such as iron oxide, are suspended in a paint-like binder and coated onto continuous plastic or other film base. When passed by an electromagnet through which an audio signal flows, the particles are magnetized in proportion to the instantaneous level of the signal. This linear magnetic "record" can then be reproduced as it in turn passes over a sensitive electromagnetic generator creates an electrical signal in proportion to the magnetism present along the length of tape. (Illustration next page).
(E)

MAIL ORDER A type of marketing in which a manufacturer ships directly to the customer by mail. Coupons advertising a record can be placed in stores or inserted in magazines or newspapers, allowing the customer to send in money and address for direct shipment. Record clubs conduct their business via mail order.
(A,R)

M&E TRACKS Music and Effects tracks of the 35mm three-track
(F,V)

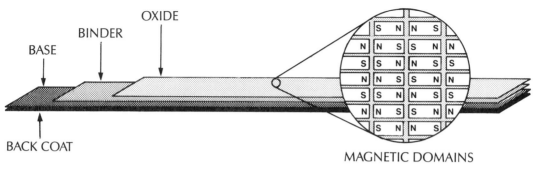

BASE BINDER OXIDE

BACK COAT

MAGNETIC DOMAINS

MAGNETIC RECORDING TAPE.

mix, which can be supplied to foreign distributors of a film so that they can dub in the appropriate language on the dialogue track.

MAIN STORAGE   The internal RAM and/or ROM of a computer, as opposed to auxiliary storage such as floppy disks.
(C)

MAJOR-MINOR   A record company that releases a substantial number of albums each year, but whose products are distributed by one of the five major U.S. labels: WEA, CBS, RCA, MCA, and POLYGRAM.
(R)

MARKET   1. The group of people that uses or purchases a specific product or service. Also called a target market. 2. Loosely, all the potential buyers of a product or service on a nationwide or regional basis. 3. The total dollar amount projected to be spent by the potential buyers of all brands of any type of product in a specific time period, usually a year. Example: The market for cosmetics in the United States is $6 billion a year.
(A)

MARKETING   The organized selling of something over an extended period of time. The entire sales effort, from design or copywriting
(A)

to final publication or broadcasting of the completed campaign. Even prior research and evaluation of audience response is a part of the marketing of a product or concept.

MARKETING MIX   The relative amount of various types of advertising used in the overall marketing campaign. Print, radio, TV, billboards, in-store promotion, etc. are all budgeted separately, and each will receive an amount that reflects its respective importance to the entire campaign. Also, the entirety of all media used in a campaign, without specific reference to the individual breakdown by medium.
(A)

MARKET POSITIONING   The use of a marketing mix to create an impression of the "rank" of a product or service relative to similar products or services by other makers. In cars, for example, Cadillac is "positioned" higher then Chevrolet, but lower than Rolls-Royce. Also used to designate the process of finding and reaching a specific target audience for a product, and establishing the "quality level" or image of the specific product with that audience.
(A)

MARK-IN/MARK-OUT POINTS (V,I)   In SMPTE video synchronization and post-production, the SMPTE code addresses selected by the editor as the beginning and end points of a loop. The synchronizer will stop master and slave transports at the mark-out point after each insert take, then automatically return all machines to the mark-in point in preparation for another take. Various synchronizers automatically add pre- and post-roll times to the mark-ins and -outs, so it is important to understand how the unit at hand internally defines all these locations.

MARRY (F)   To print sound and picture onto the same strip of film, as on an answer or release print.

MASK (F,V)   A device used in the camera or printer gate, or in front of the vidicon tube, to limit the area of the frame that will receive light from the camera lens or (in a printer) from the original exposed shot. Used to facilitate split-screen shots, to alter the aspect ratio, etc. A type of matte.

MASKING (E)   The process by which a sound becomes indistinguishable due to the presence of other sounds with similar frequency distributions, with conflicting rhythmic patterns, or other characteristics that can draw the listener's attention away from the original sound.

MASTER (G)   (noun) 1. An oft-confusing term that can be applied to an audio tape, a lacquer disc used in the pressing of records, a videotape, one fader on a console that controls all the others, etc. Make sure the context is clear before using this term.

(I,V,F)   2. In the interlock of film or video playback and audio tape machines, the single machine whose normal operating frame rate or SMPTE code readout will be followed by all the others. The SMPTE synchronizer or Sel-syn drive motor will follow every move of the master in both directions and instruct the slave machines to mimic these moves precisely. (*See* SLAVE.)

MASTER (R)   (verb) To cut a lacquer or direct metal master for a record, or make the CD master from which release pressings will ultimately be pressed. (*See* MASTERING; MASTERING LATHE; METAL PARTS; MATRIX NUMBER; DIRECT METAL MASTERING; PITS.)

MASTERING ENGINEER (R)   The person who operates the mastering lathe and makes lacquer masters, acetates, etc.

MASTERING LATHE (R)   Consists of a lathe bed (a heavy turntable) and sled or carriage (the actual cutting stylus or head, arm, and armature). Using a high-wattage amplifier to drive the cutting stylus, with a pitch/depth control computer that controls the depth, width, and spacing of grooves being cut, the mastering lathe makes the master lacquer disk from which metal parts and then vinyl records are ultimately made.

MASTER LICENSE AGREEMENT (R,B)   A legal agreement or contract by which a record company acquires the right to release an independently produced master tape (or a master originally released on a separate label in a foreign country or territory). The label normally pays a licensing fee and agrees to give the independent producer (or original label) a royalty on sales, from which the artists and sometimes the mechanical royalties are paid. The licensee label's rights may expire after a specified period of time, and may only allow the label to release the master in its own country or certain specified territories.

MASTER PURCHASE AGREEMENT
(R,B)   Similar to the master license agreement, except that the label buys the master tape and all rights to it from the independent producer or its original backer. The producer or backer is generally paid an amount called the recoupment advance, which represents the amount the label might have spent to produce the tape itself, including payment of musicians and singers according to union scales, recording costs, etc. The producer/backer will also receive points in the record's profits, from which the artist's and sometimes the mechanical royalties will be paid. (*See* ALL-IN DEAL; SCHEDULE D.)

MASTER SYNTH   The synthesizer that controls one or more other synthesizers via MIDI code outputs.
(S)

MASTER TAPE   Usually, a completed tape, used in tape-to-disc transfer, or from which other tape copies are made. The final recorded product as it is intended for duplication and/or broadcasting. Also (leading to confusion), the multitrack tape that will be mixed
(E)

down to give a final two-track master tape as described above.

MATCH CUT   An edit between two shots of the same scene or action, in which no real-time is skipped on screen. For example, if a scene was shot with two cameras (or precisely re-enacted for two sequential takes), the editor might use a match cut at the very frame where an actor slams his fist on a desk. The cut might be done to get a better view, to heighten the shock value of the action, or to show it from another actor's point of view.
(F,V)

MATCHING TRANSFORMER   Short for impedance-matching transformer. Used to interconnect devices or lines of different impedance. Necessary, for example, in order to use a low-impedance microphone with a guitar amp, which has high-impedance inputs. The transformer increases the energy transfer between mic and input and preserves high-frequency response in the signal.
(E)

MATRIXING   The three-step process in record and CD production by which metal parts are made.
(R)

MATRIX NUMBER   An identifying number engraved by the mastering engineer between successive grooves of the end spiral of a record. Since the master disk has no label and cannot be played, matrix numbers are its only identification. For example, the matrix number "RCA 3147-A-E1" would designate the record company, the release number, Side A, and the fact that this is the first master disc
(R)

---

made for the East Coast pressing plant.

MATTE
(F,V)
Any opaque object or surface which prevents light from reaching a specified area of the film frame or video receiving tube. Mattes can be located in front of the camera lens, in the camera gate, or in the gate of an optical printer or projector. (*See* TRAVELLING MATTE; BLUE SCREEN; CHROMA-KEY.)

MCU
(F,V)
Medium Close-up. A shot in which the actor's head nearly fills the screen.

M.D.
(R)
MUSIC DIRECTOR. At a radio station, the person who selects what records will be on the playlist or chart, which records will be in each rotation schedule, which will be "pick hits," etc.

MECHANICAL LICENSE
(P,R)
A written document giving a record company permission to make mechanical copies of a song. Issued by the composer, his publishing company, or Harry Fox Agency. The current statutory rate (since January 1, 1986) is 5 cents per copy of the record, cassette, or CD manufactured. Statutory rates are set jointly by the NMPA, Harry Fox Agency and the federal Copyright Tribunal. The record company is also required to make regular accountings and payments as it manufactures more copies. Publishers often grant a rate reduction or allow record companies to pay only for copies sold. Any such non-statutory arrangement must be made in writing and signed by the copyright holder. (*See* COMPULSORY LICENSE.)

MECHANICAL ROYALTY
(P,R)
The money generated for the composer and publishing company by the sale of records and tapes. The record company pays these royalties to the Harry Fox Agency or other collection agency representing the song's publisher. The agency then pays the publisher, who in turn pays the composer(s).

MECHANICALS
(P,R)
(A,R)
1. Short for mechanical royalties.' 2. The complete, camera-ready artwork for a record jacket, poster, or any item to be printed.

MEDIA
(A)
A very broad term that can collectively designate all vehicles for publication of print advertising and broadcasting of radio and television spots, or refer to a subset of all these vehicles. For instance, print media includes magazines, newspapers, billboards, flyers, etc. Television media includes network, cable, syndication, etc.

MEDIA ANALYST (MA)
(A)
An advertising agency employee who, at the request of an account executive, researches the type and amount of media exposure that is best for a finished print or broadcast campaign. The MA suggests specific magazines, radio, or TV stations that reach the target audience, the best size for print ads or times for spot broadcast, etc. This information and the client's budget then go to the media buyer.

MEDIA BUYER
(A)
The person at an ad agency who actually places orders for space in newspapers, magazines, other print media, ad time on radio or television stations, etc. He

---

specifies the size and placement of print ads, and the time and frequency of radio and television ads to be aired for the client.

MEDIA MIX   The detailed allocation of money a client will spend to (A) present visual, radio, and television ads to the public, sometimes listing the specific magazines and/or newspapers, AM and FM stations, and TV stations on which spots will run. For example, from a total media buy of $1 million, the agency may recommend a media mix of $250,000 to be spent on the print buy, $150,000 on the radio buy, and $600,000 on the TV buy.

MEDIUM CLOSE-UP   See MCU.

MEDIUM SHOT   See MS.

MEGA   A prefix meaning one million times the unit that follows—e.g., a (E,C) megabyte. Abbreviation, m.

MENC   Music Educators National Conference. Holds annual conventions (G) and monitors the progress of new educational techniques, etc.

MENU   A listing of all the options, functions, or programs available to (C) a computer operator, generally displayed on the CRT screen. Sometimes called the catalog.

MESSAGE   Any piece of information, including a request, that a computer (C) displays on the screen in the course of a program, or as a result of its operating system. It may ask for more data, tell the user he has incorrectly typed something, etc. (*See* COMMAND; PROMPT.)

METAL PARTS   Impressions—positive and negative—made from the lac- (R) quer master disc and used to produce the final pressings of a record. First the lacquer master is plated

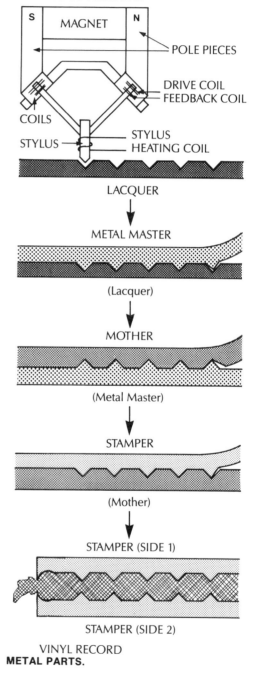

STEREO CUTTER HEAD
LACQUER
METAL MASTER
(Lacquer)
MOTHER
(Metal Master)
STAMPER
(Mother)
STAMPER (SIDE 1)
STAMPER (SIDE 2)
VINYL RECORD
METAL PARTS.

with nickel, giving a negative impression from which, when peeled off the lacquer, the grooves project upward. From this metal master a positive mother is made, again by plating and peeling. From the mother a stamper is made, which is again a negative impression. The stamper is then used in the record press to squash a lump of heat-softened vinyl into the final pressing. (*See* MASTERING LATHE; DIRECT METAL MASTERING; MATRIX NUMBER.)

dB SCALE (Top)

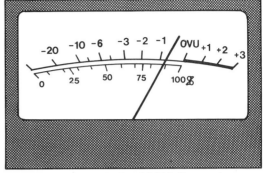

MODULATION SCALE (Bottom)

VU METER.

METER
(E)   A device for measuring voltage, current, or other electrical quantities, or for comparing two electrical signals, as in the measurement of phase relationships. (*See* BALLISTICS.)

PEAK READING METER: A level meter driven by a circuit that registers and holds transient peaks in the signal long enough for the pointer or display to show the highest instantaneous level in each peak.

VU METER: A level meter calibrated in volume units. Most VU meters are calibrated in decibels and % modulation, a linear scale defined such that 100% modulation = 0 dBVU. The ballistics of a VU meter (a function of its components and the inertia of the indicator itself) approximates the response of the human ear to sudden level changes. The ear senses the average level of sounds, not their momentary peaks. Similarly, the VU meter cannot move fast enough to indicate every peak. When the meter bounces up to 0 dBVU, the peak that caused that bounce may actually have reached +10 dBVU or more.

MIC
(E)   Short for microphone when the word is used as a noun or adjective. (*See* MIKE.)

MIC/LINE SELECTOR SWITCH   On
(E)   a recording console, the two-position switch that allows the engineer to select whether each module will control the signal from a microphone in the studio, or the previously recorded track of a tape or other signal coming into the console at line level.

MICROBAR   A unit of sound pressure,
(E)   literally one millionth of a bar, the unit by which atmospheric pressures are measured. 1 microbar = 1 dyne/cm^2. Obviously, even very loud sounds cause only small numerical changes in air pressure compared with daily atmospheric variations. In this light, one can think of atmospheric pressure changes as very loud, *very* low frequency sounds, perhaps just a few cycles per *week!*

MICRON   A standard unit of length,
(E)   equal to one millionth of a meter. Used to specify very small measure-

---

ments such as tape recorder head gap widths.

MICROPHONE (E)   Any transducer that converts acoustical energy or sound into an electrical audio signal. (*See* POLAR PATTERN, for listings by various directional characteristics.)

MICROPHONE (1) (E)   By principle of output signal derivation.

CONTACT MICROPHONE: A microphone mounted directly on a sound-producing body such as an instrument, and whose diaphragm picks up vibrations directly through the resulting vibration of the microphone's own housing—i.e., without sound being carried through the air.

DUAL DIAPHRAGM MICROPHONE: A microphone whose output signal is derived by electrically combining the outputs of two separate diaphragms. Different polar patterns can be achieved by adding various proportions of the outputs from each diaphragm, or by reversing the polarity of one diaphragm, or both. In most condenser models the DC source powers both the internal pre-amps and the mixing circuit that varies the overall pattern. Another type uses separate diaphragms for high and low frequencies, rather than to achieve different polar patterns.

PHASE SHIFT MICROPHONE: A microphone whose diaphragm movement and output is the result of acoustical addition and subtraction of sound waves entering both on-axis and through side or rear ports. These ports are located to reinforce or eliminate sounds coming from off-axis, producing the desired polar pattern and response. Most phase-shift mics are unidirectional.

DUAL DIAPHRAGM, PRESSURE, PRESSURE GRADIENT

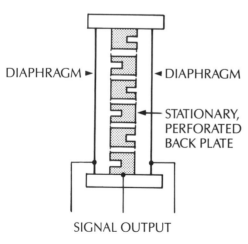

DIAPHRAGM ►   ◄ DIAPHRAGM

← STATIONARY, PERFORATED BACK PLATE

SIGNAL OUTPUT

PHASE SHIFT

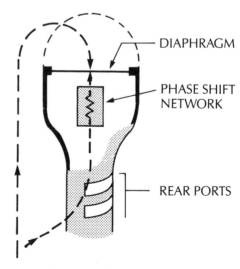

DIAPHRAGM

PHASE SHIFT NETWORK

REAR PORTS

MICROPHONES. Principle of operations. Pressure, pressure gradient, dual diaphragm: The method of combining the three output signals determines whether the specific response is pressure, pressure gradient, or dual diaphragm.

PRESSURE MICROPHONE: A microphone that produces its electrical output based on the instantaneous variations in air pressure at the diaphragm. The diaphragm covers a sealed capsule enclosure whose internal pressure remains constant. Thus, pressure mics are omni-directional microphones since the direction from which sound waves approach is immaterial.

PRESSURE GRADIENT MICROPHONE: A microphone that produces its electrical output in proportion to the difference in acoustic pressure between the front and rear of the diaphragm. A bi-directional microphone, since only the sound waves coming from the front or rear will cause the diaphragm or ribbon to move at all.

MICROPHONE (2)   By design and function of the capsule.

(E)   CONDENSER (or CAPACITOR) MICROPHONE: A microphone in which the vibrating diaphragm is electrically charged and acts as one plate of a capacitor. The movement of the diaphragm or membrane with respect to a rigid plate (charged with the opposite polarity) causes a tiny change in the potential between them. This is amplified by an internal pre-amplifier and sent to the recording console. DC power is required to run the pre-amplifier. Works like an electrostatic speaker in reverse.

DYNAMIC MICROPHONE: A moving coil or ribbon microphone, in which the movement of the diaphragm (with its attached coil of very fine wire) or ribbon through the field of a permanent magnet induces a varying output voltage.

This voltage is sent to the recording console. Works like a dynamic loudspeaker in reverse.

ELECTRET MICROPHONE: A condenser microphone whose diaphragm and plate are semipermanently charged during manufacture. The charge can dissipate after several years, which will cause a loss of output level, etc.

MOVING COIL MICROPHONE: A type of dynamic microphone in which the diaphragm is attached to a small coil of very thin wire. The motion of this coil through the field of a permanent magnet produces the output signal.

RIBBON MICROPHONE: A dynamic microphone in which the diaphragm is a metallic ribbon. The ribbon is suspended between the poles of a permanent magnet. Audio signals are generated in the ribbon itself as it vibrates through the magnetic field. Because sounds approaching the ribbon's edge (from either side along its surface) will fail to move it, ribbon mics are always bi-directional. Other patterns can be achieved by blocking sounds approaching the ribbon from various directions.

MICROPHONE(3)   Special purpose and multi-purpose.

(E)   DUAL-PATTERN MICROPHONE: A microphone with two, user-selectable polar patterns.

MULTI-PATTERN MICROPHONE: A microphone with more than two user-selectable polar patterns.

LAVALIER MICROPHONE: A small microphone intended to be worn on a cord around the neck of the singer or speaker. Many lavaliers have accentuated high-

DYNAMIC
(Side View)

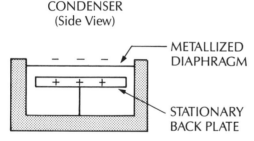

DIAPHRAGM

COIL

POLE PIECE

MAGNET

MAGNETIC
RETURN PATH

ACOUSTICAL DAMPING
MATERIAL

RIBBON
(Top View)

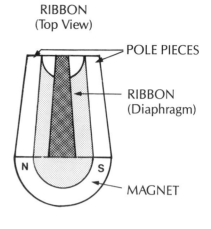

POLE PIECES

RIBBON
(Diaphragm)

MAGNET

CONDENSER
(Side View)

METALLIZED
DIAPHRAGM

STATIONARY
BACK PLATE

MICROPHONE CAPSULE DESIGNS.

frequency response to make up for their being positioned below the path by which highs leave the mouth. Lavaliers can also be clipped onto (or sometimes inside) the singer's or speaker's clothing.

PRESSURE ZONE (PZM) MICROPHONE: A type of microphone first developed and marketed by Crown Corporation, in which a dynamic or condenser capsule is mounted flush at the surface of a rigid metal plate or other plate several inches on a side. When the plate is taped to a wall, the inside of a piano lid, or other rigid surface, only direct sound can reach the capsule. This eliminates

most direct/indirect phasing problems that can be generated by virtue of mic placement itself, and (in theory) leads to a clearer sound. Many companies now make PZM mics.

SHOTGUN MICROPHONE: A highly directional microphone, generally used for film and television sound. The mic gets its name from a long tubular body, and the fact that its handgrip, resembling a pistol grip, is generally used to follow the sound source with the mic. (*See* ACOUSTIC LABYRINTH (illustration).)

STEREO MICROPHONE: A single microphone housing that

contains two completely separate transducing systems. The two outputs can be fed to two separate inputs of a console or tracks of a recorder.

MICROPHONE (or MIC) LEVEL

(E) An electronic signal level (actually a range of levels) that corresponds to the output level of the "average" microphone. Generally accepted as −50 dBV, although actual microphone output levels vary between −65 dBV for some dynamic models and −35 dBV for a few condenser types.

MICROPHONE LINE   Any cable that

(E) carries the signal from a microphone to the recording console or to another component or device in which it is amplified. Most mic lines are shielded to protect the signal from RF and ambient fields.

MICROPHONE PREAMPLIFIER   1.

(E) In a recording console, the first stage of amplification through which the signal from a microphone passes. Here, its level is raised to line level for processing or mixing with other signals. **2.** A small amplifier built into a condenser microphone to boost the tiny output level of the capsule before transmission through the mic line.

MIDDLE OF THE ROAD   See MOR.

MIDI (or M.I.D.I.)   Musical Instru-

(S) ment Digital Interface. A digital data format or scheme in which control signals generated by the keyboard commands played on one synthesizer can trigger the tone-generating circuits of other synthesizers. One player can thus simultaneously draw on the unique

sound settings or patches of several synthesizers to create combined effects that would otherwise be impossible. The MIDI system was developed by Roland Corp.

MIDI CODE   The digital data-trans-

(S) mission format by which MIDI-generating or MIDI-receiving devices communicate with each other. Exactly 31,250 BPS, with word length of 30 bits. Or the MIDI data itself.

MIDI SEQUENCER   An electronic

(S) device that generates continuous MIDI code, and using this as its time-frame for events, triggers synthesizers, drum machines, and other electronic devices capable of responding to MIDI signals. These, in turn, generate their sounds on time cues from the sequencer.

MIDI SEQUENCER, COMPUTER   A

(S,C) computer that uses a software program to emulate the operation of a MIDI sequencer, as defined above.

MIDI-THRU BOX   A circuit that

(S) divides a single MIDI signal into separate, buffered signals, each of which can drive a separate slave device.

MIDI-THRU INPUTS/OUTPUTS   A

(S) MIDI input on many synthesizers that extracts from an incoming MIDI signal the channels of data needed to control that synthesizer, regenerating and passing all other MIDI data to the output. Since data is degraded by successive regeneration, it is better to use a MIDI-thru box if several synthesizers are to be MIDI'd.

MIEA   See MUSIC INDUSTRY EDU-
(G,B) CATORS ASSOCIATION.

MIKE (verb)   To set up one or more
(E)   microphones in order to capture
the sound of something—e.g., "Have
you miked the drums yet?" In
general, in describing the use of
microphones, use the spelling
"mike." In describing the microphone itself or its accessories, use
the spelling "mic."

MIL   One one-thousandth of an inch.
(E)   Analog recording tape thickness is
measured in mils, most studio
quality tape being 1.5 mils thick.
The thinner the tape, the more will
fit on a reel, thus the longer the
reel will play or record. 1/2 mil
tape is the thinnest manufactured,
and is not recommended for professional applications since it stretches
easily and allows more print-
through than thicker tapes.

MILLI   A prefix meaning one one-
(E)   thousandth of the quantity that follows. Example: Milliseconds, the
time unit in which delay lines are
usually calibrated. Usually abbreviated by a lower case "m"
written before the specified quantity, e.g., "mm" for millimeters.

MINUTES/SECONDS/FRAMES   A
(V,I)   series of three numbers separated
by colons, indicating a particular
point in a videotape. In the United
States there are approximately 30
video "frames" photographed and
shown per second (actually 29.97
frames per second in NTSC color).
Thus, a typical video location
might be 23:14:29, or 23 minutes,
14 seconds, 29 frames after the
starting point of 0:00:00. Sometimes, a fourth pair of numbers,

representing hours, precedes the
M/S/F numbers. It is gratuitous to
use hour numbers for short
programs. (*See* COUNTS)

MIRAGE   The Quantel Corporation
(V)   model name for a very sophisticated special-effects video image
processor or manipulator. Functionally similar to the ADO, but
with far greater memory and image processing capabilities. Video
images can be topologically
mapped onto or "wrapped around"
three-dimensional surfaces such as
spheres, cones, and cubes, "peeled
away" like the pages of a book etc.
The Mirage can also perform real-
time transformations of one image
into another and create complex
combinations of various special
effects.

MITOUT SOUND   See MOS.

MIX   1. The name of the major trade
(E)   journal for the audio industry. It
publishes advances in technology,
details the work of engineers and
producers on well-known recording sessions, prints features on
major new facilities, and gives the
annual TEC Awards (for Technical Excellence and Creativity) to
the best studios, engineers, record
companies, educational institutions,
(E)   etc. 2. The composite blend of live
sounds and/or recorded tracks in
the finished audio signal or recorded
program. Used as a verb, to
produce the finished audio program
by blending all these sounds and
tracks.

MIXDOWN SESSION   A recording
(E)   session during which the separate
tracks of a multi-track tape are
processed and combined or blended

---

into two or four channels, then rerecorded onto a two- or four-track machine. The resulting tape, called the master tape, is the finished product.

MIXER **1.** The person who mixes or
(F,V) dubs all the soundtracks of a film or video production. **2.** The con-
(E) sole by which the engineer controls the relative level and sound of each track as he mixes or dubs the film. **3.** Another name for a fader.

MIXING CONSOLE(BOARD) See
(E) RECORDING CONSOLE.

MODEM Short for MOdulator/ DEModulator. Any device that
(C) allows two computers to communicate via telephone lines. If the data is transmitted via tones sent through the mouth-piece and ear-piece transducers in the phone's receiver, an acoustic coupler modem is used. If the data goes straight from the computer to the wall jack, a direct coupler is used. (*See* VIDEOTEX.)

MODES, ROOM See ROOM MODES.

MODULATION **1.** Electrically, another term for signal level. Overmodula-
(E) tion indicates that the level is too high and therefore distorting. Undermodulation indicates that it is too low to be usable. This term is used primarily in England and Europe. 100% modulation is normally defined as nominal full-level value for a signal—for example, 100% mod = 0 dBVU in line-level terms. VU meters are often calibrated in % mod and dB. (*See*
(G) IN THE MUD/IN THE RED.) **2.** In a musical performance or ar-

rangement, a change of key signature. Modulations are used to increase energy level, to avoid boredom in a repetitive arrange-
(S) ment, etc. **3.** The process of periodically changing the pitch, timbre, or other parameter of a synthesizer's output signal. Usually accomplished
(E) with an LFO or other controller. **4.** A change in an ongoing signal caused by outside stimulus—e.g., frequency modulation, bi-phase modulation, etc.

MONAURAL Literally, one ear. See
(E,G) MONOPHONIC.

MONITOR (noun) **1.** A loudspeaker in a control room or other listening
(E) area.
(C) **2.** A cathode ray tube (CRT) or, more simply, a television on whose screen programs and data can be displayed.

MONITOR (verb) To listen back to a recorded performance or a live
(E) performance in the control room.

MONITOR MODULE On a recording console, the module with the
(E) switching and master volume controls for studio and control-room monitor speakers. This module often contains master cue selector switches and cue volume level controls, and sometimes the master reverb sends and returns.

MONOCHROME Describing television images, black and white, either
(V) by virtue of having been shot with a black and white system, or by having the color or chrominance removed electronically.

MONO MODE In MIDI interconnec-
(S) tion of synthesizers, an operating

mode for multi-voiced synthesizers in which each MIDI input channel triggers notes from a separate patch or voice. Each voice, however, can only output one note at a time. Also called omni-off/mono mode.

MONOPHONIC (MONO)   Literally, single sound. In monophonic recording or playback, all sounds are blended together on one channel or track, or heard from a single loudspeaker.

(E)

MONTAGE   A rapidly cut sequence of film or video shots, often with many dissolves and/or superimpositions, used to give a generalized view of a process such as building a house, or to imply the passage of time.

(F,V,E)

MOR   Middle Of the Road. A radio programming format designating light rock, easy listening, and the like. As opposed to AOR and "Top 40," which feature hard rock and up-tempo records.

(R)

MOS   MitOut Sound. Or, more clearly, "without sound." Any shot photographed without sync sound may be designated MOS. The term originated with a German cameraman unable to correctly pronounce "without." Also called wild or non-sync picture.

(F,V)

MOST SIGNIFICANT BIT   See MSB.

MOTHER   A positive impression made by a two-step plating process, reproducing the exact shape of the grooves on a lacquer master on a metal disk. In direct metal mastering, the master itself is functionally a mother. From it, stamper and

pressings will be made directly. (*See* METAL PARTS.)

MOTION SENSING   In a tape transport, an electro-mechanical system designed to prevent damage to the tape (a) when the operator presses the play button while the transport is in a fast-wind mode, or (b) when two conflicting motion buttons are pressed simultaneously. The system brings the tape to a stop before the next operating mode is activated.

(E)

MOVIOLA   Strictly, the brand name of a prominent manufacturer of motion picture editing equipment. The term is often applied to any type of viewing and/or editing machine that runs picture and sound interlocked in sync. It is used by the film editor to decide which scenes and takes and parts thereof will be used in the workprint. The film and sound tracks (one or more of each) may run vertically on an upright moviola, (the industry standard from the 1920s through the 1960s) or horizontally on a flatbed version. (*See* FLATBED EDITING MACHINE; STEENBECK; EDIT DROID.)

(F)

MS   MEDIUM SHOT A shot showing a person from below the waist to above the head.

(F,V)

MSB   MOST SIGNIFICANT BIT. Opposite of LSB.

(D)

M-S (MIDDLE-SIDE) MATRIX   A transformer network that combines the outputs of the two microphones used in an M-S pair, sending their additive signal to one input module (for stereo left), their subtractive signal to another (for stereo right).

(E)

M-S (MIDDLE-SIDE) MIKING (E) A stereo miking technique that usually employs a cardioid microphone aimed directly at the sound source, and a bi-directional microphone, located at the same position, with its live axes pointed 90 degrees left and right of the cardioid's axis. The outputs are combined additively and subtractively (A + B and A − B) by a transformer-matrix or active-matrix circuit, giving two stereo channels that can be recorded on separate tracks. This technique provides a very spatial result, and because the mics are coincident, eliminates destructive phase cancellation. (*See* X-Y MIKING; BLUMLEIN PAIR; BINAURAL RECORDING; SPACED PAIR.)

MSO (V,A) Multiple System Operator. A cable television company that issues more than one channel of programming.

M-S MIKING.

MTV (R,V) Music Television. The major national cable television broadcaster of music videos produced as promotional vehicles for records. Formed in 1981 as an experiment without any guaranteed audience, MTV is now a major division of Warner Communications.

MULTIPLE (E) In a recording console, a group of jacks in the patch bay that are connected in parallel. A line-level signal patched into any of these jacks can then be sent to more than one destination by patching from the other jacks into separate devices or inputs. The original signal is thus multiplied or replicated for various uses. Often called a mult for short.

MULTIPLE SYSTEM OPERATOR See MSO.

MULTITAP (E) In digital delays, the ability to obtain delayed output signals (usually via patch points) at more than one point as the signal passes through a series of delay circuits or chips. The signals derived at each of these taps, each with a separate delay time, can be routed to separate destinations.

MULTI-TRACK (E) A tape recorder, console, or other device capable of handling more than two tracks of information separately. Generally, the term is applied to situations in which eight or more tracks are used. Also, the actual recording tape on which eight or more tracks are recorded.

MULTI-TRACKING (E) The use of wide-format audio recording tapes on which parallel tracks are recorded, each containing a performance by one or more instrumentalists or vocalists. A 24-track, 2″ (wide) tape may have separate tracks for kick drum, snare, tom toms, hi-hat, etc.; bass guitar, guitars, piano, etc.; lead vocal, background vocalist(s), percussion. (*See* OVERDUBBING; PUNCHING IN/PUNCHING OUT.)

MULTIPLEXER   In digital recording or computing, a device that con-
(D,C) verts parallel data to serial data. For example, each audio voltage sample taken by an A-D converter is an n-bit binary number, all of whose digits are generated simultaneously. They cannot be stored to tape simultaneously, so a multiplexer is used to sequence the bits for recording. A demultiplexer reassembles sequenced data into complete words or samples the data again.

MULTIPROGRAMMING   The capability of some computers to handle
(C) many programs simultaneously, often communicating with users at several locations.

MUSIC DIRECTOR   See M.D.

MUSIC EDUCATORS NATIONAL CONFERENCE   See MENC.

MUSIC HOUSE   A company with composers, arrangers, and producers
(F,V,A) on staff, and that has its own studios, etc. Clients in need of custom music can get it done without fear of delays caused by using multiple creative and technical sources.

MUSIC INDUSTRY EDUCATORS AS-SOCIATION (MIEA)   The
(B,G) professional association that brings together music educators and manufacturers to update the rapidly changing curriculum for all studies of music, composition, production, the music industry, and all related industries.

MUSIC TELEVISION   See MTV.

MUSIC TRACK   1. An edited track of magnetic film containing music.
(F,V) There may be more than one music track for a film, especially if the editor calls for a dissolve between two scenes, each with its own music track. 2. In the 35mm three-track mix, the recorded track that contains all the music mixed from various music tracks, as defined above.

MUSIC VIDEO   A short motion picture or video production sponsored
(V,F) by a record label in order to promote the sales of a single or album. The soundtrack of the "video" consists mainly of the song itself, perhaps in an edited or extended version, sometimes with sound effects added to complement the on-screen action. A short dramatic sequence may precede or follow the song. The entire video rarely runs more than five minutes, unless the featured artist is extremely popular. (*See* MTV.)

MUSIC VIDEO PRODUCERS ASSOCIA-TION   See MVPA.

MUSICAL INSTRUMENT DIGITAL INTERFACE   See MIDI.

MUSIQUE CONCRETE   Taped music made by recording the ready-made
(G) timbres of a group of sound sources, including instruments, sound effects, or electronic sources, then transforming or processing

---

them in various ways, and finally cutting and assembling them in a montage.

MUTE
(E,G)
To cut off a sound, input, or track suddenly. Also, to reduce monitor level by a known amount via a pre-set button on the console, normally to facilitate verbal communication in the control room.

MUTE MODE
(E)
In console automation systems, an operational write mode in which the engineer enters off/on commands for various channels, turning these off and on to avoid noise, mistakes, and any unwanted sounds.

MUTE-WRITE
(E)
The operating mode of console automation systems in which engineer mute commands are written onto tape or floppy disk so subsequent passes will be identically muted.

MVPA
(B)
Music Video Producers Association. Sets technical standards for music videos and represents producers of the videos in their dealings with the major record labels (their clients) and the major broadcasters of their products— i.e., network television, MTV, etc.

MYLAR (POLYESTER)
(E)
A strong plastic used as the base for most recording tape. Mylar is stable, easily coated, and remains supple in extended storage. The word is a Dupont Company trademark, but is used generically for any polyester base.

- N -

N.A.B. NATIONAL ASSOCIATION OF BROADCASTERS. A professional organization that sets technical standards for AM, FM, and television broadcast. The N.A.B. designed the pre- and post-equalization curves now universally incorporated into all American tape recorders. The NAB also maintains powerful political lobbies to uphold the interests of broadcasters in state and federal governmental affairs.

(E)

NABET National Association of Broadcast Employees and Technicians. A labor union formed to represent radio and television technicians. Later broadened to include motion picture technicians, especially those involved in lower budget or location shoots. In contrast, IATSE rules, including minimum calls and stiff overtime rates, were originally established to protect members from the vagaries of the Hollywood studio system. However, IATSE has now relaxed some rules in order to become more competitive with NABET.

(F,V)

NAGRA A brand of tape recorder originally designed to record on-location synchronous sound for motion pictures. It uses 1/4″ tape and is generally equipped with a crystal sync generator. These Nagras are portable, designed for use while being carried, and match the mechanical and electronic performance of the best studio recorders. There are various models and track formats, now including several made just for studio use, in making transfers, film mixes, etc. (*See* NEO-PILOT TONE.)

(F)

NAIRD National Association of Independent Record Distributors. Organized in 1972 to help small labels and their distributors share market information and increase their sales. An alternative to NARM.

(R)

NAMM National Association of Music Merchants. The association that represents all the industries that do business directly or indirectly with the music industry. Members include schools and colleges, equipment manufacturers, acoustic and electronic musical instrument manufacturers, music publishers, computer and software companies, etc. The semi-annual conventions

(B)

are spectacular marketplaces for new hardware and software of all kinds.

NANOWEBER   A unit of magnetic flux. Literally one billionth of a weber (via the "nano" prefix). On recording tape, specific or reference flux density is measured in nanowebers per meter.

(E)

NARAS   National Academy of Recording Arts and Sciences. An organization designed to promote artistic, creative, and technical excellence in the recording industry. NARAS members nominate and select Grammy recipients, etc. Members must have worked in some capacity on at least six commercially released records, and make up a very distinguished cross-section of the entire entertainment industry.

(R)

NARM   National Association of Record Merchandisers. An organization whose members are the major record companies and distributors in the United States.

(R)

NARRATION TRACK   An edited track of magnetic film that contains narrative material other than sync dialogue. This track is normally mixed in with the dialogue track in the 35mm three-track mix.

(F,V)

NARRATOR   An off-screen voice that explains what is being seen, adds commentary or information to the plot or characters, introduces various characters, or reads any material not recited by actors who are on-camera.

(F,V,A)

NARROWCASTING   As opposed to broadcasting, a type of radio or television programming that aims

(A)

to reach a selected audience with some special taste or preference.

NATIONAL ACADEMY OF RECORDING ARTS AND SCIENCES NARAS   See NARAS.

NATIONAL ACADEMY OF VIDEO ARTS AND SCIENCES   See NAVAS.

NATIONAL ASSOCIATION OF BROADCAST EMPLOYEES AND TECHNICIANS   See NABET

NATIONAL ASSOCIATION OF BROADCASTERS   See N.A.B.

NATIONAL ASSOCIATION OF INDEPENDENT RECORD DISTRIBUTORS   See NAIRD.

NATIONAL ASSOCIATION OF MUSIC MERCHANTS   See NAMM.

NATIONAL ASSOCIATION OF RECORD MERCHANDISERS   See NARM

NATIONAL ENDOWMENT FOR THE ARTS   See NEA.

NATIONAL MUSIC PUBLISHERS ASSOCIATION   See N.M.P.A.

NATIONAL TELEVISION STANDARDS COMMITTEE   See N.T.S.C.

NATIONAL CONTRACTS DIVISION   The group of AFM officials who negotiate agreements with motion picture producers, television networks, etc.

(U)

NAVAS   National Academy of Video Arts and Sciences. Analagous to NARAS in the recording industry. A highly prestigious organization

(V)

(A) = Advertising • (B) = Business & Law • (C) = Computers • (D) = Digital • (E) = Engineering & Scientific •
(F) = Film • (G) = Music & General • (I) = Interlock & Sync • (J) = Jokes & Jargon • (P) = Music Publishing •
(R) = Record Industry • (S) = Synthesizers • (U) = Unions • (V) = Video

with members from every sector of the video industry, from equipment designers to top television stars concerned with the future of the medium.

NEA (G)   National Endowment For the Arts. The federal agency that underwrites grants to artists and arts organizations working in every conceivable artform. The NEA also gives funds to the state and local arts councils, and thereby cosponsors artists, events, and products that otherwise might not come to its attention.

NEEDLE-DROP (F,V,A)   Any single section of music, no matter how short, copied from a music library for use in a motion picture or video soundtrack, or in a commercial spot. The producer or client must pay the specified fee to the library or copyright owner for each needle-drop, even when the same section is used more than once in the production.

NEGATIVE (F,V)   A photographic image in which all colors and tonalities are reversed from the way they appear in the original artwork or scene. A black line in artwork will appear white in a negative, and vice versa. All colors will appear as their complements in a negative. Thus, a red in the artwork will appear cyan or blue-green in the negative, etc.

NEGATIVE COST (F,V)   The total cost of producing a motion picture or television show, including all above-the-line and below-the-line expenses and the cost of seeking and securing distribution or exhibition of the finished program. Promo-

tion and advertising are not included in the negative cost.

NEGOTIABLE INSTRUMENT (B)   Any unconditional, written promise signed by one party, guaranteeing a specified payment to another party, either on demand or on a specified date. Bank checks and promissory notes are negotiable instruments. Invoices and bills of lading are not.

NEGOTIATED LICENSE (R)   A mechanical license in which the payment rate or other terms are specially agreed upon by the publisher and producer or record company. Not a statutory or compulsory license. (*See* GRAND RIGHTS.)

NEILSEN RATING (V)   The percentage of the entire viewing audience tuned in to a specific television program or, on average, to a particular series. Surveyed and computed by the A.C. Neilsen Company, the rating (or "share") for a particular program determines how much the broadcaster can charge to air commercials during that time slot. Ratings can be national, regional, or local. A 24-share nationally indicates that 24% of the entire viewing audience watched the program in question.

NEO-PILOT TONE (F,E)   A system for recording a sync signal on 1/4" tape in such a way that this signal will not be reproduced by the full-track playback head that reproduces the program material. Developed for use in Nagra brand recorders, the sync head records two thin tracks of sync signal near the center of the 1/4" width of the tape. The signal going to each of these

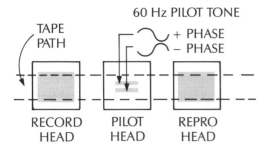

60 Hz PILOT TONE

TAPE PATH

+ PHASE
− PHASE

RECORD HEAD   PILOT HEAD   REPRO HEAD

NEO-PILOT TONE.

two tracks is out of phase with the other. Thus, when both tracks pass by the playback head simultaneously, it sums their equal and opposite signals, resulting in complete cancellation of both signals, and thus no resulting signal to the playback electronics. During sync playback, these thin tracks are read by the resolving circuits that control the motor speed to maintain correct synchronization. (*See* PUSH-PULL.)

NEW ON THE CHARTS
(R,B)
An important monthly record industry trade magazine. It lists names and addresses for all participants in records currently on the *Billboard* single or album charts (composer, publisher, artist, record company, producer, video producer, manager, agent, etc.), and has notices for deals available, ranging from publishing and subpublishing to master licenses and purchases, artist contracts now expiring, etc.

NEW USE
(U,B)
The use of a piece of recorded music in a medium other than that for which it was originally produced. Thus, if a hit record receives new use in a motion picture soundtrack, the motion picture producers must pay the original union musicians and singers again,

this time according to the appropriate music-for-film scale.

NEWTON
(E)
A unit of mechanical force, named after Sir Isaac Newton. At the threshold of hearing, sound pressure level equals 0.000000002 newtons/cm^2. (*See* DYNE.)

NIBBLE
(C)
One half a byte, or four bits of data.

N.M.P.A.
(P,B)
National Music Publishers Association. The organization that represents publishers in their dealings with the federal government foreign publishing royalty-collection organizations, and that owns the Harry Fox Agency.

NO
(J)
Used politely and defensively, the most powerful word in the language. It can protect one from naive or unintended commitments of time, money, and emotion. Use liberally until satisfied with the entirety of a proposed deal, production, etc. (*See* YES.)

NOISE
(E)
Any unwanted sound, except distortion, either in the environment, or in the sound console, recording system, etc.

(E)   AMBIENT NOISE: The inherent noise present in a particular environment. The summation of mechanical noises from heating or other systems, vibrations entering a building from nearby traffic or overhead planes, etc.

(E)   BACKGROUND NOISE: Same as ambient noise.

(E)   IMPACT NOISE: The transient created when two objects collide or strike each other.

(E)   MODULATION NOISE: Broadband electronic or tape noise produced in the recording system

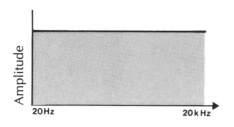

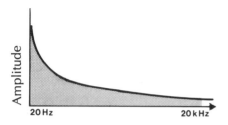

NOISE: White (top), Pink (bottom).

whenever a program signal is present. Generally heard as an added "hiss" above the normal tape noise level, in proportion to signal level.

(E)   NARROW BAND NOISE: Noise that contains only a small bandwidth of frequencies.

(E)   PINK NOISE: Broadband noise that has equal energy for each octave of its bandwidth. Used as the standard reference source for measurements of frequency response in rooms, studios, or speaker systems, microphones, etc.

(E,D)   QUANTIZATION NOISE: In digital playback, a type of distortion that is audible as a low-level, high-frequency "buzz" of varying pitch. Because the reproduced waveform is "stepped" at the sampling rate, quantization noise contains frequencies from the sampling frequency down into the audible range, its instantaneous nature depending on how rapidly the re-created sample voltages change from one stepped level to another.

(E)   RESIDUAL NOISE: The noise that remains on tape after full erasure.

(E)   WHITE NOISE: Broadband noise that has equal energy at every frequency. Used as a reference source in testing of electronic devices, etc.

(E)   WIDE BAND NOISE: Broadband noise—i.e., containing frequencies throughout most or all of the audible band.

NOISE FILTER   Generally, a narrow band or notch filter used to eliminate pitched noise. Or a broadband filter used to attenuate the entire high or low frequency range.
(E)

NOISE FLOOR   The continuous level of noise present in a specific audio signal.
(E)

NOISE GATE   An expander whose threshold can be set to totally eliminate or attenuate low-level signals, such as noise. Current models allow the user to select the threshold level (i.e., the lowest signal level that will "open" the gate or pass through it unaltered), the rates at which the gate "opens" and "closes" to allow program signal through (called attack and release times), the amount of attenuation in effect when the gate is "closed" (called the floor), and other variables. (*See* EXPANDER; EXPANSION RATIO; KEPEX.)
(E)

NOISE LEVEL   The continuous or steady-state decibel level of noise in an acoustical environment or electronic device. Same for magnetic tape.
(E)

NOISE REDUCTION SYSTEM   DOLBY, DBX, etc. An active signal-process-
(E)

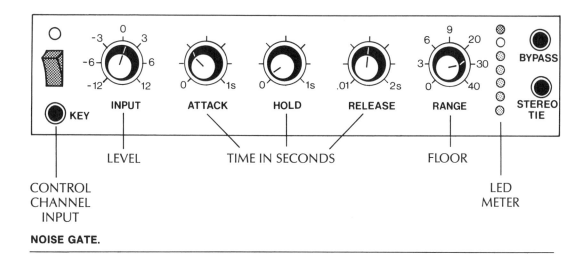

NOISE GATE.

ing device that attenuates noise added to a signal by an audio system such as a tape recorder. Almost all N.R. systems are companders, compressing one or more frequency ranges during recording or broadcast, then expanding these ranges to their original dynamics again during playback or reception. In the case of broadcasts, the compression is at the radio station, the expander in the listener's tuner.

NORMALIZE

(E)

To return all the controls of an electronic device (or an entire recording console) to the position in which they pass no signal or have no individual effect on a signal. For example, a normalized console has all faders and pots turned completely down, all pan pots set to center position, and all routing buttons or switches in the "off" or "no connection" status.

NORMALLED CONNECTION

(E)

In a recording console or other electronic device, a predesignated and continuous signal routing connection that can be interrupted by insertion of a patch cord at the cor-

responding point in the patch bay. The normalled connection is then "broken," allowing the engineer to reroute as he desires.

NOTICE

(P,R,G)

Short for copyright or patent notice, the printed or audio recitation of information concerning the copyright ownership of a composition, a recording, or other copyrighted work. Notice must contain the word "copyright" or familiar circled letter © or (for phonorecords) ℗ , the year of copyright, and the name of the copyright holder. If the work has not been registered, the owner may lose his copyright if notice is omitted in widely circulated editions or in certain other circumstances. Note that the circled letter ℗ is also used as a notice of patent.

N.T.S.C.

(V)

National Television Standards Committee. **1.** The American organization that sets broadcast and videotape format standards for the Federal Communications Commission (FCC). **2.** The format defined for U.S. color television by the N.T.S.C., specifying 525 lines of picture information per frame, 30 frames per second, two fields per frame, etc.

NULL POINT   In the update mode of console automation, the positions (E) at which all the faders are set (intentionally or not) at the beginning of an update pass through the mix. For an individual fader that happens to be at −5 dB when the update mix begins, −5 dB is its null point. Data for that channel will be copied verbatim if the engineer leaves it at −5 dB. However, any decibel movement above or below −5 dB made in the update pass will be added to the levels written on the previous pass. If that track were previously set at −10 dB, and the engineer now increases the −5 dB fader level to −1 dB, that will add 4 dB to the previously written −10 dB, giving a net level of −6 dB for the update. (*See* UPDATE MODE.)

NUMBERING SYSTEM   In mathe- (E) matics, any counting system employing a specified integer base, n. With this as a reference, any integer can be designated as a series of digits that, written from right to left, indicate the presence of various ascending powers of n in the sample integer. The right-hand-most digit represents n^0. In the decimal system (base 10) the integer "215" designates the presence of 2×10^2 plus 1×10^1 plus 5×10^0. The same number, written in the binary system (base 2) would be 11010111. This indicates the presence of 2^7 plus 2^6 plus 2^4 plus 2^2 plus 2^1 plus 2^0. Common numbering systems are: Binary, base 2; Octal, base 8, Decimal, base 10; Hexadecimal, base 16. (*See* DIGIT.)

NYQUIST FREQUENCY   The highest audio program frequency that can (D) be accurately sampled by any specific sampling rate. By definition, one-half the sampling frequency.

– O –

OCTAVE (G)   The musical interval between any two frequencies where $f_2 = 2 \times f_1$. The higher tone has a frequency exactly twice that of the lower tone. (*See* HARMONIC; FUNDAMENTAL.)

OERSTED (E)   A standard unit of magnetic force, designated by the letter H.

OFF-AXIS (E)   In a microphone or loudspeaker, not in line with the axis of maximum sensitivity or best frequency response. Opposite of on-axis.

OFF-AXIS COLORATION (E)   For a microphone, a change in its frequency response for sounds coming from directions other than the mic's axis of best response—i.e., sounds that are off-mic. (*See* POLAR PATTERN (illustrations); COLORATION.)

OFF-CAMERA (F,V)   Outside the camera's field of view.

OFF-LAY (F,V)   To separate individual sound effects, pieces of dialogue or other sounds originally on one roll of magnetic film, placing each on a separate roll to allow for individual equalization, different reverb treatment, or special effects during a mix.

OFF-LINE (V)   In videotape editing, the opposite of on-line.

OFF-MIC (G)   Not within the optimal pickup area of a microphone, and therefore not being heard clearly or at full level.

OFFSET (I)   A user-defined number of frames difference between the continuously running time codes of the master and slave machines. Usually specified and used to achieve visual sync when this is not achieved by maintaining numerical frame sync between machines.

OFFSET PRINTING (A,R)   A printing process in which ink from a cylindrical printing plate, made photographically from original artwork, is printed onto a cylindrical roller, which then rolls the ink onto the paper. Since the plate does not touch the paper, there is no impression on the paper, just ink deposited on the surface. Most printing in the record industry is done by offset, which is cheaper than letterpress and allows the plates to be used for much longer printing runs. Used to print most newspapers, magazines, album covers, etc.

OHM
(E)
The unit of electrical resistance to current flow. Used both for simple DC resistance and AC impedance measurements. Its symbol is the Greek letter omega, written Ω.

OMNI-DIRECTIONAL MICRO-PHONE
(E)
A microphone that responds equally well to sounds coming from any direction.

OMNI MODE
(S)
In MIDI interconnection of synthesizers, the operating mode in which an instrument receives notes on any of its sixteen MIDI channels, generating up to sixteen notes, all via the same patch. Also called omni-on/poly mode.

ON-AXIS
(E)
For a microphone or loudspeaker, the direction from which it has the highest sensitivity or best frequency response. Opposite of off-axis.

ONE-STOP
(R)
A type of record distributor who buys current and older releases from many labels. Smaller retailers can then make "one stop" to get all the records they need. Sometimes a large chain of stores will be supplied by a ONE-STOP established by that chain in order to get better prices for buying in large quantities from the manufac-

turers. (*See* RACK JOBBER; DISTRIBUTOR, RECORD.)

ON-LINE/OFF-LINE VIDEO EDITING
(V)
ON-LINE editing is performed by an edit programmer (a computer or CPU) that simultaneously controls several 1″ video playback decks and a 1″ master recording deck, locating takes specified in the edit-decision list (EDL) and copying them with effects onto the edited video master. The process is virtually automatic, and quite expensive on a per-hour studio rental basis. OFF-LINE editing is "hand done" by the editor, who controls one machine at a time to find takes and copy them onto the video master. OFF-LINE is generally done on 3/4″ format, is relatively inexpensive, and is used to develop the final edit-list that can program an ON-LINE edit of the original videotapes. In this context, the final 3/4″ master corresponds to a film workprint, the EDL to the film lab's cue sheet.

OP AMP
(E)
OPERATIONAL AMPLIFIER. An amplifying circuit or chip with very high gain and stability, allowing the user to apply a great deal of feedback in order to reduce gain to the desired level, even as low as unity gain. With such flexibility, op amps are used in a wide variety of audio and synthesizer applications.

OPEN-CIRCUIT VOLTAGE RATING
(E)
The output voltage of a microphone with no load—i.e., infinite resistance such as in an open circuit, or when driving a resistive load at least twenty times the microphone's internal impedance.

(A) = Advertising • (B) = Business & Law • (C) = Computers • (D) = Digital • (E) = Engineering & Scientific •
(F) = Film • (G) = Music & General • (I) = Interlock & Sync • (J) = Jokes & Jargon • (P) = Music Publishing •
(R) = Record Industry • (S) = Synthesizers • (U) = Unions • (V) = Video

One of the standard specifications of microphones.

OPEN TRACK   On a multi-track tape, any track that has not yet been used, or that may be erased and reused for overdubs.
(E)

OPERATING LEVEL   The voltage level defined for any audio system as its nominal, 100% modulation level, not including any headroom. Usually defined as 0 dBVU for a steady sine wave. (*See* DECIBEL: dBV; dBVU; dBm; VU METER.)
(E)

OPERATING SYSTEM   In computers, the software system that organizes the underlying computational and memory resources of the computer and makes them available to the user via a specific set of command names and functions called languages—e.g., BASIC, COBOL, FORTRAN, and other computer languages. Specific applications software can then be written in such a language.
(C)

OPTICAL(S)   1. Effects on 35mm film that are made in an optical printer, including dissolves, fades, superimpositions, freeze frames, matte shots, etc. Many 16mm printers allow simple effects to be made in real-time as each print is made. However, for longer print runs where higher printing speed is required (such as for theatrical features), an internegative of the effect is made on the optical printer, then spliced into the camera original. 2. Loosely, any effect used in a film or video production. (*See* STEP PRINTING.)
(F,V)

OPTICAL DISC   A type of storage medium on which massive amounts
(R,V,C)

of data can be inscribed. The data is encoded in a spiralling pattern (analogous to a record groove) by a laser that carves tiny pits into the otherwise smooth surface of the optical disc master. Each and every change from "land" to a pit indicates a change of data bits from a 1 to 0, or vice versa. Where no change occurs, the last-read digit is indicated for each increment of "groove length." When a pressing is finally made, the pitted surface is plated with metal. In the reproduction device or player, a small laser scans the groove, reading the changes from land to pits, and converting this information back into data. The data can be used to store text, visual information such as TV pictures, or digital audio. The common CD and Laserdisc are examples of optical discs.

OPTICAL SOUND   The type of sound reproduction on film that employs the photographic printing process of the optical track.
(F)

OPTICAL TRACK   1. The photographically printed soundtrack that appears either between one row of perforations and the picture in an answer or release print (in 35mm), or along the edge of the print opposite that with the perforations (in 16mm). 2. The master or original photographic soundtrack made directly from the mono mix or 35mm three-track. This strip of film has no pictorial image, but is printed along with A and B rolls onto the composite answer print or release print. The track can be a negative or positive image, depending on the type of camera original shot and print stock to be used. (Illustration next page.)
(F)

(A) = Advertising • (B) = Business & Law • (C) = Computers • (D) = Digital • (E) = Engineering & Scientific •
(F) = Film • (G) = Music & General • (I) = Interlock & Sync • (J) = Jokes & Jargon • (P) = Music Publishing •
(R) = Record Industry • (S) = Synthesizers • (U) = Unions • (V) = Video

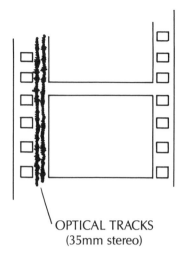

OPTICAL TRACKS
(35mm stereo)

OPTICAL TRACK.

OPTION 1. Legally, a term in a contract by which the period of the
(B) contract may be extended. A
recording contract may be for one
album, with an option by which
the record company may commission a specified number of additional albums to be completed
within specified periods of time. 2.
An agreement under which one
party, in return for a consideration, grants another party a period
of time in which he may lease or
purchase some property, or elect
to enter into some contractual
agreement with the first party. The
terms of the ultimate sale or contract must be clearly spelled out in
the option itself, or in a document
appended to it as a sample or
specimen. For instance, a record
company may buy from an independent producer a six-month
option to acquire a master tape,
obligating the producer not to sell
it to anyone else for that period.

ORCHESTRATOR A musical arranger
who specializes in writing charts
(U) for orchestral sections such as

strings, woodwinds, brass, etc. An
arranger hired for a particular job
may subcontract portions of that
job to an orchestrator. AFM payment scales for orchestrators are
very complex. Hence, many orchestrators prefer to work on a
flat-fee basis, which includes all
creative fees, but excludes copying.

ORTF STEREO MIKING A stereo
miking technique in which two
(E) cardioid microphones are placed
17 cm apart horizontally—the left
mic aimed 55 degrees to the left,
the right mic aimed 55 degrees to
the right of the axis that faces the
sound source. Developed by the
Organization of Radio and Television Français.

OSCILLATOR 1. An electronic signal
generator whose output is a pure
(E) sine wave of selectable frequency.
Standard test equipment in every
studio. Many oscillators also
produce square waves and other
waveshapes used in testing and
(S) maintenance procedures. 2. The
basic sound-generating circuit in
most traditional synthesizers. A
control voltage generated by each
key of the keyboard (or other controller) instructs the oscillator what
output frequency is required. This
can then be processed by any number of other circuits.

OSCILLOSCOPE A test instrument
that employs a cathode ray tube
(E) (CRT, similar to a black and white
television screen) to provide a
visual display of the waveform of
electrical signals. Some oscillo-
scopes can store and display
waveshapes for comparison with

others, and perform more complex analytical functions.

OUTBOARD EQUIPMENT   Any recording equipment, excluding tape recorders and noise reduction systems, not contained in the recording console, but available to patch into the signal chain in the control room.
(E)

OUT TAKE   A taped or filmed take, or section of a take, that will not be used, or may be physically removed from the recorded tape or footage by editing.
(E,F,V)

OUT TO LUNCH   The condition in which a normally reliable and predictable system (electronic or human) behaves in an erratic, misleading, or outrageous fashion. The synchronizer, for example, has gone out to lunch when it cannot interlock audio and/or video decks properly. Or, a producer may go out to lunch by exceeding his budget. Colloquial meaning: crazy, kablooey, etc.
(J,G)

OVERAGE   A cost overrun. Any amount of money spent that is in excess of the amount planned or budgeted, either in a specific category or for an entire production. (See PENALTY CLAUSE; SPENDTH.)
(B)

OVERCALL   The contractual right a producer may have to require additional money from the investors in a production, usually limited to a certain percentage of the initial investment.
(B)

OVERCRANK   Opposite of undercrank.
(F,V)

OVERDUBBING   Adding sounds to a previously recorded musical tape. In multi-track formats this is done by reproducing previously recorded tracks through the record head (in sel-sync mode), feeding these to headphones while new instrumentalists or vocalists play or sing additional parts in-time and in-tune with their headphone mix. The new sounds are recorded on open tracks. Strictly speaking, however, over-dubbing can also mean adding sound to an already mixed tape while copying it. (See PUNCHING IN/PUNCHING OUT.)
(E,G)

OVERHEAD   A major expense category in the running of any business or completion of any single production. Includes the costs of housing and providing common services and resources to all the departments of the business or phases of the production. Office and business equipment rentals, utilities and phone service, printing of letterheads and other form paperwork, general management and secretarial staff salaries—all these and more may be included in overhead. Generally considered part of a company's fixed costs. (See VARIABLE COSTS.)
(B,G)

OVERLAY   An electronic technique for combining parts of two video images, similar in effect to chroma-keying, but using specified black and white image densities to act as the "keying trigger" that will cause areas of one image to drop out and be replaced by the corresponding areas of another. (See MATTE; BLUE SCREEN.)
(V)

OVERLOAD   1. The type of distortion that occurs when an applied signal
(E)

exceeds the level at which a system will produce its maximum undistorted output level. Generally results in clipping of the waveform, since the output will be literally cut off at maximum output level. **2.** The condition that exists when this distortion is produced.

OVERSAMPLING   A process by which
(D)   each audio sample is read from a compact disc more than once, mainly to double-check the accuracy of the first reading, but also to interpolate values between samples, increasing the effective sampling rate. Oversampling rates of 88.2 kHz and 176.4 kHz are available on higher quality players, but there is no proof that the process improves the sound of the

output, at least for the average listener.

OVERTONE   An integer multiple of a
(E)   fundamental frequency. The first overtone is twice the fundamental, the second is three times the fundamental, etc. (*See* HARMONIC; PARTIALS.)

OXIDE   The actual magnetic material
(E)   applied to one side of all recording tape. It is made of small particles of iron oxide (specifically, gamma ferric oxide) or other magnetic material stirred into and suspended in viscous binder liquid, which is applied evenly to the tape and allowed to dry. (*See* MAGNETIC RECORDING TAPE (illustration).)

- P -

PACKAGING
(R)
Either the printed jacket and wrapper of an album, or the actual shipping boxes in which records are delivered to distributors or stores. (*See* SPECIAL PACKAGING or PROMOTION.)

PACKAGING DISCOUNT
(R)
A reduction in royalties by which some recording contracts allow the label to deduct a fixed percentage of all gross receipts from a record before computing artist and/or producer royalties. Also called a container charge. (*See* BREAKAGE ALLOWANCE; ROYALTY BASE RATE.)

PAD
(E)
An attenuator that can be switched or plugged into a signal path to reduce signal level and prevent overload or distortion. (*See* ATTENUATION PAD.)

PAINTBOX
(V)
A digital video image processor and computer-image generator used in post-production, made by Quantel Corp. The operator can modify a pre-shot video image by loading it into computer memory, using a light pen and a "palette" of electronic colors to recolor and shade areas in the original scene, add animated objects, etc. The completed images can then be retransferred onto tape and edited normally. (*See* MIRAGE; DUBNER; BOSCH.)

PAL
(V)
PHASE ALTERNATING LINE. The European standard color television format, established by the E.B.U. It specifies 625 lines of picture information per frame, 25 frames per second, etc. (*See* N.T.S.C.)

P&L
(B,G)
See PROFIT AND LOSS STATEMENT.

PAN POT
(E)
A multiple pole potentiometer used to vary the proportion of an incoming signal sent to two or more separate outputs. Generally used to position sounds left to right in a stereo mixdown, or to distribute one signal to two tracks in a multi-track recording. Stereo and quad pan pots are common in audio applications. (*See* GANG; JOYSTICK)

(A) = Advertising • (B) = Business & Law • (C) = Computers • (D) = Digital • (E) = Engineering & Scientific •
(F) = Film • (G) = Music & General • (I) = Interlock & Sync • (J) = Jokes & Jargon • (P) = Music Publishing •
(R) = Record Industry • (S) = Synthesizers • (U) = Unions • (V) = Video

PANCAKE   A roll of recording tape wound only on a hub, without reel flanges.
(E)

PANNING   Splitting the output of a single mono channel or track between the stereo left and right channels of the studio monitors, or the two-track master tape that results in a mixdown, usually via a pan pot.
(E)

PARALLEL   In the connection of one signal or power source to more than one device or destination, the wiring configuration in which the input leads of all the devices meet at a common electrical point. Signal or power routed to this point flows directly to each device. Opposite of series wiring, in which the source is wired to the input of one device, whose output becomes the input for the next, etc.
(E)

PARALLEL ACTION   The dramatic action occurring in two separate
(F,V)

scenes whose conclusions will (a) be in the same location, or (b) bring one or more of the characters from each scene together. Shots from both scenes are generally intercut to allow the viewer to see both "simultaneously."

PARALLEL INTERFACE   In computers, the multi-pin connector and associated cable through which parallel data flows. The Centronics Corporation defined the current standard parallel interface. (*See* PARALLEL OUTPUT; MULTIPLEXER.)
(C)

PARALLEL OUTPUT   An output with one pin for each digit of an n-digit word, all digits of which will simultaneously be transmitted to another device. (*See* SERIAL OUTPUT; MULTIPLEXER.)
(C,D)

PARITY CODE/PARITY CHECKING   In digital recording, one or more bits of data derived from
(D,C)

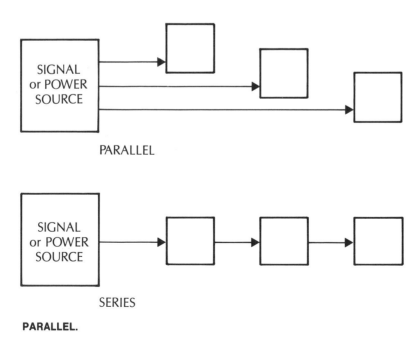

SIGNAL or POWER SOURCE

PARALLEL

SIGNAL or POWER SOURCE

SERIES

PARALLEL.

---

the audio sample and appended to it as a part of the 16-bit word. The parity code allows error-detection circuitry to determine whether the audio bits are correct, and therefore whether they should be sent on for D-A conversion, discarded or "repaired." The same system is used to check for errors in each byte of computer data.

PARTIALS (S)   The upper harmonics or overtones in a complex waveform or sound. The partials of a flute, for example, include the sound of the player's breath passing over the embouchure or mouthpiece, in addition to the higher frequencies emanating from the instrument's body.

PASS (or PASS ON) (verb) (B,G)   To turn down or reject an offer, a song, or recorded submission, etc.

PASS BAND (E)   In an electronic filter, those frequencies allowed to pass through without attentuation. (*See* EQUALIZER.)

PASSIVE DEVICE (E)   A circuit or network that operates without need for any outside power supply—AC components—i.e., resistors, capacitors, and inductors, and as a result of their internal consumption of some of the signal's energy, the audio output level of the device will be lower than the input level. (*See* ACTIVE DEVICE.)

PASTE-UP   See CAMERA-READY.

PATCH (noun) (S)   A particular sound produced by a synthesizer, either preset at the factory, or programmed by the performer. Example: A clarinet or harpsichord patch—i.e., the

synthesized sound of that instrument.

PATCH (verb) (E)   To route a signal in via a desired path, usually by use of the patch bay and patch cords.

PATCH BAY (E)   In a recording console or equipment rack, one or more rows of female input and output jacks, used in conjunction with patch cords to route signals through outboard signal processing gear, or to reroute signals inside the console itself. Synonym for jack bay.

PATCH CORD (E)   A short length of audio cable with an audio plug on each end, used for signal routing in a patch bay.

PATCH POINT (E)   A location in a flow chart or the corresponding electronic circuit at which access to the circuit is provided by a jack in the patch bay.

PATENT NOTICE (P,R)   The circled letter ℗ or the word "patent," and name of the patent holder, which must appear on copies or specific examples of a mass-produced tangible product in order to secure the patent holder's proprietary ownership of its design and/or manufacturing process. In record or compact disc manufacture, for example, the composition and recorded performance are protected by copyright law. However, the actual physical shape of the groove or sequence of data pits that encodes the copyrighted sounds must be separately patented in order to provide full protection from piracy. On records, the circled ℗ thus serves a dual function, giving notice of patent and copyright of a "phonorecord." (*See* NOTICE; PHONORECORD.)

PATH LENGTH   The distance between a sound source the and listener or microphone.
(E)

PAYMASTER   A person or company who, as a service to a client or ad agency, acts as the legal employer of musical or vocal talent. The paymaster bills the agency or client for the total talent expense, then accepts responsibility for paying each musician or singer according to union or individual contract, withholding taxes, pension and welfare payments and other deductions, etc. The paymaster, in return for all these bookkeeping and accounting functions, collects a percentage of the whole talent payment due each person before deductions. The paymaster may also perform similar services for actors or other on-camera talent in filmed or videotaped ads.
(A,F,V)

PCM   See PULSE CODE MODULA-
(D)   TION.

P.D.   1. Program Director. At a radio
(A,R)   station, the person in charge of what type of music or other shows
(P)   are broadcast. 2. Public Domain.

PEAK LEVEL   The instantaneous highest level of the transient in any signal or series of signals. Because these transients are so short, meters designed to read peak levels have circuitry built in that remembers and holds the level on display long enough for the meter itself to reach the peak's full level and be observed by the engineer.
(E)

PEAK-TO-PEAK VALUE   A measure of the highest positive-to-negative voltage swing in any specified segment of program signal. Twice the absolute value of the greater voltage reached by an adjacent positive or negative transient peak. (*See* RMS VALUE (illustrations).)
(E)

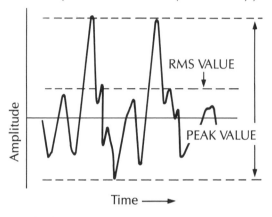

PEAK-TO-PEAK VALUE.

PEANUT MICROPHONE   Colloquial term for any of the miniature lavalier microphones popular in film and video shoots.
(F,V,E)

PEGBAR   A metal strip mounted on an animation stand, with three metal pegs on which the pre-cut alignment holes in animation cels or artwork are fitted. This ensures exact registration of all layers of artwork.
(F,V)

PENALTY CLAUSE   Any clause in a contract that specifies some financial or other penalty to be imposed on one of the parties if he fails to fulfill one or more of his responsibilities—e.g., if he misses a deadline, goes over budget in some expense category, etc.
(B)

PER DIEM   An amount of money, over and above normal wages and
(F,V,R)

---

benefits, paid by the producer or production company to employees (union technicians or talent) who must live away from home while employed on a film, TV, or musical production. A $40 per diem given to each crew member on a film shoot will cover expenses for meals (except those served during the workday), personal travel, or phone expenses, etc. Hotel expenses and travel between home and locations are separate line items, not paid for by per diems.

PERFECT PITCH   The ability to remember a standard frequency (such as concert A) and accurately judge the pitch of other musical sounds heard in any context. A person with perfect pitch can tell when an instrument is out of tune with concert pitch, for instance, or tell what note is being played, without any reference other than memory. (*See* RELATIVE PITCH.)
(G)

PERFORATION   1. Evenly spaced holes punched along one or both sides of all motion picture film. The holes are engaged by the teeth of sprocket wheels, the claws of intermittent movements, and other devices that move film through cameras and projectors. Also called sprocket hole. (*See* PITCH.) 2. A type of medieval torture still used by some clients on producers who go over budget. (*See* SPENDTH.)
(F)
(J)

PERFORMANCE   In royalty collection, any use of a composition or recording for which royalties are due and collectable. A live performance in a signatory hall, or a radio or television broadcast of a record, commercial spot, etc. AS-CAP or BMI collects such royalties
(U,P)

due to publishers and composers; AFTRA collects residuals due to singers. (*See* CATEGORY; USE WEIGHT.)

PERFORMANCE CREDIT   A payment unit used by ASCAP to determine how much a surveyed broadcast performance of a composition will earn for its writers and publisher. The number of performance credits ascribed to a specific broadcast is the product of several factors: Station Weight (in radio) or hook-up weight (in TV), Use Weight, Feature Multiplier and Strata.) (*See* CATEGORY; UNIT.)
(P,A)

PERFORMING RIGHTS ORGANIZATION OF CANADA   See PRO CANADA.

PERIPHERAL   Any device connected to a computer—e.g., a monitor, terminal, printer, keyboard, etc.
(C)

PHANTOM POWER SUPPLY   A type of microphone power supply that raises the voltage potential of both conductors in a balanced line to the same DC value, the opposite voltage being applied to the shield. Because both signal leads are identically charged, the input channel that receives the mic's output cannot sense a polarizing voltage at all. Hence the name "phantom." Many consoles have internal phantom supplies, individually assignable to any or all mic input lines.
(E)

PHASE   The time relationship of two or more sound waves reaching the same point in space simultaneously, or of two or more signals passing through the same point in an electronic circuit simultaneously. If the two sounds or signals are of
(E)

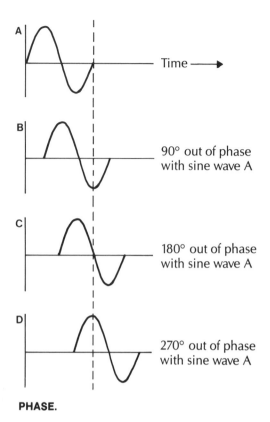

A

Time ⟶

B

90° out of phase
with sine wave A

C

180° out of phase
with sine wave A

D

270° out of phase
with sine wave A

PHASE.

identical frequencies, they are "in-phase" if the peaks and troughs of the waves occur simultaneously. They are "out-of-phase" if the peaks of one partially or fully cancel the peaks of the other. The degree of "out-of-phaseness" is designated in degrees (x°) such that 0° phase difference indicates two sounds or signals exactly "in-phase," and 180° phase difference indicates the two are completely "out-of-phase," cancelling each other completely. (*See* PHASE DIFFERENCE (illustration).)

PHASE ALTERNATING LINE   See PAL.

PHASE CANCELLATION   The attenuation that results when two acoustic or electric waves of the
(E)

same frequency but opposite or nearly opposite polarity combine. (*See* COHERENT SIGNALS.)

PHASE COHERENCY   A condition encountered in the summation of two or more signals, in which the signals combine constructively, with little or no cancellation. (*See* COHERENT SIGNALS.)
(E)

PHASE DIFFERENCE   Defined most simply with respect to pure sine waves, the measure of time delay with which two identical signals reach a common electrical or acoustic point. Since the sine wave is defined as the graph of the height of a point on the perimeter of a uniformly rotating circle with respect to time, one complete cycle of a sine wave results when the circle has rotated 360 degrees. Thus, for a pure tone of F Hz, 360 degrees of phase difference, D, represents one full cycle. If F = 1,000 Hz, then a D of 360 degrees takes exactly 0.001 seond. For any F, the number of degrees phase difference, D, between two sources whose identical outputs arrive at a common point with a time difference of T seconds, is: D = F × T × 360.
(E)

PHASE METER   An electronic circuit and display that compares two incoming signals and shows the phase difference between them.
(E)

PHASE REVERSAL   In electronic signals, changing the polarity of the signal from positive to negative or vice versa, thereby causing a reversal in polarity of the signal. When viewed on an oscilloscope, the waveform "flips" with respect to
(E)

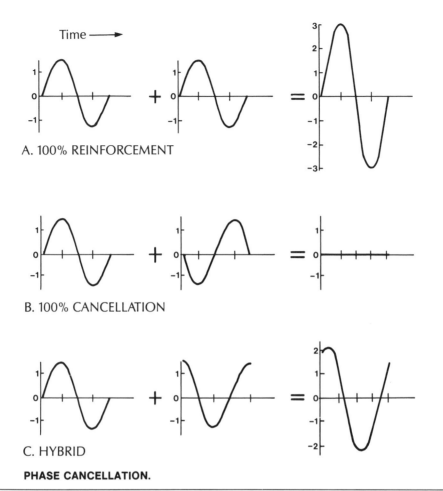

Time ⟶

A. 100% REINFORCEMENT

B. 100% CANCELLATION

C. HYBRID

PHASE CANCELLATION.

the horizontal or time axis. Also called phase inversion.

PHASE REVERSAL SWITCH (E) A switch (almost always) in a balanced line that allows the user to interchange the two conductors, thereby causing a 180 degree shift in the phase of the signal passing through them. Often incorporated into recording consoles to allow the engineer to obtain the best overall phase relationship among several mics used to record the same instrument or section—e.g., a drum set.

PHASE SHIFT (E) Synonym for phase difference.

PHASE SYNC (I) In SMPTE synchronization, an option by which the slave machine is speed-controlled in such a way that the phase of its bi-modulated code wave is held in-phase with the code wave on the master machine. This provides much closer alignment of the two than in frame sync. However, because the synchronizer must make continuous adjustments to the slave's speed, phase sync can introduce noticeable flutter when the audio machine is slaved to video. In some synchronizers, only sub-frame information is used to achieve interlock, giving 1/100 frame accuracy between machines.

PHASING (E)   The variable comb filter effect that occurs when a direct signal is mixed with a phase-shifted (or slightly delayed) copy of the same signal. Sometimes used to mean flanging.

PHLANGÈR (J)   Southern French dialect form of flanger.

PHON (E)   A standard unit of loudness, originally defined in relation to an average listener's sensitivity at 1,000 Hz. By definition, at this frequency the number of phons equals the dB SPL reading. For other frequencies, the SPL that to the listener seems just as loud as the sample 1,000 Hz tone is rated as the same number of phons. The equal loudness curves thus relate phons to dB SPL. (*See* EQUAL LOUDNESS CONTOURS.)

PHONE JACK (E)   A type of audio jack that accepts a 1/4″ male plug, generally with a single mono channel of signal. There are stereo phone jacks, and mini- and microphone jacks, which look similar but are much smaller than the original.

PHONOGRAPH RECORD LABOR AGREEMENTS (U,R)   The industry-wide agreements developed by various unions (AFM, AFTRA, etc.) that bind signatory record companies, producers, television stations, etc. to pay union scale wages to member musicians, vocalists, narrators, etc. AFTRA calls its contract with signatories the "CODE OF FAIR PRACTICE."

PHONORECORD (R)   Legally, any fixed recording of a musical composition or other copyrightable work that may be stored as proof of copyright, or that is manufactured for sale to the consumer. Conventional phonograph records, reel-to-reel or cassette tapes, compact discs, or any standard-format digital tape are all phonorecords in the eyes of the law.

PICKUP (E)   **1.** A type of microphone that attaches directly to an instrument and is sensitive to the vibrations of a part or all of the body of the instrument itself. It does not sense vibrations carried by the air. Contact mics are one type of pickup. In magnetic pickups, such as those that sense the vibration of metal guitar strings, the signal is induced by the movement of the steel strings through the magnetic field (G) of the pickup itself. **2.** In music production, a short segment of music by which musicians or vocalists find their place when overdubbing sections of a chart. The recording engineer may give a four-bar pickup before the section to be dubbed in. This allows players or singers to find their place, get pitch and tempo together, then begin singing or playing. (*See* PRE-ROLL.)

PINCH ROLLER (E)   The rubber wheel that holds the recording tape firmly against the capstan during record or playback. The capstan idler, pressure roller, or puck. (See ALIGNMENT, TAPE HEAD (illustration).)

PING-PONG To bounce tracks in mul-
(E) ti-track recording.

PINNING Referring to audio level
meters, a condition in which the
(E) signal is too high, causing the indicator to hit the top of its scale.
This can damage the meter in addition to producing distortion in
the program.

PIRACY The act of making copies of
copyrighted songs, records, video-
(P,R,G) tapes, etc., for sale, rental, or paid
exhibition to the public (a) without
obtaining legal permission from the
copyright holder to make these
copies, and (b) without any intent
of paying the statutory or other
royalties and fees to the lawful
copyright holder. For several years
in the late 1960s and early 1970s,
record pirates got away with their
misdeeds by claiming that they
made no copies of any copyrighted
work, but only duplicated the
shape of a physical groove, not
realizing that music could be ex-
tracted from it by placing it on a
turntable! Soon thereafter, embar-
rassed record companies began
putting patent notices on their releases. (*See* NOTICE; COPY-
RIGHT NOTICE; PATENT
NOTICE.)

PITCH 1. The distance between two
perforations or sprocket holes along
(F) a strip of film. Camera original is
generally "short pitch," and print
film is generally "long pitch," the
difference in these lengths being
on the order of .0006″ per frame.
The two different pitches are
necessary to prevent slippage between original and print film as
they wind around various sprocket
wheels in the contact printers used
(R) to make most prints. 2. The number of grooves per inch on a record,
measured along its radius. Singles
may be cut as low as 90 pitch, soft
or long classical LPs as high as 400.
The lower the pitch number, the
shorter the side, and více versa.
However, lower pitch means
greater spacing between adjacent
grooves, which allows greater level
(G) to be cut on the disc. 3. The subjective impression of the frequency,
or musical tone of a sound, expressed in the latter case by a capital letter and number (e.g., A2, the
second A above middle C on the
piano). Also, the frequency of a
musical note—e.g., 880 Hz, indicating the same pitch as A2 cited
(B,A) above. 4. To sell a service or
product to a prospective client. An
ad agency may pitch a new account; a song plugger may pitch a
song to a recording artist.

PITCH TRANSPOSER An electronic
device or signal processor with
(E) which the engineer can raise or
lower the frequencies of incoming
signals. (*See* HARMONIZER.)

PITS On a compact disc, microscopic
depressions laser-burned into the
(D) surface on which the digital data is
stored. Each pit-edge encodes a
"1" in the data stream. Incremental
lengths of flat disc surface (either
land between pits or the bottom of
an extended pit) designate 0s in
the data. Audio samples, location
and synchronization information,
bands and indexing, visual information, etc. are all encoded in the
pits. (*See* LAND.)

PIXEL Short for PIXure ELement.
The smallest visible element of a
(F,V) picture or image, corresponding in

(A) = Advertising • (B) = Business & Law • (C) = Computers • (D) = Digital • (E) = Engineering & Scientific •
(F) = Film • (G) = Music & General • (I) = Interlock & Sync • (J) = Jokes & Jargon • (P) = Music Publishing •
(R) = Record Industry • (S) = Synthesizers • (U) = Unions • (V) = Video

video to the brightness and color information for one location on a single line of the video image.

PLASTIC LEADER   Usually, white or yellow leader tape (with no oxide) in between various songs on a master tape. Plastic leader can pick up static, which can create clicks or pops on the master tape. For that reason, paper leader is generally used on master tapes. There are special types of plastic leaders, made of an anti-static base, that are used for archival storage where paper leader, which changes shape in varying humidity and deteriorates with age, will not suffice.

(E)

PLATE REVERBERATION SYSTEM   A sheet metal plate, vertically suspended by shock-mounts in a frame, into which sounds are introduced by a contact transducer or speaker. These sounds then disperse through the plate, bouncing back and forth from the edges, and are picked up by one or more contact transducers or microphones. The resulting sound simulates echo that would be regenerated when the sound might have bounced around in a reverberant room. The decay time is most often varied by changing the position of one or more dampers in contact with the plate. Almost all plates have stereo outputs.

(E)

PLATING   Short for electroplating, the process by which a lacquer master is coated with nickel in order to make the metal master, one of the metal parts that will eventually lead to vinyl release pressings of a record. (*See* MATRIXING.)

(R)

PLATINUM   Used to describe a record (single or album) that has sold one million units in the North American territory. Certification of sales and awarding of the platinum ranking is done by the RIAA.

(R)

PLAYBACK   1. The amplified reproduction of any type of sound recording. 2. The reproduction of a recorded take immediately after it is recorded. Done to make aesthetic and technical judgements about the performance and recording quality. 3. On a motion picture set, the reproduction of music or other sounds recorded previously under studio conditions, to which the actors, singers, and dancers in a scene mime and move in exact synchronism. Called shooting to playback.

(E)

(F,V)

PLAYLIST   The list of songs a radio station has scheduled for broadcast. Or the list of music videos a station plans to air during a program. (*See* CHART; ROTATION.)

(R,V)

PLOSIVE   Any speech sound that begins with a sharp transient—e.g., words or syllables beginning with "p" or "b".

(E,G)

POINT OF PURCHASE   See POP.

POINT OF VIEW SHOT   See POV SHOT

POINT SOURCE   A theoretically perfect source of sound—i.e., one that is infinitely small and suspended in free space. Most problems in sound propagation are calculated assuming the source is of this type, just to simplify the calculations.

(E)

POINT(S)   **1.** A point equals one percent of either wholesale or retail
price of a record, and royalties are
generally specified in points. For
example, a producer may be paid
20 points of wholesale (usually considered equal to 10 points of retail),
from which he then pays the artists and others points for their
respective contributions. **2.** In
general, a percentage of the profit
derived from any venture or
product. (*See* ROYALTY; ALL-IN
DEAL)

(R)

(B)

POLAR PATTERN   The graph of the
sensitivity of a transducer (i.e., the

(E)

output level of a microphone, or
measured SPL output from a
loudspeaker) at a specific frequency, plotted as a function of
the angular direction from which
sound approaches, or (in the case
of loudspeakers) the direction in
which sound propagates. A composite polar pattern often contains
several graphs representing response
at various frequencies, all inscribed
on the same set of polar axes. For
speakers, the ideal polar pattern
would be omni-directional, indicating that sounds of all frequencies
are propagated equally in all directions. This is the theoretical pat-

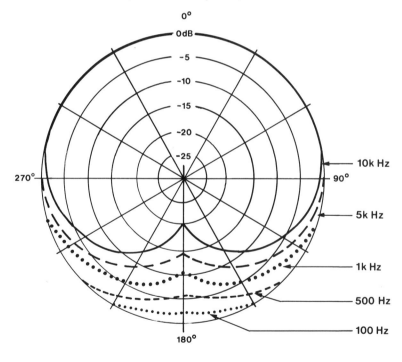

POLAR PATTERN. Complete polar pattern showing directional frequency responses for an inexpensive
cardiod microphone.

tern of the legendary point source. Alas, no speaker even comes close.

Common Polar Patterns for Microphones

BI-DIRECTIONAL MICROPHONE: The axes of maximum sensitivity are at 0° and 180°; minimum sensitivity is at 90° and 270°. In three dimensions, the pattern resembles two eggs end to end—maximum sensitivity along the line through their long axes, minimum sensitivity along the plane between them.

CARDIOID MICROPHONE: A uni-directional pattern, with the axis of minimum sensitivity at 180°. The pattern derives its name from its heart-shaped appearance.

COTTAGE LOAF MICROPHONE: Colloquially, a super-cardioid or hyper-cardioid polar pattern.

HYPER-CARDIOID MICROPHONE: The narrowest of uni-directional patterns, narrower even than super-cardioid, indicating very low off-axis sensitivity. There is usually a small lobe of sensitivity around 180°. Thus, minimum sensitivity occurs at about 110° and 250° away from the axis.

OMNI-DIRECTIONAL MICROPHONE: A nearly circular pattern, indicating equal sensitivity to sounds approaching from all directions around the microphone.

SUPER-CARDIOID MICROPHONE: A unidirectional pattern narrower than cardioid, but broader than hyper-cardioid. Minimum sensitivity occurs at about 135° and 225° off-axis.

UNI-DIRECTIONAL MICROPHONE: Any pattern in which the microphone exhibits more sensitivity to sounds ap-

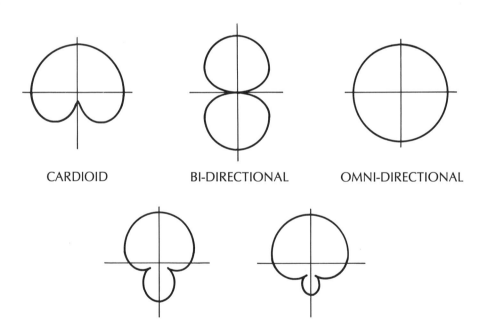

CARDIOID   BI-DIRECTIONAL   OMNI-DIRECTIONAL

HYPER-CARDIOID   SUPER-CARDIOID

COMMON POLAR PATTERNS FOR MICROPHONE.

Comparison of Microphone Specifications

Polar pattern	Other name	Minimum sensitivity at	No. of rear lobes
Omni-directional	Non-directional	No minima	None
Bi-directional	Figure-8	90° and 270°	One, equal
Uni-directional*	Cardioid	180°	None
Super-Cardioid	Cottage Loaf	135° and 225°	One small
Hyper-Cardioid	None	110° and 250°	One large
Shotgun	Interference	70°, 130°, 210°, and 290° approx.	Three or more**

*Uni-directional is used to designate any of the cardioid variety of microphones.
**Due to specific internal design features, shotgun mics may have several lobes, even different numbers in separate frequency ranges. No standard definition will fit each make or model.

proaching on-axis—i.e., any variation of the basic cardioid pattern.

POLARITY   Designation of the direction of flow for an electrical or magnetic force.
(E)

POLARIZING VOLTAGE   The DC voltage supplied in opposite polarities to the plate and diaphragm of a condenser microphone or electrostatic speaker.
(E)

POLYESTER   See MYLAR.   (E)

POLY MODE   In MIDI inter-connection of synthesizers, the operating mode in which an instrument can receive several notes on one specified MIDI channel, generating a polyphonic output with all notes sounding the same patch. Also called omni-off/poly mode.
(S)

POOR MAN'S COPYRIGHT   Same as common law copyright.
(P)

POP   Point of Purchase. The store or retail outlet where the consumer buys goods or services. Advertising agencies and jingle producers try to create visual and auditory impressions of the product the buyer will recall at the POP. Good
(A)
(A)

jingle weighs heavily in POP buying decisions.

POP FILTER   A microphone wind screen specifically designed to prevent bursts of air from reaching the diaphragm—e.g., those produced by vocal plosives.
(E)

PORT (or I/O PORT)   A jack or plug by which another device or computer can be connected to the computer at hand.
(C)

PORT, SPEAKER   An opening in the front surface or baffle of a loudspeaker enclosure.
(E)
     REAR- (and/or SIDE-) ENTRY PORT: One or more openings on the body of a uni-directional microphone. Passing through the port(s), sound waves can reach the rear side of the diaphragm and, through acoustic cancellation or reinforcement, contribute to its polar pattern. (Illustration next page.)
(E)

POST (or POSTING)   To post-produce a film or video production.
(V,F)

POST-DE-EMPHASIS   In a tape recorder, the playback equalization applied internally to all output signals. (See PRE-EMPHASIS (illustration).)
(E)

(A) = Advertising   •   (B) = Business & Law   •   (C) = Computers   •   (D) = Digital   •   (E) = Engineering & Scientific   •   (F) = Film   •   (G) = Music & General   •   (I) = Interlock & Sync   •   (J) = Jokes & Jargon   •   (P) = Music Publishing   •   (R) = Record Industry   •   (S) = Synthesizers   •   (U) = Unions   •   (V) = Video

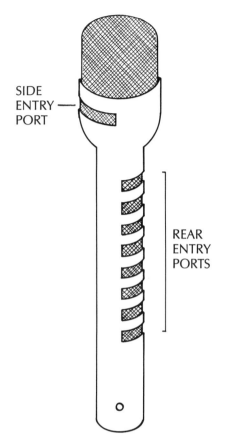

SIDE
ENTRY —
PORT

REAR
ENTRY
PORTS

REAR AND SIDE ENTRY PORTS.

POST-ROLL   In SMPTE synchroniza-
(I)   tion for videotape post-production,
a number of seconds and/or frames
specified by the engineer, which
he desires to be automatically
added to any code address he may
subsequently specify as a record-
out point. Thus, when inserting
dialogue or music, on each take
master and slave machines will
continue to roll for the post-roll
duration after recording is stopped.
This prevents the type of wow that
occurs when a transport is stopped
while the electronics are still recording. Note: Some brands of synchronizer add the post-roll to the
mark-out rather than the record-
out location. (*See* PRE-ROLL.)

POST-PRODUCTION   Everything that
is done once the original footage
(F,V)   for a motion picture or video
production is shot, or "in the can."
Includes looping, editing, sound
cutting, scoring, making of titles,
etc.

POST-SCORE   To compose and/or
produce a musical score or jingle
(F,V,A)   after the film or videotape for the
production has been shot, and
usually after a fine cut is completed. The composer can then
take counts, locate hits, and really
tailor his music to the visuals.

POST-STRIPE   To re-lay the mixed
soundtrack onto the edited video
(V)   master, or onto a copy made from
it.

POST-SYNCHRONIZATION   The
recording of sound that will replace
(F,V)   or add to the synchronous sound
recorded at the time of filming or
videotaping. (*See* LOOPING.)

POTENTIOMETER   POT for short.
A device to vary the voltage al-
(E)   lowed to pass through itself. The
simplest type consists of a resistor
and a movable metal arm. Depending on the position of the arm
along the length of the resistor, the
resistance itself can be varied,
which allows more or less voltage
to pass. Also, used generally to
designate any electronic component
that controls signal level. (See PAN
POT.)

POV SHOT   Point of View Shot. A
shot that shows the scene through
(F,V)   the eyes of its main character. The
audience sees what the character
sees. (*See* SUBJECTIVE CAMERA
ANGLE.)

POWER   In general, the rate of energy
flow produced by an acoustical or
(E)   electrical system or device.
Specified in watts. Technically,
this should be measured per unit
of time, but is often specified as a
continuous value without time
reference.

ACOUSTIC POWER: The
number of watts of energy
produced by any sound source or
transducer. (See ACOUSTIC IN-
TENSITY.)

ELECTRIC POWER: The
number of watts of electric energy
produced by a source or dissipated
in a device. Many electronic devices
consume only a few milliwatts.
Motion picture lighting fixtures can
consume tens of kilowatts.

POWER OF ATTORNEY   Collectively,
the ability to exercise the legal
(B)   rights of ownership concerning all
or a portion of one's business,
financial holdings, career, etc.
When one person appoints another
as his "attorney in fact," he grants
the second party power of attorney, which allows him to make
legally binding decisions and sign
all contracts on behalf of the first
party. One may grant limited
power of attorney to a manager or
business agent, allowing a lawyer,
manager, or agent to make decisions or sign agreements concerning specified areas of the music
industry, for a limited period of
time, etc. Power of attorney should
be granted with extreme care, and
with all limitations and contingent
terms defined clearly and completely.

POWER SUPPLY   A circuit or device
that supplies DC power to an
(E)   amplifier or other electronic device.

It often includes three circuits, one
that converts alternating current to
direct current, then a second that
transforms the DC from its original
voltage to that required by the
device. The third smoothes out any
fluctuations in current caused by
any unevenness in the original AC
source. These operations are often
performed in a different sequence.

MICROPHONE POWER
SUPPLY: The device or circuit that
supplies the polarizing voltage to a
condenser microphone, and that
powers its internal pre-amplifier.
(See PHANTOM POWER SUP-
PLY.)

P.R.   See PUBLIC RELATIONS.

PREAMBLE   In digital recording, a
defined digital word which is in-
(D)   serted into the data stream at
regular intervals to act as a start
marker for each block of data. On
playback this allows the proper
grouping and de-multiplexing of
audio data prior to D-A conversion. (See DATABLOCK; WORD.)

**PRE-AMPLIFIER (or PREAMPLI-
FIER)**   In a console or other
(E)   audio system, the first stage of
amplification, in which very low
level input signals, such as from a
phonograph cartridge or microphone, are boosted to line level (or
some usable level). Many pre-am-
plifiers contain circuits to equalize
signals whose source has a known
imbalance in frequency content,
again such as a phonograph record.

PRE-ECHOES   In room acoustics, any
early reflections of sound that oc-
(E)   cur within about 40 milliseconds,
the shortest time for which the
human ear can distinguish two non-

(A) = Advertising • (B) = Business & Law • (C) = Computers • (D) = Digital • (E) = Engineering & Scientific •
(F) = Film • (G) = Music & General • (I) = Interlock & Sync • (J) = Jokes & Jargon • (P) = Music Publishing •
(R) = Record Industry • (S) = Synthesizers • (U) = Unions • (V) = Video

simultaneous sounds. Some digital reverberation devices produce pre-echoes as a part of their hall simulation program.

PRE-EMPHASIS   1. Generally, the process of equalizing a signal to increase the content of a desired band before the signal is sent to another device. 2. In tape recording, a standardized equalization (high-frequency boost) applied to an audio signal before biasing and record pre-amplification. Done both to help achieve flat high-frequency response on tape, and to reduce tape noise, which occurs as a complementary post-de-emphasis curve is applied to the signal read by the playback head. Pre- and post-emphasis curves are different for each standard tape speed, and standardized by the NAB, CCIR, and IES for their respective countries. High-frequency boost is least in the IES curve, greatest in the CCIR. (*See* RIAA CURVE.)

(E)

PREMIUM   The annual cost of an insurance policy (blanket producer's policy), or the one-time cost of adding a floater to that policy to cover a special situation or specific production, etc.

(B)

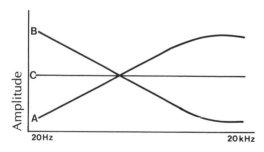

PRE-EMPHASIS. Average playback EQ curve: (A) Shows the frequency response of the electrical output of a playback head. It must be equalized by a complimentary curve (B) to yield a flat frequency response (C) on playback.

PREMIUM RATES   1. In AFM payment schedules, rates for sessions booked between midnight and 8 AM on weekdays, between 1 PM Saturday and 8 AM Monday, or on specified holidays. Premium rates are 50% higher than normal rates, except on holidays, which command double scale payment. 2. Loosely, the higher rates that well-known musicians often charge to play in recording sessions. Double scale, triple scale, and even higher rates are common.

(U)

PRE-MIX (noun)   If many tracks of sound effects (or music) are required for a specific scene, the mixing engineer may want to mix all these effects together onto a single strip of magnetic film (or onto a single track of the sync multi-track master), then use this one track during the final mix rather than the individual effects tracks. Because this effects mix is done before final mix, it is called a pre-mix.

(F,V)

PRE-MIX (or PREMIX) (verb)   To blend or mix and bounce two or more tracks of a multi-track tape before making the final mix of all tracks. Done to free up tracks for additional instruments or voices, or to save time in the final mix by having sections already blended.

(E)

PRE-PRODUCTION   Everything done in any production before the actual recording or shooting of original footage. Composing or writing, arranging, scheduling, budgeting, hiring of crew, casting, location scouting, etc. Rehearsals are also sometimes included. Production per se begins on the

(F,V,R)

morning when tape or film rolls. (*See* POST-PRODUCTION.)

PRE-ROLL (I)   In SMPTE synchronization for videotape post-production, a number of seconds and/or frames specified by the engineer, which he desires to be automatically subtracted from any record-in point he may subsequently select. (**Note:** Some brands of synchronizer subtract the pre-roll from the "mark-in" point rather than the "record-in" point.) The synchronizer will then return master and slave machines to a point located ahead of record-ins by the duration of the pre-roll. This assures that all machines will be up to speed, properly interlocked, and that actors or musicians can find their place and be ready to perform by the actual record-in point. For example, when the engineer directs the video deck to return to a begin recording at 20:10:00 (the record-in point), if he has previously specified a pre-roll of 5:00, the deck will actually stop at 20:05:00, precisely five seconds before the record-in. (*See* POST-ROLL.)

PRE-SCORE (F,V,A)   To compose and/or produce a musical score or jingle before the film or videotape has been shot. Almost all animated films are pre-scored (with all dialogue and effects added), after which frame counts are taken from hits in the music so that the animators can time actions to fit the soundtrack.

PRE-SCORING (F,V)   The technique of recording the music for a scene or entire film before the film itself is shot. This can be done in anticipation of filming live actors to playback, or in animation to provide the animator with exact scene lengths, cue points, and other information by which he will match the animated scene to music.

PRESENCE (E)   A subjective term describing the amount of middle to upper-middle frequencies (2 kHz to 4 kHz) contained in a sound source. Up to a certain point, more of this range will give the impression of a speaker or singer being "present" or near the listener, simply because these frequencies increase intelligibility. A presence control on an amplifier will allow adjustment of this frequency range.

PRESS KIT (A,R)   A selection of printed material used to promote and publicize a record or other product. Usually, aside from pictures and reviews, etc., the press kit also contains a factual mini-story of who made the product, why, where, with whom helping, playing, singing, etc. Often used by critics and reviewers in writing articles or doing broadcast reviews of records, shows, etc.

PRESS RELEASE (A,R)   A written information sheet or news bulletin about a record, cassette, group, event, etc., including its name or title; principal musicians or other participants; a brief description; the most important features, songs, etc.; prices; and how to buy the record, tickets, or whatever is being sold. A mini press kit.

PRESSURE ZONE MICROPHONE (E) (**PZM**)   See MICROPHONE.

PRESSURE SENSITIVITY (S)   A type of touch sensitivity by which the syn-

---

(A) = Advertising • (B) = Business & Law • (C) = Computers • (D) = Digital • (E) = Engineering & Scientific •
(F) = Film • (G) = Music & General • (I) = Interlock & Sync • (J) = Jokes & Jargon • (P) = Music Publishing •
(R) = Record Industry • (S) = Synthesizers • (U) = Unions • (V) = Video

thesizer registers how hard each key is being depressed by the player. This information can be used to vary some parameter of the instrument's output or sound. Similar to velocity sensitivity.

PREVIEW   In video editing, to rehearse
(V)   an edit without actually recording it. (*See* REHEARSE MODE.)

PREVIEW HEAD   In the making of
(R)   lacquer masters or acetates, a playback head installed on the reproducing deck a distance ahead of the program playback head that corresponds to the time it takes for one revolution of the cutting lathe bed. The signal from the preview head tells the variable pitch circuitry the sound level that it will cut one groove later. This allows the unit to space the grooves so that they do not intersect due to

sudden, unanticipated level changes. In quieter passages, it allows the circuit to pack the grooves closer together, minimizing land. (*See* MASTER; LACQUER.)

PRIMARY   1. Short for Primary Market.
(A)   The main target market for a
(R)   product or service. (*See* SUB-SIDIARY MARKET.) 2. The largest radio station in a geographical area, or the largest station of a certain format—e.g., a primary AOR station.

PRIME TIME   The hours of the even-
(A)   ing during which the largest number of television viewers are tuned in, usually between 7 PM and 11:30 PM. These are the hours during which broadcasters can charge the highest price for airing commercials. (*See* DRIVE TIME.)

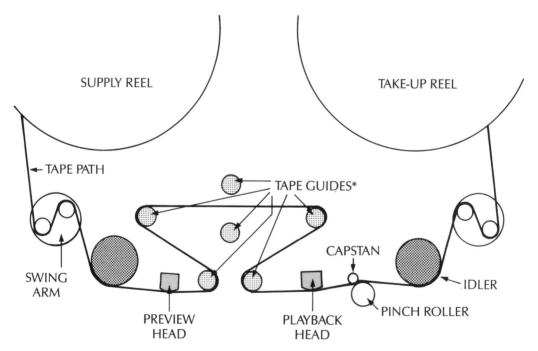

PREVIEW HEAD. Typical mastering playback path. The extra tape guides are used for longer and shorter tape paths to accommodate different tape speeds.

PRINT-THROUGH (E)   The unwanted transfer of signal from one layer of magnetic tape to another. Noticed particularly when a very loud sound on one layer of tape can be heard during very soft sounds or pauses on the adjacent layers. (*See* GHOST.)

PRO CANADA (R)   Performing Rights Organization of Canada. Formerly BMI Canada, the second-largest performing rights organization in Canada, CAPAC being the largest.

PRODUCER (F,V, R,A)   In film or video, the boss, responsible to the financial backers of the production for its completion on time and budget, and consequently the person who does all hiring and firing of creative and technical personnel, including the director. In music productions, the producer is also personally responsible for all creative decisions. In any medium, the producer generally accepts a fee for services, plus points in the finished musical or visual production. In radio or TV spots, the producer must be content with his fee and any residuals he may deserve for performing in his spots. (*See* EXECUTIVE PRODUCER; LINE PRODUCER.)

PRODUCER'S DESK (E)   A flat surface on the recording console that can be used by the producer for note-taking, following a score, etc. Usually located in front of the patch bay.

PRODUCER'S BLANKET POLICY (B,G) See BLANKET POLICY.

PRODUCTION (F,V,R)   That phase in the making of a musical master tape, motion picture, or video project during which the music is actually recorded, or the original film or videotape footage is shot. (*See* PRE-PRODUCTION; POST-PRODUCTION.)

PRODUCTION COMPANY (A,F,V)   A company that acts as producer for radio or television ads, or for video or motion picture projects, dividing specific responsibilities among its employees, one of whom is named producer or line producer.

PRODUCTION MANAGER (F,V)   In a film or television production, the person on the set who administers the producer's decisions. He schedules and hires most technicians, approves rentals, establishes the overall shooting schedule, is actually in charge of all technical crews, and keeps the production rolling accordingly on a daily basis. Everyone except cast and director are under the production manager's control from the first crew call through cast call, at which point the director takes charge until a wrap is declared.

PRODUCTION MEMORANDUM (U)   See SCHEDULE A and B; DEAL MEMO.

PRODUCTION STUDIO (A,F,V)   A type of recording studio designed to facilitate the making of master tapes for sales and educational presentations and radio or television spots in which the music has already been recorded elsewhere. Production studios include a narration or sound effects booth, several two-track playback decks, cart machines and other playback sources, a multi-track machine on

---

(A) = Advertising • (B) = Business & Law • (C) = Computers • (D) = Digital • (E) = Engineering & Scientific •
(F) = Film • (G) = Music & General • (I) = Interlock & Sync • (J) = Jokes & Jargon • (P) = Music Publishing •
(R) = Record Industry • (S) = Synthesizers • (U) = Unions • (V) = Video

which individual sounds and segments can be assembled, a substantial mixing console (sometimes automated), and a hearty sprinkling of outboard equipment and special effects devices.

PRODUCT SHOT   In a TV spot, a shot that features the product being advertised.
(A)

PROFESSIONAL MANAGER   The publishing company employee who is responsible for persuading artists to record compositions, and for selling compositions for use in other royalty-earning or fee-earning contexts—e.g., synchronization and advertising licenses, etc. The formal job title of a "song plugger."
(P)

PROFIT   The money that remains after the producer or production company have paid for all expenses in planning, recording, filming or taping, and editing a radio or television ad, a video, or a motion picture project, etc. These expenses may include research, creative fees (composers, arrangers, etc.), talent payments, recording or TV studio costs, production personnel, materials, etc. The list is very long, and one omission at the budgeting stage can cost the producer his entire profit on a job. Be careful—and don't forget the contingency.
(B,G)

PROFIT AND LOSS (P&L) STATEMENT   A report prepared periodically for the investors in a business, showing not only summarized cash flow figures, but the unrealized profit or loss from changes in the value of assets like real estate, inventory, etc. Anything that will help the company justify
(B)

its decisions to distribute or withhold dividends, issue or buy back stock, etc. (*See* CASH FLOW.)

PROGRAM   The desired audio or video signal passing through any system or stored on any medium such as tape. As opposed to noise and other undesired signals.
(E)

PROGRAM DIRECTOR   See P.D.

PROGRAMMABLE   Containing memory circuits that allow the user to select all the parameters of a new patch, then store these parameters (via battery-powered memory chips) so that he can recall them when he next uses the instrument.
(S,E)

PROGRAMMING GUIDE   A type of trade journal whose major subscribers are radio stations. Over 500 new records are released weekly, too many for any radio station to preview individually. The guide reviews new releases, helping stations decide which will fit into their broadcast format, then tracks the progress of records already in release, and sometimes publishes feature articles on hot producers, artists, labels, studios, etc. The *Friday Morning Quarterback* and *The Gavin Report* are the most important guides, for FM and AM stations, respectively.
(R)

PROJECTION SYNC   The relative location of picture and sound in a motion picture print that produces proper synchronization during projection. Since each frame of picture must be held still while light shines through it and illuminates the screen, and since quality sound can only be read from film moving smoothly and
(F)

continuously past an optical or magnetic playback head, the picture frame and sound frame corresponding to the same event on film must be separated by a distance on film that will allow proper conditions for image projection and sound reproduction. In 16mm, answer and release prints of films are made with the soundtrack advanced 26 frames ahead of the picture. At 24 frames per second projection speed, this distance represents over one second in film "footage." 35mm prints are made with the sound advanced 20 frames. (*See* EDITORIAL SYNC.)

PROJECTOR (F,V)   A machine that throws an image onto a screen for viewing by a group of people. The motion picture projector throws the individual images or frames of film in a sequence for continuous action. The video projector accomplishes the same effect, but creates an image itself from magnetic information encoded on video tape, or recreates the image from electrical signals it receives direct from the video camera, or from reception of a signal transmitted from a distance.

PROMISSORY NOTE (B)   A written I.O.U., specifying the amount of money owed and the date it is due. Sometimes other conditions of payment are specified, with a payment being due only after break-even sales have been achieved. If payment is unconditional, promissory notes are considered negotiable instruments.

PROMOTION (A,B)   The process of letting people know about, and getting them excited about acquiring or using a product or service. Effective promotion conveys both factual information about the product or service and creates the need for it in the viewers' or readers' mind, generally by telling him how he will feel or benefit by having it. (*See* INDEPENDENT PROMOTION; SPECIAL PACKAGING or (PROMOTION).)

PROMPT (C)   A message that asks the user to input data, choose between options, etc.

PROSPECTUS (B)   A description of a planned artistic or business venture. A business plan.

PROTECTION (E)   Short for protection copy. Synonym for safety copy.

PROTOCOL (C)   A predetermined procedure or series of rules that ensures sending and receiving units pass data efficiently and accurately.

PROXIMITY EFFECT (E)   A rise in the low-frequency response of all non-omni directional microphones, caused when the mic is used very close to the source—e.g., when a singer "swallows" the mic.

PSYCHOACOUSTICS (E)   The study of the brain's perception of and reaction to all aspects of sound—i.e., intensity, time of arrival differences, reverberation, etc. The subject encompasses the definition of what the brain thinks it hears, and the analysis of how it reacts subjectively to these sounds—even emotionally—inasmuch as certain genres of sound are known to cause identifiable physical or emotional responses.

PSYCHOGRAPHICS   Similar to demographics, except that the psychographics of an audience or market defines their social attitudes and mores, political views, or other opinions that may be important for advertisers or their clients. Overlaps with some characteristics of sociographics, ethnographics, etc.
(A)

PUBLIC DOMAIN (P.D.)   A legal term applied to any composition or recorded performance whose copyright protection has expired. Anyone can record, perform, or duplicate such materials without payment to the original author(s) or copyright owner(s).
(P,R)

PUBLIC RELATIONS (PR)   The efforts of a company or public figure to establish good rapport with various sections of the public. Generally, a company will have one or more people in charge of PR, making the "neighborhood" aware of and supportive of what the company does, and running interference in cases where the public or any interest group may try to restrict the company's activities. PR people try to uphold a company's good image. (*See* PROMOTION.)
(B,A)

PUBLISHING COMPANY   A company, usually a member affiliate of either ASCAP or BMI, that acts as agent for composers and lyricists. For a percentage of the gross receipts from the sale of recordings of a composition, the publisher promotes the composition, tries to get artists and record companies to record it or perform it, seeks to get the composition used in films, television, shows, etc., then collects the royalties and/or fees for
(P,R,B)

such use through ASCAP, BMI, Harry Fox Agency, etc., and distributes them to the composer(s) and lyricist(s). (*See* ADMINISTRATION; MECHANICAL LICENSE; MECHANICAL ROYALTY; PROFESSIONAL MANAGER.)

PUCK   See CAPSTAN IDLER.

PULL FOCUS   To make a focus pull.
(F,V)

PULSE CODE MODULATION (PCM)   The method used in most digital recording systems to repetitively sample the analog signals and directly produce the binary code equivalents of each sample. PCM is loosely used to designate the digital recording process, without regard to specific sampling rate or any other parameters. (*See* DELTA MODULATION.)
(D)

PULSE WAVE   An oscillator output signal in which a high steady-state voltage alternates with a lower one.
(S)

PULSE WIDTH   Same as duty cycle.
(S)

PUMPING   Noticeable or annoying changes in level caused by the action of a compressor. Usually occurs when one loud sound source, such as bass guitar, causes severe gain reduction in the compressor. With each bass note the level of the other instruments will decrease sharply. Pumping occurs during program material. Breathing occurs when the program stops long enough for the compressor to cease its gain reduction, suddenly boosting the noise floor of the program. (*See* BREATHING.)
(E)

PUNCH MARKS (F)   Holes punched in the academy leader of a workprint and its corresponding magnetic film tracks such that the projectionist will know how to thread up the various picture and tracks for proper synchronization. (*See* SYNC MARK;) PROJECTION SYNC; EDITORIAL SYNC.

PUNCHING IN/PUNCHING OUT (E)   Placing one or more tracks of a multi-track recorder in record, and taking them out again, recording a small section of an already-recorded track. Done to add a note or phrase, or to replace one sung or played badly. Many artists literally assemble their performances by punching in small segments one at a time until the performance is perfected. Usually done during overdubbing.

PURE TONE (E,G)   A single sine wave, without harmonics. A sound containing only one frequency, generally produced by an oscillator.

PUSH-PULL (E)   A type of electronic circuit with two identical signal paths, but whose inputs and/or outputs are reversed in phase to reinforce some signal components and cancel others. The Nagra neo-pilot tone sync circuit, for example, records two narrow push-pull sync tracks near the center of the full-track program. In playback, the sync signal can be retrieved and resolved from either of these tracks. Since their sum is 0, neither will be audible to the audio playback head that reads the entire tape width.

PZM (E)   See MICROPHONE, PRESSURE ZONE.

-Q-

Q **(E)** 1. Loosely, a measure of the bandwidth of frequencies a circuit such as an equalizer will affect. Generally specified in octaves, an equalizer will have a Q of one octave centered at 1 kHz if it boosts incoming signals between about 700 Hz and 1.4 kHz. On a parametric equalizer, the Q of each band of boost or cut can be varied. 2. In a bandpass filter, mathematically defined as the center frequency of the pass band divided by bandwidth—i.e., the highest frequency present minus the lowest.

Q-LOCK **(I)** A brand of electronic synchronizer used for interlocking various audio and videotape recorders. Manufactured by Audio-Kinetics Corporation. The name is sometimes used generically for any such synchronizer. (*See* SYNCHRONIZATION; SMPTE CODE; BTX.)

QUADRUPLEX RECORDER **(V)** A VTR recording configuration in which four heads are mounted around a wheel that turns in contact with 2″ tape. This system has largely been replaced by helical scan formats.

(*See* HELICAL SCAN; FORMAT, 5. (illustrations).)

QUANTIZATION **(D,E)** Generally, the process of assigning each of the sequence of samples taken of an analog waveform to one of a number of discrete levels, each of which can have one value from a number of predetermined possible "steps." Each stepped value is thus the nearest approximation of the actual analog voltage at that instant.

(D,E) N-BIT QUANTIZATION: The process of representing each voltage sample as an n-bit digital word. The number of bits determines how many fixed, stepped levels are available to represent each sampled voltage in the original signal. In most professional recorders, n = 16, a format that provides wide dynamic range, plus plenty of bits for error detection and correction schemes, and allows manufacturers to use data-processing chips developed for standard computing applications.

QUANTIZING INCREMENTS **(D)** 1. The total number of stepped levels (from noise level to saturation) that the A-D converter has available for assignment of the continuously varying analog input voltage with each sample taken. For example, if each sample occupies 10 bits of data, there will be 2 raised to the 10th power, or 1,024 quantizing increments. **2.** The voltage or decibel difference between any particular quantizing step and the next step higher or lower. In a system with 1,024 discrete steps, if signal voltage from noise level to saturation varies from 0.0 to 1.0 volt, each quantizing increment will correspond to about 0.001 volt.

QUARTER-TRACK   A recording format on 1/4″ tape in which two tracks are recorded, each a bit less than one quarter of the tape's width. The left stereo track lies along one edge—the first quarter of the tape width. The right stereo track occupies the third quarter of the tape's width. Since there are still two quarters of the tape's width unrecorded, the tape may be turned over and used in the other direction too. (*See* FORMAT (illustration).)

(E)

-R-

R.A. (or R/A) Recording Authorization. A form used by major record
(R,A) labels, filled out by the A&R man and/or producer of a single or album project before recording begins. It is basically a proposed budget for all expenses necessary on the project, with a brief description of the musical nature of the completed tape(s). Once signed by a label executive, the form authorizes the producer to spend amounts listed in each category—i.e., studio costs, union wages, rentals, creative fees, etc. R/As are also used by some jingle production houses.

RACK A type of shelving, usually with
(E) enclosed sides and back, to which a variety of audio components can be attached vertically, one over the other. Components are normally screwed into front-mounted, tapped metal strips with holes closely spaced to allow adjustment of the height of each component.

RACK JOBBER A type of record dis-
(R) tributor who stocks only current hit record releases and a few "classic" oldies. He sells to department stores and other retailers who have no record buyer on staff. The rack jobber fills the stores racks or bins with the "Top 40" (for instance), replacing these as the charts change. Because the rack jobber decides what his customers will buy, he generally has to accept up to 100% returns, unless the retailer agrees to pay for a certain minimum total number of albums, regardless of the artists or labels represented.

RADIAN In mathematics, an acute
(E) angle containing $360/2\pi$ degrees, or approximately 57.29 degrees. The angle of a circle that is subtended by a curved line segment equal in length to the radius. (*See* STERADIAN.)

RADIATION PATTERN The polar
(E) pattern that graphs a speaker's directional characteristics for a group of specific test frequencies. Also, the three-dimensional graph of the intensity with which any sound source emits various frequencies at all angles around itself.

RADIATOR, DIRECT/INDIRECT A
(E) loudspeaker whose cone or

diaphragm is coupled directly to the air in the listening environment is a direct radiator. A compression driver or any type of loudspeaker that uses a horn or other device to match its acoustic impedance to that of the listening environment is an indirect radiator.

RADIO AND RECORDS   The name of a weekly newspaper and trade journal that tells what's happening nationwide in AM and FM programming, publishing charts of a wide variety of stations, listing charts, pick hits, etc. for many types of music. A very important force in the record industry.
(R)

RADIO FREQUENCY   See RF.

RAM   See RANDOM ACCESS MEMORY.

RAMP WAVE   A sawtooth wave.
(S)

R&D   Research and Development. A major category of expenses in the development of a new product, or in the operation of companies that bring many new products to market. Strictly speaking, all A&R activities of a record company are a form of R&D—i.e., finding and developing new artists and their products—master tapes.
(B)

RANDOM ACCESS MEMORY (RAM)   A type of computer memory in which the user can send data to or retrieve it from any single memory address, independently of all other addresses. The number of Kbytes in a computer's RAM limits the complexity of programs to be run, the size of matrices established for spreadsheets, and the amount of
(C)

text data instantly available for review or editing. (*See* READ-ONLY MEMORY; CPU; ALU.)

RAREFACTION, AIR   The spreading apart of air molecules (which lowers the local air pressure) during the second half of each complete cycle of a sound wave. This corresponds to the portion of the wave that appears below the axis when graphed. Opposite of condensation or compression of air.
(E)

RASTER   The characteristic patterns of horizontal lines formed by the scanning beam of the TV picture tube: 525 lines in the U.S. NTSC system, 625 in the European PAL system, etc. Also, the actual electronic circuit that creates the scanning spot that traces these lines on the TV screen.
(V)

RATE   In a digital delay or flanger, a circuit and control that enable the engineer to vary the length of time during which the depth circuit completes one full increase/decrease cycle of the nominal delay time. To the ear, the rate control varies the speed of the apparent vibrato added to the input signal by the depth circuitry. (*See* DEPTH.)
(E)

RATE CARD   A small card or single sheet on which a person or company lists their standard "list" prices for services and materials, at least for those services most often provided. A recording studio's "card rate" is their highest rate, which is normally reduced for regular clients or especially long projects involving large numbers of hours for recording or mixing, block bookings, etc.
(B)

(A) = Advertising • (B) = Business & Law • (C) = Computers • (D) = Digital • (E) = Engineering & Scientific •
(F) = Film • (G) = Music & General • (I) = Interlock & Sync • (J) = Jokes & Jargon • (P) = Music Publishing •
(R) = Record Industry • (S) = Synthesizers • (U) = Unions • (V) = Video

RAW STOCK   See FILM STOCK; NEGATIVE; REVERSAL.

RCA JACK (or PLUG)   A type of audio connector developed by RCA, and in common use on most home audio equipment. A 1/2″ long, thin metal pin projects from the center of a cylindrical group of metal leaves about 1/4″ in diameter. The pin carries the signal; the leaves act as ground.
(E,G)

R-DAT   Recording Digital Audio Tape. A consumer system developed to allow some digital recording of various audio material. The R-DAT standard adopted by some 80 equipment manufacturers employs a miniature "VCR"-like recorder, with a rotating head drum inscribing the signal on a cassette somewhat smaller than the standard audio cassette. By agreement of manufacturers, R-DAT recorders will not be able to record with a 44.1 kHZ sampling rate. This prevents direct digital copying of material from compact discs.
(D)

REACTION SHOT   A shot that shows one or more characters reacting to something that just happened, on- or off-screen.
(F,V)

READ   To retrieve information or data from a disk or other storage medium. Opposite of Write.
(C)

READ MODE   In console automation, the operational mode in which automation data concerning the fader level or other parameter for each channel is read back from data storage and used to reproduce those settings in real-time, actually controlling each parameter exactly as the engineer did while writing
(E)

the data. (See CONSOLE AUTOMATION; UPDATE MODE; WRITE MODE.)

READ-ONLY MEMORY (ROM)   A type of computer memory into which data has been factory-stored. Hence the user can only read the data. He cannot rearrange or replace it. Used to store programs that (a) comprise the machine's operating system, (b) translate between user languages such as FORTRAN, BASIC, etc. and machine language, (c) telecommunications programs any basic program the user needs in order to run applications software. ROM cartridges and/or cards also store factory-designed patches for many synthesizers. (See RANDOM ACCESS MEMORY; CPU; ALU.)
(C,S)

READY   An operational mode of tape recorder electronics. For any tracks placed in ready mode, the record circuits are enabled. When the engineer presses the master record button and tape begins moving, the "ready" tracks begin recording. Opposite of safe mode.
(E)

REAL-TIME ANALYSIS (RTA)   The process of continuously measuring the signal level present in each of many separate bandwidths in a complex waveform. Professional analyzers divide the input signal into third-octave bands (usually from a precisely calibrated microphone), the level of each of which is then displayed in real-time by a series of peak-reading LED meters. RTAs are particularly helpful in adjusting the combined monitor speaker response and acoustics of control rooms to deliver flat frequency response to the engineer.
(E)

Pink noise is sent to the monitors, and the RTA mic is placed at the engineer's position. The output of the mic is displayed on the RTA. A stereo third-octave equalizer installed between the console and monitor amps can then be used to adjust the overall speaker/room response until the desired curve is achieved.

RECAPTURE (P,R,B)   To take control of a copyright back from the publisher or other agent who has administered it. If a composer has signed a publishing contract giving the publisher one year to secure a mechanical license or other income-earning use of a work, and the publisher fails to do so, the composer will recapture the copyright. An independent producer will recapture a master tape after a label's option to purchase it expires. (*See* REVERSION; ASSIGNMENT.)

RECORD-IN/RECORD-OUT (V,I)   In SMPTE synchronization for videotape post-production, the user-specified SMPTE code addresses at which the synchronizer will automatically place the audio or video recorder in record mode (thereby punching in), and subsequently cancel the record mode (thereby punching out). (*See* PRE-ROLL; POST-ROLL; MARK-IN/MARK-OUT.)

RECORDING AUTHORIZATION   See R.A.

RECORDING DIGITAL AUDIO TAPE   See R-DAT.

RECORDING ENGINEER/PRODUCER   See RE/P.

RECORDING FUND (R)   General form of an album fund.

RECORDING GOAL (P)   The sales or song-placement goals a publisher must meet in the first term of a publishing contract, without which it loses its rights to renew. If the publisher promises to secure two mechanical licenses for a composer within one year of signing a publishing contract, and fails to do so, the company has not met its recording goal. (*See* RECAPTURE; REVERSION.)

RECORDING INDUSTRY ASSOCIATION OF AMERICA   See RIAA.

RECORDIST (F,V)   The chief sound technician on a motion picture or television set, responsible for the technical and dramatic quality of all sound recorded. Also called sound mixer, or on smaller productions, simply sound man.

RECOUPABLE (R)   The total amount of money spent by a record company on all phases of a specific single or album release, the entirety of which is usually paid back to this company from the artist's royalty account—that is, if the record sells well. (*See* CHARGE-BACK.)

RECOUPMENT (R,F,V)   The process of taking back money advanced by a record or film company during the making of any particular production. For example, a record company will advance all money necessary to produce, release, and promote an album, then take recoupment for all these expenses from the artist's royalties when and

---

if the album sells. (*See* CHARGE-BACK.)

RECOUPMENT ADVANCE   Money paid to an independent record producer by a record company, specifically to repay him for expenses made in the production of one or more master tapes the company wants to purchase and release. The amount of this advance is normally what the record company feels it would have to spend to produce the same master tapes in good recording studios, using all union musicians, etc., which may be far more than the producer actually spent. (*See* MASTER PURCHASE AGREEMENT; MASTER LICENSE AGREEMENT; SCHEDULE D.)
(R)

RED-GREEN-BLUE   See RGB.

REDUCTION PRINT   A step print of film footage made on print stock of smaller gauge than the camera negative. 70mm films are often reduction workprinted on 35mm for easier editing. Likewise, 35mm films can be reduction printed to 16mm, primarily to save money.
(F)

REED-SOLOMON CODE   An error detection and correction scheme that, combined with cross interleaving, is used in compact disc reproduction. Together they are called CIRC.
(D)

REEL MOTOR   In a tape recorder, the motor that controls the motion of either the feed or take-up reel. Some machines use one motor for both.
(E)

REEL SIZE CONTROL   On a tape transport, the control that maintains proper tape tension by accomodating for various size feed and take-up reels (which have different amounts of angular momentum). Some machines have separate controls for feed and take-up. Newer machines use an infrared or other beam to automatically measure and accommodate various reel sizes.
(E)

REFERENCE LEVEL   A standard level, such as 0 VU, +4 dBm, 0 dBV, to which other levels can be compared.
(E)

REFERENCE (TEST) TAPE   A recorded tape containing a series of pure tones at various frequencies, all recorded at a known, standard level or fluxivity. The test tape is used to verify the performance of the recorder's playback system. Once this is done, the record system is adjusted to produce signals that, when played back, are identical with the input.
(E)

REFERENCE TONE   A single-frequency tone, recorded at the head of a tape, and used to check the alignment of the tape at a later date, or when played on a different recorder. Also, to establish the relative level at which each of the tracks on the tape should be reproduced or copied. In professional studios, it is customary to record 1 kHz, 100 Hz, and 10 kHz reference tones on the head of every reel of multitrack or 1/4" tape. These are usually called "tones" for short.
(E)

REFRACTION   The bending of sound waves as they pass from one medium into another, or as they encounter the corner of a barrier.
(E)

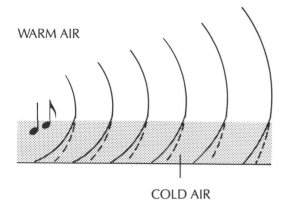

WARM AIR

COLD AIR

REFRACTION. The dashed lines show the direction of the sound wave if its speed remains constant. The speed of sound slows in colder air. If the air is cooler near the ground, refraction occurs as shown by the solid lines.

Exactly analogous to the refraction of light. Often confused with diffraction. (*See* DISPERSION.)

REGENERATING TIME CODE   In
(V,I)   copying a video or audio tape with SMPTE time code, the process of reading the code from the master tape and creating a perfect electronic duplicate of it for recording on the copy. The new code is created by a separate device, and is necessary to ensure that the audio or video copy is free of timing errors and drop-outs.

REGENERATION   A repeated delay
(E)   produced when the output of a digital delay is routed back to its input. Or, generally, any type of feedback.

REGISTER   A temporary storage area
(C)   in the CPU, used to briefly hold data and commands before they are used or executed. (*See* BUFFER MEMORY.)

REGISTER OF COPYRIGHTS   The
(P,R)   office in the Library of Congress that issues copyright forms to writers and publishers, then accepts scores, manuscripts, tapes, and records for permanent storage. These can later be used as proof of authorship and date of registration in cases where copyright infringement is claimed. This office makes no comment on the originality of each work received, but merely certifies what is received from whom, and when.

REGISTRATION   1. The correct align-
(F,V)   ment of (a) the frame lines of motion picture film with the center of the sprocket holes in 16mm, or with the midpoint between two sprocket holes in 35mm stock, which in turn ensures the proper placement of the photographic image on the camera original and the printed image on the release print and movie screen; or (b) the three colors (RGB) projected on a color television picture tube, ensuring a single, focused image. Also called
(P,B)   convergence. 2. See COPYRIGHT REGISTRATION; PATENT NOTICE; NOTICE.

REGULAR SESSION   The term used
(U,R)   by the AFM for a three-hour recording session for master tapes of records, etc. The standard sideman's scale payment is for one regular session in weekday hours. In sessions for phonograph records, only 15 minutes of different music can be recorded during any regular session. (*See* PREMIUM RATES; SPECIAL SESSION.)

REHEARSE MODE   In SMPTE
(I)   synchronization for videotape postproduction, a synchronizer mode that simulates the engineer-specified operations (including record-in and

record-out commands) at the designated code addresses, but does not actually punch in and out. (*See* PREVIEW.)

REINFORCEMENT   An increase in acoustic or electric amplitude that occurs when the peaks and troughs of two or more waves combine additively.
(E)

RE-LAP   To regrind and polish the front surface of worn tape heads. The abrasion of thousands of hours of recording tape can wear a deep path across the head gap. To maintain proper tape-head contact, and to ensure that the heads can be properly aligned, they are periodically sent for re-lapping, done on high-precision equipment at the factory or qualified labs. Most heads have to be replaced after two or three re-lappings.
(E)

RE-LAY   To post-stripe a video master tape, recording the mixed soundtrack back onto the tape after it has been stripped for post-dubbing or the addition of narration, music, and/or effects. (*See* LAYBACK RECORDER.)
(V)

RELATIVE PITCH   The ability to judge one pitch by reference to another. The total lack of this ability is tone deafness. (*See* PERFECT PITCH.)
(G)

RELEASE   1. A short legal agreement by which someone whose voice and/or picture appears in a recording or visual presentation being made for broadcast, public exhibition, or commercial sale allows the producer to use the tape or footage of him for a specified consideration or payment. 2. Any agreement
(F,V,B)

by which, for a consideration, one person or company releases another party from any future responsibility for further payment or any damages that may result from the use of his likeness, voice, or performance in an audio or visual presentation. 3. In a song, a section that is neither verse nor chorus, in which the lead vocalist or instrumentalist is released from the overall structure for a period. A bridge. 4. The fourth and final segment of a sound's envelope, following the attack, decay, and sustain. The release of an instrumental sound begins when the player stops depressing a key, blowing into the mouthpiece, etc.
(G)
(S,E)

RELEASE PRINT   A composite print of a film made for general exhibition purposes. Release prints are generally made using the same exposure, color balance, and effects information employed in the final or "approved" answer print. Can also be made from internegatives or CRIs exposed as approved answer prints.
(F)

RELEASE TIME   The length of time it takes for a signal processing device (generally a compressor, limiter, or expander) to return to its nominal gain before threshold, once the input signal level no longer meets threshold conditions. (*See* ATTACK TIME.)
(E)

RELUCTANCE   The opposition to a magnetic force or field, exhibited by another field and its source (such as an electromagnet), or by unmagnetized but potentially magnetic objects such as the oxide domains on recording tape.
(E)

(A) = Advertising • (B) = Business & Law • (C) = Computers • (D) = Digital • (E) = Engineering & Scientific •
(F) = Film • (G) = Music & General • (I) = Interlock & Sync • (J) = Jokes & Jargon • (P) = Music Publishing •
(R) = Record Industry • (S) = Synthesizers • (U) = Unions • (V) = Video

REMANENCE (or REMANENT FLUX)

(E)   The amount of magnetization left on recording tape when an applied magnetic force is removed. Measured in lines of force per quarter inch of tape width. (*See* FLUX DENSITY; HYSTERESIS LOOP.)

REMEDY

(B)   The cure for a problem, default, or breach that occurs in the execution of a contract.

REMOTE

(E)   1. An audio and/or video session or a live broadcast done away from the normal studio—i.e., on location. 2. A piece of equipment controlled at a distance, either through a supplied remote control device, or by using the controls of another device. One can play a remote synthesizer using MIDI codes, for example, or operate certain sync tape machines as remotes by transmitter control.

RE/P

(E)   Recording Engineer/Producer. An American trade journal that tracks the latest developments in recording technology, interviews noted producers and engineers on techniques used in specific projects, and follows developments of interest in related fields such as film and video production, etc.

REPORTING STATION

(R,V)   A radio or television station that reports its weekly playlists, requests, and pick hits to *Billboard, Radio & Records,* a programming guide, or other record industry trade magazines. Certain record stores in each area also report to these magazines. These stores and stations together determine the national charts.

REPRO

(E)   One of the operating modes of tape recorder electronics. Tracks placed in repro mode will play the tape via the normal playback head—i.e., not via sel-sync. Alternative to sync mode.

REPRODUCING CHARACTERISTIC

(E)   In tape playback, the standardized equalization curve introduced by post-de-emphasis. (*See* PRE-EMPHASIS.)

RE-RECORDING

(F,V)   The process of mixing (or remixing) all the edited sync and non-sync audio tracks of a motion picture or video production to mono, stereo, four-track, or whatever final audio format is needed for theatrical or television exhibition. (*See* DUBBING THEATER.)

RESEARCH AND DEVELOPMENT

See R&D.

RESIDUAL MAGNETIZATION

(E)   Similar to remanence, but generalized to designate the magnetism remaining in any magnetic material once the applied magnetic field is removed.

RESIDUALS

(U,A)   Payments made by clients or advertisers to talent for the reuse of radio or television ads. Talent payments for the initial ad cover its use in specified markets for a specified number of broadcasts during a specified period of time, usually thirteen weeks. Residuals are due to talent when any of these constraints is exceeded—i.e., showing the ad in new markets, or more frequently than originally planned, or for a longer time. Also called re-use fees. (*See* PERFORMANCE; PERFORMANCE CREDIT; CATEGORY.)

(A) = Advertising • (B) = Business & Law • (C) = Computers • (D) = Digital • (E) = Engineering & Scientific •
(F) = Film • (G) = Music & General • (I) = Interlock & Sync • (J) = Jokes & Jargon • (P) = Music Publishing •
(R) = Record Industry • (S) = Synthesizers • (U) = Unions • (V) = Video

RESISTANCE (E)   The opposition of an electric component or circuit to the flow of direct current. Specified in basic units called ohms, symbolized by the Greek capital letter omega, Ω. Calculated by the formula $R = E/I$, where E is the voltage and I is the current flow (in amps) through the component or circuit. (*See* IMPEDANCE.)

RESISTOR (E)   An electronic component that opposes current flow.

RESOLUTION (F,V)   1. Generally, the measure of photographic sharpness of any image. 2. In motion picture film, this depends on the quality of lenses, the accuracy and stability of registration in the camera and projector, and the grain structure of the emulsion itself. 3. In video, the number of pixels into which a horizontal line of picture is accurately divided. This presumes that the system in use is capable of supplying distinct picture information to all 525 lines (if it is an NTSC system). Home televisions, for example, can deliver no more than 325 lines of vertical resolution, with about 250 pixels per line.

RESOLVER (F,V)   The electronic circuit within or connected to a Nagra or other synchronous tape recorder that controls motor speed on playback to maintain proper synchronization of sound with picture. It keeps the recorded sync tone in phase with the 60 Hz AC powering the recorder and projector, or can sync the playback with a crystal or outside 60 Hz reference source. (*See* ERROR SIGNAL; SERVO-CONTROL; SELSYN MOTOR.)

RESONANCE (E)   1. A reinforcement of signal caused when the incoming frequency is equal to the natural frequency of vibration of the acoustic or electric system through which it passes. 2. A specific frequency at which a resonant condition exists.
(E)   ROOM RESONANCE: Any frequency whose half-wavelength is equal to one or more dimensions of a room. When propagated in the room, this frequency will cause a resonant condition.

RESONANT PEAK (E)   An increase in amplitude or intensity that occurs when a resonant frequency passes through an acoustic or electronic system. Measured in dB above nominal signal level or SPL for other frequencies.

RESTORED TIME CODE (V,I)   In SMPTE synchronization, a newly generated continuous time code that will maintain sync with an external reference code. Used to replace a discontinuous code—e.g., one that includes unrelated segments of code, perhaps copied from video shots from several origins.

RESULTANT (E)   The note or frequency heard as the difference of the frequencies of two tones played simultaneously. Essentially, the frequency of beating between two tones.

RETENTIVITY (E)   The flux density present on a specific type of magnetic tape after a magnetic field of saturation strength is removed. The maximum flux density the tape can store.

RETURNS   Records or cassettes a
(R)   dealer feels he cannot sell, and that
he may return to the record com-
pany for credit against future orders. Record companies have varying policies about the percentage
of any order that may be returned,
except as defective copies. Before
1979 most record companies would
accept 100% returns. Since that
time, return policy has varied from
10% to 30% among major labels. It
can also vary with individual albums or any part of a company's
catalog.

RE-USE FEES   Synonym for residuals.
(A)

REVERBERATION   Numerous repeti-
(E,G)   tions of an acoustic sound or audio
signal, becoming more closely
spaced (denser) with time, and
generally decaying within a few
seconds to silence or zero level.

REVERBERATION SYSTEM   Any
(E)   electronic or acoustical device used
to simulate the natural reverbera-
tion of a large hard-surfaced room,
or to produce reverberant effects
of any type at all. The reverb may
be produced in a chamber, a plate,
springs, or digitally.

REVERBERATION TIME   Generally,
(E)   the length of time it takes for a
sound to become inaudible once
its source stops vibrating. Often
called T-60, the time it takes for
the sound pressure level to drop to
one millionth of its original intensity, a decrease of 60 dB.

REVERSAL FILM   Motion picture
(F)   raw stock (developed for and used
mostly in 16mm low-budget
productions) that produces a posi-

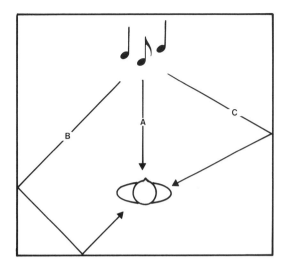

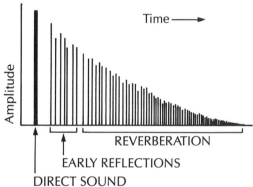

REVERBERATION. Top view of room, sound
source and listener, showing the direct and south
path (A) and reflections (B), and (C).

tive image when exposed and
processed. As opposed to the traditional camera negative stock used
in most film production.

REVERSION   The returning of rights
(P)   to a composition or other
copyrighted work to their former
owner or controller. If a master
license is issued for a three-year
period, the rights to that recording
will revert to their original owner
after three years. In any contract,
one may insert reversion clauses
by which granted rights automatically return to their original owner

if the other party fails to achieve specified goals, or if the term of the contract expires, etc. (*See* RECAPTURE.)

REWIND   A geared crank used to wind
(F)   film onto reels or cores (using split reels), or used in pairs to wind film from one reel to another.

RF   Radio Frequency. Used generically for any type of electromagnetic
(E)   interference picked up by audio or video cables. (*See* SHIELD; SHIELDED CABLE; BALANCED LINE.)

RGB   1. Red-Green-Blue. The three
(F,V,E) primary colors, and, more importantly, the colors whose individual exposure or density is adjusted (a) in the timing of motion pictures, and (b) in the scene-to-scene color correction of videotaped programs. The timer or video engineer can change the overall exposure of a shot by changing the RGB settings equally, up or down. Or he can alter the color balance of the shot by raising or lowering one or two
(V)   of the RGB settings. 2. A video signal or system in which red, green, and blue information is transmitted or stored separately for each field or frame—e.g., the 1/2″ Betacam format.

RHYTHM TRACKS   Basic tracks usu-
(E)   ally recorded first in a multitrack session. These are generally played back through headphones to musicians and singers who later overdub various parts of a complex arrangement. (*See* BACKING TRACKS.)

RIAA   Recording Industry Association
(R)   of America. The professional or-ganization that certifies figures for record sales and establishes technical standards for record mastering and production, among other things. The RIAA certifies the sales levels required for so-called "gold" and "platinum" records.

RIAA CURVE   An equalization curve established by the RIAA and ap-
(E)   plied to all music as it is transferred from master tape to master disc. This pre-emphasis curve introduces about 20 dB skew in frequency content of the program, decreasing bass content and increasing treble around a 500Hz turning point. The opposite post-de-emphasis curve is applied by the phono pre-amp during reproduction. Since groove width increases in proportion to low frequencies in the program, greatly reducing the the program-time that can be cut on a master, and since surface noise is most noticeable in the high frequencies, RIAA curve encoding allows grooves to be closely spaced, while decoding during reproduction reduces surface noise.

RIDER   In a contract or legal agreement, one or more paragraphs or
(B)   clauses added to the main body of the text by written consent of all parties. A rider may limit or modify a part of the contract, or contain some completely new material. (*See* SCHEDULE; TECHNICAL RIDER.)

RIFF   A short, catchy musical phrase usually played between lyric lines
(G)   in a song, and often repetitively, thereby acting as a hook. The Beatles often used guitar riffs as signatures for specific songs.

(A) = Advertising   •   (B) = Business & Law   •   (C) = Computers   •   (D) = Digital   •   (E) = Engineering & Scientific   •
(F) = Film   •   (G) = Music & General   •   (I) = Interlock & Sync   •   (J) = Jokes & Jargon   •   (P) = Music Publishing   •
(R) = Record Industry   •   (S) = Synthesizers   •   (U) = Unions   •   (V) = Video

RINGING   An unwanted resonance produced by a sharp cutoff or brickwall filter near its turnover frequency. In digital reproduction, this can cause severe phase distortion in the high frequencies, which accounts for the "edginess" or brittleness many listeners noticed in first-generation CD players.
(D)

RING MODULATOR   A signal processing circuit that accepts two signal inputs, then produces an output containing only the sums and differences of all the original harmonics present in the inputs. Used to create strange hollow and metallic sounds.
(S)

RIVAS SPLICER   A brand of tape splicer preferred by some film editors. (See GUILLOTINE SPLICER).
(F)

RMS VALUE   Root Mean Squared Value. One of a number of ways of measuring continuous signal level or power output of an amplifier or other device. RMS measurements are considered the most accurate indication of continuous power handling capacity of a piece of equipment, or the level of acoustic energy. (See PEAK-TO-PEAK VALUE.)
(E)

ROBINSON-DADSON CURVES   A new type of equal loudness curve (slowly replacing the Fletcher-Munson curves) made from surveys of a large sampling of listeners, and using very sophisticated testing and evaluations software.
(E)

ROCK AND ROLL   A system used in dubbing or mixing by which the projector, dubbers, and recorder can run in synchronization in reverse. Thus, if a mistake is made
(F,V)
in mixing a particular scene, the mixing engineer can roll all materials back past the mistake and try another pass at the proper mix, punching in before the mistake. Also called ROLLBACK. Selsyn motors on all machines involved make rock and roll possible.

ROLLBACK   See ROCK AND ROLL.

ROM   See READ-ONLY MEMORY.

ROOM ACOUSTICS   Properties of a room that affect the quality of sounds heard in the room. The main properties are reverberation and resonance modes, which in turn are affected by the room's surfaces, dimensions, and overall shape.
(E,G)

ROOM MODES (EIGENTONES)   The acoustic resonances in a room caused by similarity of the wavelengths of these frequencies and the dimensions of the room itself.
(E)

ROOM SOUND   The characteristic ambient sound of a concert hall or other listening room. (See ROOM ACOUSTICS.)
(E)

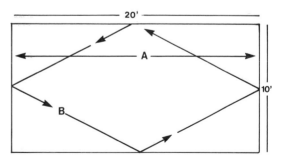

ROOM MODES. (A) A simple standing wave results in a room mode, or resonance, at 28 Hz and its harmonics; 56 Hz, 84 Hz, and 112 Hz; (B) A complex standing wave.

ROOM TONE   The ambient sound of
a location or set, interior or exterior, usually recorded as wild
sound for later use in editing the
dialogue or effects track. If, for
instance, someone bumped a light
during a shot, but between lines of
dialogue, a length of room tone
can be substituted for the uninten-
tional bump. Also called ambience
or simply tone.

(E)

ROOT MEAN SQUARED VALUE
See RMS VALVE.

ROS   See RUN-OF-SCHEDULE.   (A)

ROSTRUM CAMERA   A motion picture or video camera that shoots
one frame at a time, mounted vertically above an animation stand
or other table used for the photography of artwork, titles, etc. (*See*
PEGBOARD; ROTOSCOPING.)

(F,V)

ROTATION (HEAVY, MEDIUM, LIGHT)
At a radio station, the measure of
how many times certain records
are played on a daily basis. Records in heavy rotation receive the
greatest number of daily plays;
those in light rotation the least.
(*See* PLAYLIST; CHART.)

(R)

ROTATION POINT   In a compressor
or expander, the input signal level
at which the graph of the device's
output vs. input (its transfer characteristic) intersects its unity gain
curve. At this level, there is no net
change from input to ouput level.
(*See* COMPRESSOR (illustrations).)

(E)

ROTOSCOPING   A technique used in
producing special effects, primarily the addition of animated charac-

(F)

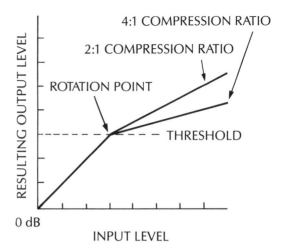

ROTATION POINT.

ters to live action footage and vice
versa. A light source is placed
behind the gate in a rostrum
camera, so that the frame held still
in the gate will be projected onto
the surface of the animation table.
The animator then creates artwork
on cels properly registered with
each frame via the pegbar. The
artwork can later be matted into
the live scene. Also used to make
travelling mattes, etc.

ROUGHT CUT   A stage in the editing
of the workprint or videotape at
which the scenes and shots are in
order and cut approximately to
their correct length. Between an
assembly and a fine cut.

(F,V)

ROUTINE/SUBROUTINE   Any set
of computer instructions (or codes)
that performs a task. A subroutine
is a small set of instructions that
accomplishes one of many tasks to
be done by the whole routine or
program. The subroutine, when
finished running, returns the computer to the point in the program
from which it originally came.

(C)

(A) = Advertising • (B) = Business & Law • (C) = Computers • (D) = Digital • (E) = Engineering & Scientific •
(F) = Film • (G) = Music & General • (I) = Interlock & Sync • (J) = Jokes & Jargon • (P) = Music Publishing •
(R) = Record Industry • (S) = Synthesizers • (U) = Unions • (V) = Video

ROYALTIES Monies paid by record
(R,P,G) companies, broadcasters, and other
users of songs and specific performances released on records, tape,
compact disc, etc. Royalties are
paid by record companies to
publishers for use of songs, who in
turn pay the writers. The record
company also pays the producer a
royalty, a part of which he may
pay to the artists, arranger, or
whoever has points. Sometimes all
parties are paid directly by the
record company. It depends on
who initially paid for the recording of the master tapes and the
order in which various participants
became involved in the project.
(*See* AIRPLAY ROYALTIES; ME-
CHANICAL ROYALTY; RESID-
UALS; ALL-IN DEAL.)

ROYALTY ARTIST In the record in-
(R,U) dustry, the person or group of
people who have signed a production or recording contract with the
record company. Generally, in addition to their union scale payments for playing and singing on
their own records, royalty artists
receive a percentage of the profits
(called points) from sales of the
records, cassettes, CDs, etc. Because
of this additional payment, the
AFM and AFTRA limit the amount
of scale payments record companies must pay to royalty artists.
AFM musicians are limited to one
scale payment per Side or song
recorded, while AFTRA singers
are limited to three scale payments
per Side, regardless of how many
parts or tracks are played or sung
or how long it takes to record
them. (*See* SIDE.)

ROYALTY BASE In calculating artist
(R) and producer royalties from record
sales of a specific release, the dollar amount remaining after the
record company's total wholesale
receipts, minus the recoupable or
all chargebacks, have been multiplied by the royalty base rate. This
figure may then be multiplied by
the artist and producer royalty
rates, checks then being issued in
the resulting dollar amounts. The
latter calculation can have other
variables in some recording contracts.

ROYALTY BASE RATE In calculat-
(R) ing artist and producer royalties
from record sales, a fixed percentage that is multiplied by the total
units sold, and that thereby reduces
the amount of royalties actually
paid. Originally intended to help
labels avoid paying royalties on
records broken in shipment (which,
before vinyl became the standard
pressing material, used to be 10%
of all records shipped), the standard royalty base rate was 90%.
These days record companies also
deduct a packaging discount or
container charge of between 10
and 25%, bringing the base rate
down to perhaps 65%. (*See* PACK-
AGING DISCOUNT; BREAKAGE
ALLOWANCE.)

RS-232 PORT A 25-pin connector
(C,S) and/or socket used in computers
and some synthesizers for transmitting serial data. Many auxiliary
slots are the RS-232 type.

RTA See REAL-TIME ANALYSIS.

RUBATO A musical term indicating
(G) that a conductor or musician may
take expressive liberties with the
tempo (slowing down and/or

speeding up) during the designated section of a chart or score.

RUMBLE
(E)   Unwanted low frequencies present, due to mechanical vibration of motors, heating systems, the proximity of roads, etc. Rooms and many turntables have significant rumble problems.

RUN
(C)   In computers, to execute an entire program, drawing data from all designated sources and calculating all the requested answers, etc.

RUN-OF-SCHEDULE (ROS)
(A)   If an advertiser or media buyer does not want to pay a premium to have a spot aired at specific times, he will simply order so many airings per evening or other period of time. The broadcaster will then fit these airings in at his discretion, or "run-of-schedule."

RUSHES (or RUSH PRINTS)
(F)   Same as dailies.

- S -

SABINE
(E)
A unit of measure for sound absorbency, equal to 100% broadband absorbence over a 1 ft² area. (*See* ABSORPTION COEFFICIENT; INERTANCE.)

SACEM
(P)
Societé des Auteurs, Compositeurs et Editeurs de Musique. The French performing rights organization, formed in 1851 (making it the first anywhere) that licenses and collects royalties and fees both for recordings and performances of copyrighted works.

SAFE
(S)
One of the operating modes of tape recorder electronics. Any tracks placed in safe mode are prevented from entering record mode, even if the engineer accidentally depresses the record-ready buttons or master-record button. Opposite of ready mode.

SAFE ACTION AREA
(V)
The portion of the video screen in which it is safe to assume, while shooting original videotape, most televisions will display anything of importance happening on-screen. About 90% of the entire screen area, measured from the center out, vertically and horizontally. All video and many motion picture cameras have safe action areas etched in their viewfinders.

SAFE TITLE AREA
(V)
The portion of the video screen in which written titles can be located. About 80% of the area of the video screen, measured from the center out, vertically and horizontally.

SAFETY
(E)
Short for safety copy or safety master, a duplicate of any audio or video tape made in case the master itself is damaged or lost. Also called a protection copy.

SAMPAC
(A)
Society of Advertising Music Producers, Arrangers and Composers. The professional organization that represents the makers of musical spots in dealings with the Four As and their members, the AFM and AFTRA, the government, and other organizations that regulate advertising or represent anyone whose services are used in the making of musical spots.

SAMPLE
(D)
1. To take regular measurements of the instantaneous voltage

of an analog signal. **2.** Any single measurement of such a voltage. (*See* QUANTIZATION; CLOCK; LSB; MSB.) **3.** To digitally record one or more sounds intended as a sound source for playback via keystrokes on a synthesizer or other device. One might, for example, sample a frog croaking, and later reproduce the croak at any desired pitch through the various keys of a synthesizer.

SAMPLE AND HOLD CIRCUIT Any electronic circuit that can take a measurement of the instantaneous voltage (or other parameter) of a signal and hold the value for processing and/or display until the next sample is requested. The time at which the sample is taken may be manually designated, as in certain test equipment, or programmed to happen in response to certain signal events (e.g., as in a peak-reading meter), or repeatedly with respect to time (e.g., in the D-A or A-D circuits of a digital recorder. See CLOCK; PULSE CODE MODULATION
(E,D)

SAMPLING RATE (or SAMPLING FREQUENCY) The number of samples a digital recorder takes per second for each signal channel or track. Expressed in hertz, although this term does not exactly apply, since sampling, though a repetitive process, has nothing to do with audio frequencies per se. Various professional digital recorders sample at 48,000 or 50,000 Hz. CD players have a 44.1 kHz sampling rate, while digital audio recorded on NTSC video formats is sampled at 44,056 Hz (due to the corresponding 29.97 frame per sec-
(D)

ond rate of the NTSC standard itself).

SASE Self-Addressed Stamped Envelope. Publishing and record companies, who get so many unsolicited submissions of material, generally require that those submissions be accompanied by an SASE, or they wont' be returned.
(P,R)

SATURATION In magnetic tape, the condition in which full retentivity has been reached—i.e., the oxide is fully magnetized. (*See* COERCIVITY; HYSTERESIS (illustration).)
(E)

SATURATION DISTORTION The distortion that results on magnetic tape when the applied audio signal is greater than its saturation point.
(E)

SATURATION POINT The input signal level to a tape recorder that will cause the record head to produce saturation on the magnetic tape.
(E)

SAVE To send the contents of a file, data base, or program from a computer's working memory to a disk or other permanent storage medium. Opposite of load.
(C)

SAWTOOTH WAVE One of the three basic types of waveforms produced by most synthesizers, then modified or processed to create the finished sound. A true sawtooth wave contains the fundamental and all of its harmonics, and gets its name from the way it looks on an oscilloscope. Also call a ramp wave. (*See* SINE WAVE (illustration); SQUARE WAVE.)
(E,S)

SCALE
(U,B)   The standard payment rate or fee specified in labor agreements for the basic services of musicians, singers, or other talent used in commercials. In phonograph recording sessions, each musician is paid scale for a standard three-hour session, plus overtime at another rate. Jingle session players are paid by the hour, with different overtime rates. Similar rules apply to singers, actors, etc. Soloists, featured actors, etc. have higher scales or, in certain cases, individually negotiated payments depending on their stature in the industry. Check the current appropriate AFM or AFTRA labor agreements for each specific type of ad when budgeting. (*See* SCHEDULE A AND B. REGULAR SESSION, SPECIAL SESSION; SIDE; CONTINGENT SCALE.)

SCAN
(G)   The way melody and lyrics are phrased together. A good scan means words and music fit well together and are easily sung and understood. Bad scan may occur when words such as "a" or "the" are sung on high notes or emphasized notes of the melody, sounding awkward or misphrased.

SCANNING
(V)   The movement of an electron beam in the video camera pickup tube or the television set's picture, forming (in NTSC format) the 525 lines of picture known collectively as the raster.

SCENE
(F,V)   In the script, the entirety of action and dialogue that takes place in one location and in one continuous period of time. Also a numbered section of the script that can be filmed or taped continuously without stopping the camera.

SCENE-TO-SCENE COLOR CORREC-TION
(V)   In a video editing session, the process of separately adjusting the color balance (RGB content) of each shot to maintain consistent brightness and flesh tones within each scene of a videotaped show. Analagous to "timing" in the making of answer prints of motion pictures. (*See* COLOR TEMPERATURE.)

SCHEDULE
(B)   A list of information appended to a contract, detailing some data called for in one of its paragraphs or clauses. Usually capitalized, Schedule A, for example, might list the names, addresses, and phone numbers of the members of the band called "artist" in the contract. Schedule B might list their previous releases, including date of release and record label. Schedule C might list the songs to be recorded under the present contract. (*See* RIDER.)

SCHEDULE A AND B
(U)   The AFTRA reporting form that must be filed by any signatory who employs union singers in a recording session. It lists all singers, the type of performances, and the various amounts due for scale wages, overtime, benefits, etc. Penalties are imposed if the signatory does not file this form within 48 hours and submit full payment within 21 days of the session. Also called a production memorandum.

SCHEDULE D
(U,R)   An AFTRA reporting form that must be filed with the union by any signatory label when releasing a master tape acquired from an independent producer. It warrantees that all singers who performed on the tape have been paid

---

(A) = Advertising • (B) = Business & Law • (C) = Computers • (D) = Digital • (E) = Engineering & Scientific •
(F) = Film • (G) = Music & General • (I) = Interlock & Sync • (J) = Jokes & Jargon • (P) = Music Publishing •
(R) = Record Industry • (S) = Synthesizers • (U) = Unions • (V) = Video

according to AFTRA scale, with all benefits. The record company, in turn, usually requires that the independent producer submit this form or sign it before submitting it to AFTRA. (*See* MASTER PURCHASE AGREEMENT; RECOUPMENT ADVANCE.)

SCHEMA   The data organizing system used to establish and work with a data base. It includes the names of each column and row of the matrix, their principal attributes, and the equational relationships between them.
(C)

SCHMOOZE   To chat with someone informally before entering into a business deal or collaboration, often in preparation for a negotiation.
(J,B)

SCORE (noun)   **1.** The conductor's chart, containing all parts of a musical arrangement. Also, the chart derived from the conductor's, embodying only the part for a single instrument. Example: a piano score. **2.** Collectively, all the music composed and recorded for use in the soundtrack of a motion picture or television production. **3** (verb). To write the music for a motion picture or television production soundtrack.
(G)
(F,V)

SCORING PAPER   Music paper with several (usually five) lines printed above each staff for other information needed by the composer while writing a score or jingle. These lines may contain elapsed time counts or SMPTE locations, summaries of on-screen action, dialogue and/or narration, required sound effects, etc.
(F,V,A)

SCORING STAGE   A large recording studio equipped with synchronous multi-track or other recording equipment, interlocked film and video playback, and large-screen projection in the studio itself. Motion pictures and video productions are scored here, the conductor watching the image and footage or SMPTE data and conducting performers so that the finished recording aligns properly with the footage.
(F,V)

SCORING WILD   The recording of a motion picture or television score using non-synchronous recorders. The conductor derives timings for each part of the score from footage counts of the edited film, and seeks a performance that approximates the required timing to a close tolerance, perhaps 1/2 second. The wild score can be made to fit exactly if its playback speed can be adjusted during transfer, or by editing out short pauses, etc.
(F,V)

SCRATCH DEMO   A quick and inexpensive demo, usually done in a home studio, to give a client a rough idea of what type of music is being composed or produced for him.
(A,R, F,V)

SCRATCH PRINT   Another name for slop print or dirty dupe.
(F)

SCREEN   One complete video frame, consisting of two fields, or a full 525 lines in NTSC broadcast standard.
(V)

SCREENPLAY   See SCRIPT.

SCRIPT   The plot, action, and dialogue of a motion picture or video production, written out in full detail as a series of numbered
(F,V)

(A) = Advertising • (B) = Business & Law • (C) = Computers • (D) = Digital • (E) = Engineering & Scientific •
(F) = Film • (G) = Music & General • (I) = Interlock & Sync • (J) = Jokes & Jargon • (P) = Music Publishing •
(R) = Record Industry • (S) = Synthesizers • (U) = Unions • (V) = Video

SCORING PAPER.

(A) = Advertising • (B) = Business & Law • (C) = Computers • (D) = Digital • (E) = Engineering & Scientific •
(F) = Film • (G) = Music & General • (I) = Interlock & Sync • (J) = Jokes & Jargon • (P) = Music Publishing •
(R) = Record Industry • (S) = Synthesizers • (U) = Unions • (V) = Video

scenes. Also called screenplay. The shooting script is written in shot-by-shot detail, with specific notes on lighting, camera movements, and technical aspects not included in the screenplay.

SCROLL   Referring to the titles or credits in a video or film produc-
(V,F)   tion, to move smoothly upward (or through the frame in any direction), passing smoothly onto and finally off-screen. (*See* CHARACTER GENERATOR.)

SEALED ENCLOSURE   A loudspeaker cabinet with no vents or ports—e.g.,
(E)   an acoustic suspension system or an infinite baffle.

SEARCH, COPYRIGHT or PATENT
(P,B)   The process of checking with the Library of Congress or U.S. Patent Office to make sure that the ownership of a copyright or patent is clear and unencumbered. Music publishers, record companies, or any manufacturing firms that want to buy or license a copyright or patent should hire a lawyer or search company to verify that the rights are available and actually belong to the seller. Otherwise, one may buy the proverbial Brooklyn Bridge.

SEARCH FEE   1. An hourly fee paid by an ad agency or film/TV
(F,V,A)   producer to a music producer for looking through available music libraries and other sources to find the right music to go with visuals.
(P,B)   2. The fee paid to a lawyer or company who conducts a copyright or patent search by a company wishing to acquire license to a copyright or patent.

SEARCH-TO-CUE   A feature in auto-locators that allows the engineer to
(E)   instruct the recorder to find a designated time location on tape and stop there and await further instructions.

S.E.C.   Securities and Exchange Com-mission. The federal agency (es-
(B)   tablished after the stock market crash of 1929) that protects inves-tors against unscrupulous practices of companies issuing stocks or sell-ing any investment vehicles—e.g., limited partnership shares, etc. The S.E.C. also monitors the operation of brokerage houses, financial managers, many banking opera-tions, etc.

SECONDARY   1. A smaller or sub-sidiary market—i.e., not the primary
(A)   market. 2. A smaller radio station in a major geographical area, or a smaller station in any format—e.g., a secondary AOR station.

SECONDARY KEY   A user-specified data attribute for which a com-
(C)   puter can search in the entries of a data base. The user might define secondary keys that ask to find and printout all the people in the particular data base who live in New York, or who are more than six feet tall, etc.

SECONDARY STORAGE   See
(C)   AUXILIARY STORAGE.

SECONDARY TRANSMISSION   The broadcast on cable TV of program-
(B,A)   ming originating at a commercial station, network, etc.

SECURITIES AND EXCHANGE COM-MISSION   See S.E.C.

SEG   See SPECIAL EFFECTS GENERATOR.

SEGUE   Pronounced "seg-way". The playing of two songs (or any recordings) one right after the other, with no pause or band between them.
(G)

SELF-CONTAINED GROUP   A performing ensemble the members of which play and sing all the main parts heard on most of their master tapes and records. Outside string, winds, or other sections may be used on certain Sides, but the group can duplicate most of its recordings in live performance without help.
(R)

SELF-ERASURE   In a tape recorder, the tendency of a record head to partially erase a high-level, high-frequency signal as it is being recorded. Caused as the changing polarity of the right pole piece reverses the magnetism applied to the section of tape just recorded in the head gap.
(E)

SELF-FINANCING   Providing the money oneself for the recording of a master tape or other production. Obviously risky, but generally the best way of doing an independent project, since it involves no sale to, or partial ownership by, outside parties at least until the project is completed.
(B)

SELLING   The process of making prospective buyers aware of the product or service and generating within them the need to acquire the product or service. Marketing and selling are often used interchangeably, although marketing implies a longer term process with
(A)

greater attention to the client's competition. (See MARKETING; MARKET POSITIONING; PROMOTION.)

SEL-SYNC   1. Short for Selective Synchronization. The process of using one or more channels of a record head to play back track(s) already recorded on a magnetic tape. Ampex Corporation has this term trademarked, since it developed the process first. Other manufacturers trade names for the same process: Sel-Rep (Otari), Sync (Studer), Cue (MCI), etc. 2. The process of recording new tracks on a multi-track tape while listening to previously recorded tracks via playback through other channels of the record head.
(E)

SELSYN MOTOR   The trade name for a type of synchronous motor used to drive the projector, dubbers, and recorder in the dubbing, mixing, or rerecording theater. These motors, when connected to the generators and drive motors, will run in rigid interlock with one another, starting, running, slowing down, and running in reverse without loss of sync.
(F)

SEMI-PRO EQUIPMENT   Recording equipment capable of high technical performance, but generally not built as ruggedly as fully professional equipment. Built primarily for use by a single engineer who cares for his gear.
(E)

SEMI-VARIABLE COSTS   See VARIABLE COSTS.
(B)

SENSITIVITY   1. In general, all information about a transducer's response characteristics to incom-
(E)

ing sound waves, or about an electric circuit's response to input signals. **2.** With reference to microphones, a standard performance specification that indicates the output voltage generated when a sound of known SPL and frequency arrives at the diaphragm. Given in millivolts by most manufacturers, and generally specified for broadband response to pink noise. (*See* TRANSFER CHARACTERISTIC; REMANENCE; RETENTIVITY; EFFICIENCY.)

SEPARATION   **1.** The degree of isolation between signals flowing in (E)   two paths. Specified in decibels, indicating the level of a signal induced by one signal path in the other. A separation of 70 dB indicates that a signal at 0 dBVU in one path would be present at −70 dBVU in the adjacent path. (*See* (A)   CROSSTALK.) **2.** Short for color separation.

SEQUENCE   **1.** A specific list or order of keystroke commands, control (S)   voltages, and the times at which they are to be issued, all stored in a sequencer. **2.** To edit the master tapes of an album, putting the songs in the desired order, prior to cutting acetates and lacquer masters, etc.

SERIAL INTERFACE   A single-wire plug and associated cable through (C)   which serial data flows, one bit after another. The RS-232 connector is the current industry standard serial interface. (*See* SERIAL OUTPUT; MULTIPLEXER.)

SERIAL OUTPUT   A data transmission mode in which each bit of an (C)   n-bit word is delivered to a single-pin connector one at a time, in sequence. Opposite of parallel output.

SERIES   A wiring configuration by which several circuits or devices (E)   may be connected. A signal or power source is first routed to the input of one device. Its output then becomes the input for the second device, and so on. Opposite of parallel wiring.

SERVO-CONTROL   A type of speed control employed in DC motors (E,V)   for audio-tape and videotape recorders, turntables, etc. Actual motor speed is compared with and varied to match a reference source, either to maintain a more constant overall speed than is attainable with standard multi-pole AC motors, to adjust the motor's speed to maintain SMPTE or other synchronization with an external source, or to change the musical pitch to match an instrument that cannot easily be tuned, etc. (*See* ERROR SIGNAL; RESOLVER; SELSYN MOTOR.)

SESAC   Society of European Stage Authors and Composers. A per- (P)   forming rights organization like ASCAP and BMI, formed in 1931 and operating in the United States and Europe. Unlike ASCAP and BMI, SESAC also handles mechanical rights and royalties for its members. It is the only privately owned rights organization, and features gospel and serious music in its catalog.

SET-UP   The part of a recording session in which the engineer places (E,F)   various instrumentalists or vocalists, sets up the microphones, and gets

---

basic sounds through the recording console.

SFX
(A,F,V) Slang "abbreviation" for sound effects.

SHELF EQUALIZATION
(E) Any type of equalization in which the boost or cut levels off to a constant shelf of the specified number of decibels. A shelf equalization of +5 dB at 5 kHz implies that from 5 kHz to 20 kHz all frequencies will be boosted by 5 dB. The curve by which frequencies below 5 kHz increase from unity gain to +5 dB varies according to the design of the circuit. (*See* TURNOVER FREQUENCY (illustration).)

SHIELD
(E) Any material or device used to inhibit the destructive effects an ambient magnetic or electric field may have on a signal path or an entire electronic system. (a) In tape recorders, the heads may be shielded by plates of mu-metal, an alloy impervious to magnetic fields. (b) In electric signal paths, the signal conductors may be wrapped in a thin metallic sheath, either of foil or fine wires, etc.

SHIELDED CABLE
(E) Any audio cable in which the conductors are protected from ambient fields by a surrounding braided or foil metal shielding.

SHOCK MOUNT
(E) A microphone suspension system that prevents mechanical vibrations of the stand from reaching the mic. Usually made of elastic bands mounted on a metal frame, which together hold the mic in position without rigid mechanical contact with the stand.

SHOOT
(F,V) 1 (verb). To take motion picture or videotape footage, either in the studio or on location. 2 (noun). A motion picture or videotape production—i.e., the actual day(s) in which the original footage is shot. Example: "I have a three-week shoot coming up in July."

SHOOTING SCRIPT
(F,V) The version of a screenplay used on the set or location during filming or taping. It contains all dialogue, blocking, camera directions, and notes of important off-camera effects. All of the information needed by the director to put each scene together properly.

SHOP (verb)
(R,B) To sell or attempt to sell songs, tapes, ideas, etc. A rock group shops its tapes to record companies, for example.

SHOTGUN MICROPHONE
(E) A highly directional mic with a long tubular body, used mainly for sync recording of film dialogue and distant miking, especially for television. Its directionality is produced by an internal acoustic labyrinth. (*See* MICROPHONE, SHOTGUN; POLAR PATTERN.)

SHRINK WRAP
(R) A clear cellophane wrapping that is heat-shrunk around album covers, cassettes, and other products to protect them from damage before purchase.

SHUTTLE
(E) To move recorded tape forward or backward past the playback or sync reproduce head, either by hand winding or motor drive, in order to locate a certain spot on the tape. Shuttling may be done slower or faster than playback speed, but in any case is not ac-

complished by use of the normal capstan drive.

SIBILANCE   High frequencies pro-
(E,G)   duced by the human voice, and most noticeable on words with pronounced "s" sounds. Many voices contain enough sibilance to cause overload distortion when recorded at full levels. Equalization or "de-essing" must be used to prevent this in recording.

SIDE   1. Any master tape of one song,
(R)   whether recorded for inclusion in an album, or as the A or B Side of a single. Always capitalized, Side is used in recording contracts, so precise definition is important. **2.** In the AFTRA Code of Fair Practice, a Side is a master tape of no more than 3 1/2 minutes. If the total length of the tune is longer than this, AFTRA singers must be paid another 50% of their normal scale for every additional minute.

SIDE CHAIN   In an electronic circuit,
(E)   a secondary signal path in which the condition or parameter of an audio signal that will cause a processor to begin working is sensed or detected. For example, in a Dolby B circuit, frequencies over 1 kHz are separated from lows by a low-pass filter. When the level of this side chain signal falls below -10 dBVU, the highs are then companded and finally re-mixed with the unprocessed lows.

SIDEMAN   A union musician, or
(U)   (loosely) any musician other than the contractor or leader.

SIGNAL   The electric current that
(E)   carries audio information.

SIGNAL FLOW CHART   The block
(E)   diagram that shows all the possible signal paths in a recording console or other audio system. The flow chart is *not* a circuit diagram, which would show every electric and electronic component in the console or device.

SIGNAL GENERATOR   A test instru-
(E)   ment that produces one or more of the following types of waveforms through a wide range of frequencies: sine wave, square wave, sawtooth, ramp voltage, etc. (*See* SINE WAVE (illustration).)

SIGNAL PROCESSING DEVICE   Any
(E)   audio system used to alter the characteristics of a signal passing

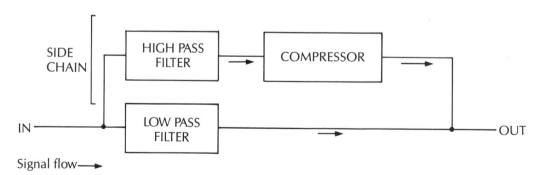

SIDE CHAIN (Dolby "B"). In dolby b, the side chain feeds any signals above 3 kHz to the compressor.

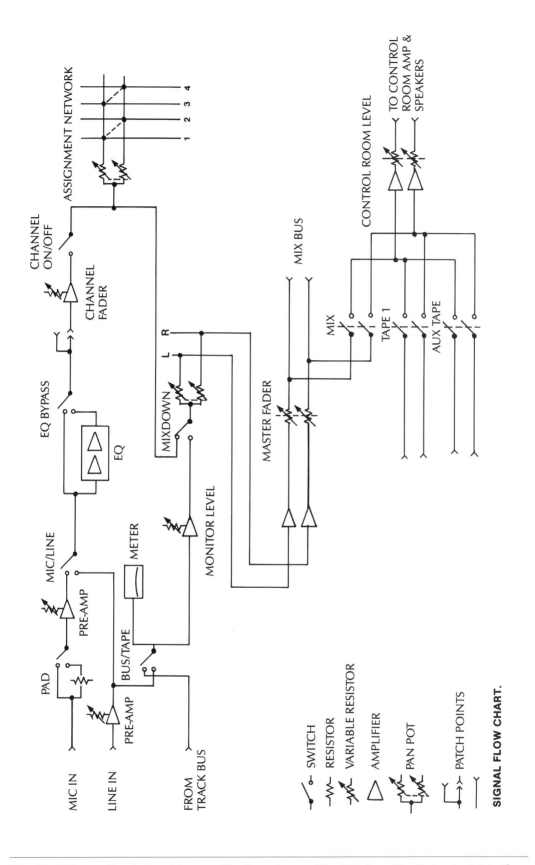

SIGNAL FLOW CHART.

through it. Examples: equalizer, compressor, noise gate, etc.

SIGNAL-TO-NOISE RATIO   For any audio system, the ratio of maxi-
(E)   mum undistorted signal voltage level to noise voltage level, usually expressed as the decibel difference between these two levels. This quantity can be measured for any single piece of audio equipment, or for a number of processes performed sequentially on a signal, such as recording and reproducing it. (*See* DYNAMIC RANGE; HEADROOM; DISTORTION, THIRD HARMONIC.)

SIGNATORY   Generally, anyone who has signed a contract. In the music
(U)   industry, any person or company who employs union musicians or singers, and who has signed the applicable AFM Labor Agreement, the AFTRA Code of Fair Practice, or other union employment contract. The signatory agrees to pay union members wages according to union scale, with all appropriate overtime and benefits fees, and to abide by the working conditions stipulated in each contract. Finally, he agrees to use only union performers. (*See* SCHEDULE D; UNION STEWARD.)

SIGNATURE, MUSICAL   An short audio logo or tag heard (a) on the
(A)   end of all spots made for a certain company, (b) at the end of every program produced by a certain company, or (c) at the end of each broadcasting day—e.g., when a TV station "signs off" for the night. (*See* LOGO; DEALER TAG; ID.)

SINE WAVE   The waveform of pure
(E,S)   tone or single frequency. One of the three basic waveforms produced by synthesizers, the others being square and sawtooth waves. (*See* PHASE DIFFERENCE.)

SINGLE MARKET   1. A specific ur-
(A)   ban area or other geographic area in which potential buyers of a product or service are concentrated.
(U)   2. The AFTRA payment category that corresponds to local broadcast of a spot. Used in calculation of singers' residuals.

SINGLE-SYSTEM   A system by which
(F)   sound is recorded optically or magnetically onto motion picture film inside the motion picture camera while the film is being shot. Sound and picture are thus on a single strip of film from the start, with image and sound in projection sync with respect to each other. This system is primarily used for news or sports coverage, where the limited sound fidelity of single-system cameras can be tolerated. Double-system shooting, with the camera recording only images and a separate sync recorder taping the sound, is used for almost all motion picture production.

SKEW   A deflection or dislocation of
(E)   the proper path for magnetic tape as it passes over a misaligned tape head, guide, or roller. (*See* ALIGNMENT, TAPE HEAD (illustration).)

SLAP-BACK   An unwanted and dis-
(E)   tracting echo caused by a reflective surface in any environment—e.g., a large window in a recording studio. 2. A tape delay, or the effect it creates.

SLATE   1. A board held in front of the
(F,V)   camera usually before each shot,

SLATE.

with information such as the scene and take number, title of the film or television production, etc. written on it. A clapstick is often hinged to the top of the slate, so that the shot can be identified and synched efficiently. Same as clapper board. **2.** The photographed image of the information written on the slate. A headslate is photographed before the action on the shot. A tailslate is photographed after the action, but before the camera is turned off. Tail slates are often held upside down for easy identification on the editing bench. **3.** The recorded announcement of the title and take number at the beginning of a recording. **4.** The button on a recording console that allows the engineer to put this information on tape via the talkback mic, without its being heard through the studio monitors. Sometimes called the cue button.

(E)

SLAVE (or SLAVE TRANSPORT)   An audiotape or videotape transport, motion picture projector, or mag-

(I,V)

netic film recorder or dubber whose movements of tape or film are electronically made to follow the movements of a single, master transport. Accomplished by electronic synchronization of SMPTE codes present on the slaves with that of the master, or by electro-mechanical linkage of sprocketed machines' motors to provide identical movement of all sprocket drives. (*See* MASTER.)

SLICK   The printed paper cover with front (and sometimes back) artwork for an album. Slicks are often sent to distributors or stores for use in wall or window displays.

(R)

SLIDE CHAIN   Same as a film chain, but for transfering 35mm slides or other transparencies onto videotape.

(F,V)

SLIDING SCALE   **1.** In wholesale record sales, a variation in the unit price that depends on the number of units ordered by the retailer. The unit price is reduced as the number ordered increases. **2.** In royalty calculation, a variation in royalty rate that depends on the number of units sold. The artist's or producer's basic royalty rate generally increases as sales increase.

(R)

SLIP CUE   In playing records, the process of locating the first note of music in any band, holding the record motionless while the turntable rotates beneath it, then releasing the record so that music begins precisely when the DJ releases it. This is done either to effect precise segues, or to align the rhythm of one record with another one already playing—called mixing.

(R)

(A) = Advertising • (B) = Business & Law • (C) = Computers • (D) = Digital • (E) = Engineering & Scientific •
(F) = Film • (G) = Music & General • (I) = Interlock & Sync • (J) = Jokes & Jargon • (P) = Music Publishing •
(R) = Record Industry • (S) = Synthesizers • (U) = Unions • (V) = Video

SLOP PRINT
(F)   Generally, a black and white print made from the edited workprint. The workprint, with many tape splices, can tear under the stress of repeated rollback during the mix. The slop print, with no splices at all, will save costly mixing time. Also called a dirty dupe or scratch print.

SLUG
(F)   A short length of blank leader or filler spliced into an edited workprint to (a) replace a section of damaged workprint, or (b) fill in for a scene that has not yet been shot but whose precise length is predetermined, perhaps by an existing soundtrack, as in an animated cartoon, etc.

SMALL RIGHTS
(P)   Collectively, those performing rights in a composition for which payment rates are set by the federal government, by industry agreement or convention, etc. Specifically, mechanical rights, radio and TV broadcast, etc. All other rights in the composition are called grand rights.

SMPTE
(F,V)   Society of Motion Picture and Television Engineers. Like the AES, it sets standards for hardware and software design and operation in motion picture and television industries.

SMPTE CODE
(V,I)   A high-frequency signal that permits the accurate interlocking of motion picture, videotape, and audio equipment. Usually generated at the picture source—i.e., the SMPTE generator that drives the film or television camera system—the signal is recorded onto the videotape or along the edge of motion picture film, and sent simultaneously to the audio recorder.

The signal contains encoded numerical information allowing the same point in film or tape time to be located on the separate strips of film/videotape and audio tape, for proper alignment or lip sync. The playback operator can select an SMPTE code number that instructs videotape and audiotape machines to locate a certain point and begin playing in sync from there. The coded information contains eight digits: two each for hours, minutes, seconds, and frames.

SOCIETE DES AUTEURS, COMPOSITEURS ET EDITEURS DE MUSIQUE   See SACEM.

SOCIETY OF ADVERTISING MUSIC PRODUCERS, ARRANGERS AND COMPOSERS.   See SAMPAC.

SOCIETY OF EUROPEAN STAGE AUTHORS AND COMPOSERS   See SESAC.

SOCIETY OF MOTION PICTURE AND TELEVISION ENGINEERS   See SMPTE.

SOCIETY OF PROFESSIONAL AUDIO RECORDING STUDIOS   See SPARS.

SOFT CUT
(F,V)   A very short dissolve used, instead of a straight cut, to edit two shots together smoothly, but without implying the passage of time.

SOFT TALK
(A)   A group vocal track sung in breathy, transparent tone. Used to "fatten" the apparent orchestral size of a track or make it more

lush. Often sung in "aah" or "ooh" syllables.

SOFTWARE
(C)
The instructions that tell the computer what to do, provided either by a manufacturer or the user. Programs and data.

SOLID-STATE
(E)
Characterizing types of electronic circuits that use transistors, integrated circuits (ICs), and chips as their active components. Characterized by small size, low power consumption, and high reliability.

SOLO
(G)
(E)
1. (noun). Musically, a section of a recording in which the lead musician or singer improvises freely over a predetermined set of chords. 2. (or SOLO BUTTON). In a recording console, a switch that disconnects the output of the normal monitor system from the monitor amp input. Instead, it routes the signal passing through the circuit or module containing that solo button directly to the monitor amp. The result is that only the signal from that source or module will be heard. All others are muted. 3. (verb). To press a solo button on a recording console in order to hear only the signal passing through one module or channel.

SOLO-IN-PLACE
(E)
In a recording console, the function that allows muting all input signals except one, and permits that one to pass through to the monitor or mix buses exactly as heard in the composite mix, preserving its level, equalization and other processing, and stereo position.

SONE
(E)
A standardized unit of perceived loudness. A graph of sones vs. SPL shows for any constant SPL the relative loudness the ear perceives at each frequency—i.e., the inverse of the equal loudness curves.

SONEX
(E)
A brand of open-cell foam that is popular as a sound-absorbent material used in studios, rehearsal rooms, etc. Available in a variety of thicknesses, colors, and surface textures.

SONG CASTING
(P)
The process of deciding what artists might be interested in recording compositions in a publisher's catalog. Normally a part of the professional manager's duties, although casting suggestions can come from anyone.

SONG DOCTOR
(P,R)
A composer or arranger called in by a publisher or record company to polish a composition the company represents or wishes to record, making it more applicable to the current marketplace or a specific artist, or repackaging it via a new arrangement or lyrics to appeal to a new medium, such as musical drama. The song doctor is paid a fee for his work, or may receive a cut-in if the publisher succeeds in generating income from the reworked composition.

SONG PLUGGER
(P)
See PROFESSIONAL MANAGER.

SONG SEQUENCE
(R)
The order in which various songs are edited for the final album.

SONG SHARK
(P)
A record or publishing company that offers worthless

---

deals to writers in order to gain rights to good songs.

SOPHISTICATED INVESTOR   Any

(B)   person or company who has previously invested money in a venture similar to one currently being proposed. The law expects such an investor to be familiar with the risks, jargon, and potential scams associated with his area of sophistication. An investor sophisticated in oil wells may be totally unsophisticated in entertainment ventures, etc. Federal law provides more protection for unsophisticated investors.

SOUND ABSORPTION COEFFI-

(E,G)   **CIENT**   See ABSORPTION COEFFICIENT.

SOUND BLANKET   A thick, sound-

(F,V)   absorbent blanket, often a mover's packing quilt, that can be spread on the floor of a set or hung anywhere just outside camera range. Its purpose is to stop unwanted sound reflections, echoes, or reverberation on the set, or to keep unwanted outside sounds from reaching the microphone(s) during shooting of film or videotape.

SOUND CUTTING   See TRACK LAY-ING.

SOUND DROID   A sophisticated, com-

(F,V,E)   puter-based audio editing system manufactured by the Droid Works, a division of Lucasfilm, Inc. Similar in function to the Edit Droid, the unit has a large internal memory capable of storing (digitally) all the sounds required for a scene. Any sounds that do not have SMPTE code already (corresponding with visual footage) are as-

signed codes. The operator selects and assembles sounds by their quality and function only, "marking" the beginning and end of each segment desired, designating any fades or other effects, and assigning it to a particular "track" for later mixing. He thus spends all his time making creative decisions, since the machine handles the SMPTE data internally. The Droid then allows each assembled track to be recorded onto mag film or other hard copy.

SOUND READER   A magnetic

(F)   playback head mounted either directly on a sync block, or on a freestanding metal base with alignment rollers. Used by film editors to check sync of all effects and music, they slowly hand-crank the workprint and various rolls of magnetic film through a sync block on the editing bench. Signal from the sound reader is amplified by a squawk box.

SOUND STAGE   A soundproof room

(F,V)   or building in which film or television shooting can take place without interference from outside noise.

SOUND PRESSURE LEVEL   (SPL)

(E)   The decibel rating of acoustic pressure of a sound wave. The threshold of hearing is defined as 0 dB SPL. The threshold of pain for most people is near 140 dB SPL. SPL meters are often equipped with filters to give weighted, as well as flat readings. (*See* ACOUSTIC INTENSITY.)

SOUND PRESSURE LEVEL (SPL)

(E)   **METER**   A device used to measure sound pressure levels in any environment, calibrated in decibels, and usually offering a selec-

---

(A) = Advertising • (B) = Business & Law • (C) = Computers • (D) = Digital • (E) = Engineering & Scientific •
(F) = Film • (G) = Music & General • (I) = Interlock & Sync • (J) = Jokes & Jargon • (P) = Music Publishing •
(R) = Record Industry • (S) = Synthesizers • (U) = Unions • (V) = Video

tion of "weighted" scales that allow reading of levels in specific frequency ranges, such as the high frequencies, which can damage the ear at high levels. 0 dB SPL is defined as the threshold of hearing. 140 dB SPL is the threshold of pain.

SOUND WAVE   The cyclic variations in air pressure that radiate spherically away from a sound source. (*See* SINE WAVE.)
(E)

SOURCE   Another name for the input mode of tape recorder electronics.
(E)

SPACED PAIR   Two microphones separated by a distance, used to pick up stereophonic sound. Closer than two feet, the pair will pick up noticeable off-axis cancellation of midrange or high frequencies. Farther than five feet, their signals begin to exhibit a "hole in the middle." (See COINCIDENT MICROPHONES; M-S MIKING; BINAURAL RECORDING.)
(E)

SPARS   Society of Professional Audio Recording Studios. An organization whose members include prominent studios, individual engineers and producers, many manufacturers of professional equipment, recording schools and colleges, etc. The goal of SPARS is to promote worldwide communication among all those who make and use professional equipment, to foster high-quality educational programs for future engineers and producers, and to promote the economic well-being of the recording industry as a whole.
(E)

SPEC   Short for speculation. Any work done without the guarantee of
(B)

being paid. Creative artists from songwriters to motion picture directors often take projects on spec, with a written contract guaranteeing them (a) a deferred payment of some salary and/or expenses, and/or (b) points, or a percentage of the profit that is ultimately made from the products to which they contribute.

SPECIAL EFFECTS GENERATOR   (SEG) The video control unit that performs fades, dissolves, wipes, and other optical effects on live or taped video signals. Often called a switcher, since most shots in a film or videotape have straight cuts between them. (Illustration next page.)
(V)

SPECIAL PACKAGING (or PROMOTION)   Expenses incurred by a record company over and above the amount budgeted in these categories for the average single or album release. These extra amounts become charge-backs against the artist's royalties. (*See* INDEPENDENT PROMOTION.)
(R)

SPECIAL SESSION   Under AFM rules, a recording session of 1 1/2 hours, in which no more than 7 1/2 minutes of finished music can be recorded. A producer may call a special session rather than the regular 3-hour session if the charts at hand are short or simple. Rates for special sessions are about 2/3 those of regular sessions, but a special session with 1 1/2 hours overtime is more expensive than the regular session it might replace.
(U,R)

SPECTRUM, FREQUENCY   The distribution of frequencies present in a specific sound, or reproducible by a certain medium or device.
(E)

(A) = Advertising • (B) = Business & Law • (C) = Computers • (D) = Digital • (E) = Engineering & Scientific •
(F) = Film • (G) = Music & General • (I) = Interlock & Sync • (J) = Jokes & Jargon • (P) = Music Publishing •
(R) = Record Industry • (S) = Synthesizers • (U) = Unions • (V) = Video

WIPE PATTERN SELECTION

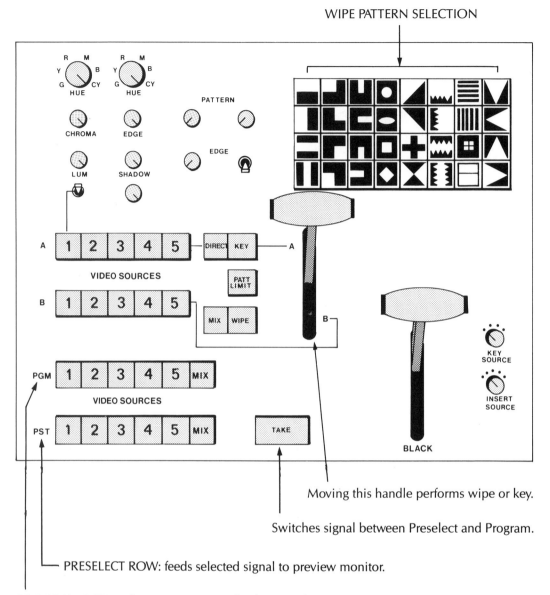

Moving this handle performs wipe or key.

Switches signal between Preselect and Program.

PRESELECT ROW: feeds selected signal to preview monitor.

PROGRAM ROW: selects main output of video switcher to feed recorder.

SPECIAL EFFECTS GENERATOR.

SPEED! (F,V)   An exclamation shouted by the on-location soundman, indicating that the sound recorder or sync playback machine has achieved stable operating speed of 24 fps. The director can then give the cue for action.

SPENDTH (B,J)   Opposite of thrift. The tendency of music producers to go over budget on professional recording projects. Caused by one or more of the following: insufficient attention to budgeting, scheduling and planning; slow in-studio controls; self- or client-generated need for changes or redos; or surcharges necessitated on rush jobs.

SPINNER (R)   Slang term for disc jockey. Someone who "spins records."

SPIRAL (R)   The widely separated grooves that follow the last selection on a record, leading the stylus quickly toward the center groove. Also called the tail-out on mastering lathe controls. The less widely separated grooves preceding the first selection on a record are called the lead-in.

SPL (E)   Sound Pressure Level. (*See* SOUND PRESSURE LEVEL METER; DECIBEL.)

SPLICE (E,F)   The joint made between two pieces of magnetic tape or motion picture film in the process of editing. Or the point in audio or screen time at which this joint occurs.

SPLICING BLOCK (E)   A device used to position and hold down the two pieces of magnetic tape to be joined by a splice.

SPLICING TAPE (E)   An adhesive-backed tape, usually slightly narrower than the magnetic tape with which it is meant to be used, for making splices.

SPLIT (COPYRIGHT or PUBLISHING) (P)   The business situation in which the writer or publisher of a song shares his royalties and credits with one or more other people or companies. The division need not be equal, and in the case of publishing, administration must reside with one of the co-publishers. (*See* SUBPUBLISHING; CUT-IN.)

SPLIT FEED (E)   The process of routing the same signal to two or more separate outputs, modules, or devices, or the actual device that allows the signal to be routed to more than one destination.

SPLIT KEYBOARD (S)   A technique for assigning different sounds, effects, or patches to single keys or one or more sections of the entire synthesizer keyboard. The lower octaves may generate a viola sound, while the upper octaves generate synthetic vibes.

SPLIT REEL (F)   A film reel that can be separated into two separate flanges, so that the film itself, wound on a plastic core, can be stored without reels. Used constantly in editing pictures and magnetic film.

SPOT (noun) (A)   A radio or television ad, usually specified by its duration (10 sec, 20 sec, or 60 sec) and perhaps its area of exposure (i.e., local or "single-market," regional, or national). One might produce a 30-second regional TV spot.

SPOT (verb) (F,V)   In scoring, to identify the scenes for which music cues will be written, write down their length, footage numbers, or SMPTE data, and decide what type of music for each cue will best suit the director's intentions. The composer may spot a film, then respot it later if more music is required.

SPOT-ERASE (E)   To erase a very small segment of a recorded tape, on one track or all. Most accurately done by slowing down the tape via vari-speed, enabling the engineer to go in and out of record mode at exact points marked on the tape itself.

SPREADSHEET   A type of data-based applications software that es-
(C,B) tablishes a matrix in the computer's RAM or CPU. Used mostly for business applications such as budgeting, cost monitoring and control, scheduling, and inventory. The user can assign names and values (costs, number of items required or available, time or scheduling factors, etc.) to the items in each position of the columns and rows of the matrix. He can also define equational relationships between the items in various columns and rows. By plugging in different test values for each entry, the user can predict how various factors will affect the outcome of the overall program. He can thus computer-optimize cost, time, and other factors in order to achieve specific business goals. (*See* APPLICATIONS SOFTWARE.)

SPRING REVERBERATION SYSTEM
(E) A signal-processing device that uses springs to simulate natural room or hall reverberation. Spring reverbs work basically like plate systems, but are much smaller and generally considered inferior.

SPROCKET   A toothed wheel used in
(F) motion picture cameras, projectors, mag film dubbers, etc. to pull the perforated stock through the mechanism. Each tooth engages one sprocket hole or perforation.

SPROCKET HOLE   See PERFORA-
(F) TION; PITCH.

SQUARE WAVE   A waveform containing a fundamental sine wave
(S,E) frequency and all of its odd-numbered harmonics. Called square because of its flat, horizontal posi-

tive and negative plateaus, connected by vertical voltage jumps, when viewed on an oscilloscope or graphed on paper. One of the three basic waveforms produced by most synthesizers. (*See* SINE WAVE (illustration); SAWTOOTH WAVE.)

SQUAWK BOX   A small tabletop amplifier and speaker used for
(F) playback of magnetic film passing through a sound reader. The poor sound quality gives rise to the name.

STAGE   In an electronic device when a signal is repeatedly amplified, any
(E) portion of the circuit in which one "boost" is achieved. In a console, for instance, there is generally a stage of pre-amplification after each fader or pot.

STAMPER   The negative metal impression made from the "mother" in
(R) matrixing. The stamper is placed in the record press and actually squeezes the lump of heat-softened vinyl into a release pressing for sale in stores, etc. (*See* METAL PARTS; DIRECT METAL MASTERING.)

STANDARD OPERATING LEVEL   A reference level by which various
(E) pieces of equipment can be adjusted to produce identical output levels or meter readings. In professional recording, it is defined as 0 VU = +4 dBm. In broadcasting, 0 VU = +8 dBm. (*See* CALIBRATION; SENSITIVITY; RETENTIVITY; DECIBEL.)

STAND-BY   Another name for the auto-
(E) input operation mode of multi-

---

track tape recorders. (*See* AUTO-INPUT.)

STANDING WAVE   A waveform that appears to be stationary, created by the interference of a sound source and its reflection off a surface. When peaks and nodes in both directions line up for specific frequencies, these high and low points in the waveform seem to remain stationary, when in fact the waves are going through that point in both directions, reinforcing each other.
(E)

STATIC SIGNAL PROCESSING   Signal processing in which the nature of the input signal has no effect on the type or amount of processing applied to it. (*See* DYNAMIC SIGNAL PROCESSING.)
(E)

STATION WEIGHT   One of the factors used by ASCAP in calculating
(P,A)

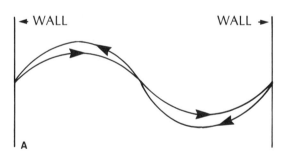

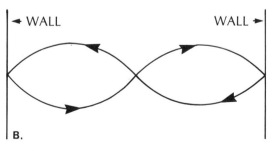

STANDING WAVE. (A) A standing wave resulting in reinforcement of the frequency; (B) Standing wave resulting in cancellation of the frequency.

the number of performance credits ascribed to a radio broadcast of a composition. It reflects the number of listeners the station reaches, which is a function of its location, wattage, and broadcast frequency.

STATUS BYTE   1. In MIDI Code, the group of 8 bits in each message or "note on" transmission, identifying the type of data and instructions that will follow. 2. Lunch at a chic restaurant.
(S)
(J)

STEADICAM   A device worn by the cameraman, on which he mounts the film or video camera, and which gyroscopically stabilizes its motion as he walks or runs while shooting. Although Steadicam is a trademark of the manufacturer of this device, the term is used generically for any camera mount that reduces jitter in hand-held shots.
(F,V)

STEENBECK   A German-made brand of flatbed or horizontal editing machines. Because Steenbeck was the first manufacturer of horizontal editing machines, the name is often used generically to denote any such device. (*See* MOVIOLA.)
(F,V)

STEPPING OUT   In AFTRA rules, if a group singer is asked to sing a solo or duo line of more than sixteen bars, he has "stepped out." The producer must pay this singer (or duo) the soloist's rate, rather than the group rate at which he may have been originally booked.
(U)

STEP PRINTING   Any copying of an exposed strip of movie film done in a printer with an intermittent movement, holding the exposed film and raw stock still during exposure of each frame.
(F)

STERADIAN   A solid angle on a sphere, conical in appearance, that sub-
(E)   tends on the sphere's surface an area equal to the square of the radius. Used as a mathematical unit in calculations of propagated wave intensities. (*See* RADIAN.)

STEREO MIKING TECHNIQUES   See
(E)   BINAURAL MIKING; BLUM-LEIN PAIR; CALREC SOUND FIELD MICROPHONE; COIN-CIDENT MICROPHONES; M-S MIKING; ORTF MIKING; SPACED PAIR; X-Y MIKING.

STEREOPHONIC   A type of audio
(E)   system that uses two or more speakers or channels to reproduce spatial information, giving the listener the illusion of lateral placement of sounds between two speakers and their relative distance from the listener.

STEWARD   See UNION STEWARD

STINGER   In a misical score, a short,
(F,V)   accented chord played to underscore a specific dramatic event on-screen. (*See* HITS.)

STOCK   See FILM STOCK.

STOCK ARRANGEMENT   A com-
(G)   mercially published chart or arrangement of a song, not a custom-written chart.

STORAGE MEDIUM   Any type of
(E,D,   material on which analog record-
C,V)   ings or digital data is permanently saved—i.e., recording tape, floppy disk, hard disk, optical disk or CD, punched paper tape, etc. Technically, even a common LP is a storage medium for analog information.

STORYBOARD   A sequence of illustra-
(F,V)   tions (like frames of a comic strip) made by a graphic artist from the (shooting) script of a motion picture or video production. Each "frame" of the storyboard shows what the director wants to see in a particular shot, usually with the accompanying dialogue, narration, or music and sound effects noted in a box beneath the frame. Some directors, particularly of TV spots, use the storyboard as the actual shooting script during production.

STRAIGHT CUT   A normal cut from
(F,V)   the last frame of one shot to the first frame of the next, with no optical effects between shots. Also called a hard cut. (*See* SOFT CUT; FADE; DISSOLVE.)

STRATA MULTIPLIER   One of the
(P,A)   factors used by ASCAP in calculating the number of performance credits ascribed to a specific radio or TV broadcast of a composition. Represents the ratio of blanket licensing fees received from all broadcasters in that medium to AS-CAP's total income from all licensees.

STRETCHED   A descriptive term for
(E)   an encoded signal, as in a noise-reduction system. Sometimes used to describe the signal after subsequent decoding.

STRIKE   To take down or disassemble
(F,V)   a set used in a motion picture or video shoot. Once the director has called a wrap, the production manager may call for a strike.

STRIPPING   1. The insertion of
(A,R)   photographic or other pictorial material into the line-art composite

---

negative for artwork. This is done by the graphic designer or printer, prior to making either printing or color separations. **2.** Recording the sync sound from the edited video master onto an external sync recorder, usually to build music and effects tracks, add narration, loop or post-dub some or all of the dialogue, etc. When all the resulting tracks have been re-mixed, the mix is then re-layed or post-stripped onto the video master, hopefully still in sync.

(V)

STUDIO MUSICIAN   A professional musician who specializes in performing for recording sessions. Since the techniques of playing for tape are different than those for good live performance, experienced studio musicians can help producers save time (and ultimately money) in the studio.

(U)

SUBCODE   In compact discs, various bits of data appended to the audio data to encode information such as band and index numbers, beginning and end points of each band, video information, etc. The subcode data is assigned to separate "tracks" designated by the letters P, Q, R to W, etc.

(D)

SUBFRAME   In SMPTE synchronization, a unit of time smaller than a frame, generally 1/100 of a frame in length. Synchronizers are designed to maintain synchronization to within a small number of subframes. (*See* FRAME SYNC; PHASE SYNC.)

(I,V)

SUBJECTIVE CAMERA ANGLE (or SHOT)   A shot made from the point of view of one of the charac-

(F,V)

ters in a scene, showing the action or setting exactly as he sees it, perhaps even "walking" through the action. A POV Shot.

SUB-MASTER   **1.** Any tape used in the making of a master tape, but representing an earlier generation number of some or all of the material included in the final master. **2.** In recording consoles, the fader that controls the gain of a summing amp whose input is the combined signals from a group of other faders. Generally, each of these individual faders still controls the proportion of its own signal in the combined signal or submix. Also called a group master. (*See* SUBMIX.)

(E)

SUBMIX   A group of tracks in a multi-track mix that are all assigned to a single mono or stereo sub-master fader, so that their level can be varied together. A drum submix will enable the engineer to fade the entire drum kit in or out, or to cut it off instantly in order to create a break that was not originally a part of the arrangement.

(E)

SUBPUBLISHING   A portion of the publishing rights, responsibility and/or rewards, delegated by the original publisher or composer to another person or company. The subpublisher may be responsible for publishing in a foreign territory, or may only represent synchronization rights to the composition. Or, because of a special expertise in merchandising, the subpublisher may take over all the sales functions, leaving only the administration to the original publisher. (*See* SPLIT COPYRIGHT.)

(P)

(A) = Advertising • (B) = Business & Law • (C) = Computers • (D) = Digital • (E) = Engineering & Scientific •
(F) = Film • (G) = Music & General • (I) = Interlock & Sync • (J) = Jokes & Jargon • (P) = Music Publishing •
(R) = Record Industry • (S) = Synthesizers • (U) = Unions • (V) = Video

SUBSCRIPTION PAPERS In a limited
(B) partnership, the document by
which shares of ownership are actually transferred from the general
partners to limited partners. In effect, they are the bill of sale and
receipt that says who has bought
what from whom, and at what
price. (*See* OFFERING.)

SUBSIDIARY MARKET Less important than, with smaller sales poten-
(B,G) tial than, or considered as a part
of, a major or primary market. For
example, in the record industry,
cities of under 500,000 are considered subsidiary or secondary
markets. Larger cities are called
primaries.

SUBSIDIARY RIGHTS Some rights
derived from or separated from
(P,R) the primary rights in or to a song,
recorded performance, or other
copyrighted work. For example,
the company that owns the rights
to a Broadway show may license
subsidiary rights to a motion picture studio to film the show,
separate subsidiaries to a doll company to make dolls named after
the show's characters, etc. In each
case, the licensee may only use the
name and contents of the show to
make products in its own industry.
Also called derivative rights.

SUBSTRATE In production of lacquer
masters or reference acetates, the
(R) flat, circular aluminum disc on
which the lacquer is coated. The
substrate must be machined until
absolutely flat. Otherwise, the cutting stylus will carve grooves of
irregular depth.

SUBTITLE The process of adding
(F,V) written words across the bottom
portion of a motion picture or
television image, most often to
translate soundtrack dialogue that
is in a foreign language. Or the
actual words added.

SUBTRACTIVE SYNTHESIS The
process of creating sounds by tak-
(S) ing some of the overtones or partials out of a very complex original
signal, such as a square or sawtooth wave. Most analog synthesizers generate sounds subtractively.

SUMMING AMP A circuit or device
that combines or mixes signals
(E) from several sources, then amplifies
the resulting blend for routing to
another device. For example, Aux-
send #1 controls on all channels of
a console feed a summing amp,
whose output can be routed to a
reverb system, cue or headphone
amp, the monitor amp, etc. (*See*
COMBINING AMPLIFIER.)

SUPER Short for superimposition. An
effect in which two or more im-
(F,V) ages are combined and seen simultaneously. These can be separate
scenes, or titles superimposed over
action, etc.

SUPERTHEME One of the four use
weights that determine the pay-
(P) ment rate for use of a copyrighted
song or recorded musical performance in a broadcast performance.
Supertheme is the second highest
payment category, indicating that
the song or tape will be used
repeatedly as the theme of a series,
mini-series, etc. (*See* PERFOR-
MANCE CREDIT; CATEGORY.)

SUPPLY MOTOR In a tape transport,
(E) the motor that establishes proper

---

tape tension on the supply side of the capstan, and drives the fast rewind mode. Also called the rewind motor. (*See* TENSION, HOLD-BACK/TAKE-UP.)

SUPPLY REEL   On a tape recorder, the reel from which tape winds before passing over the heads.
(E)

SURROUND TRACK(S)   In 35mm and 70mm projection from release prints with magnetic sound, one or two of these tracks is amplified through speakers mounted at the sides, rear, or on the ceiling of the auditorium. Sound effects such as thunder, by appearing on this track, will seem to envelop the audience. (*See* FORMAT (illustration).)
(F)

SURVEY   The process by which AS-CAP and BMI estimate the total number of performances of an individual song or composer's work (in order to pay broadcast and performance royalties) by recording and actually counting the number of broadcasts of songs on a set of test radio and TV stations. ASCAP says it records 60,000 hours of programming per year, computing royalty payments based on the songs logged from these tapes. (*See* CATEGORY; PERFORMANCE.)
(P,B)

SUSTAIN   The third portion of a sound's envelope, after its attack and decay, but before its release. The continuous portion of the sound of any instrument—e.g., a prolonged note played on a clarinet. (*See* ENVELOPE (illustration).)
(E,S)

SWARF   See CHIP.
(R)

SWEEP WEEK   A seven-day period (usually occurring once in each quarter year) during which research firms such as A.C. Neilsen or ARB conduct surveys of the listening or viewing audience to determine station and series program ratings. (*See* ARBITRON.)
(A,V,B)

SWEETEN   To add strings, horns, percussion, soft-track vocals, etc. to the existing basic tracks of a musical recording. A sweetening session may be booked to add production value, lushness, to smooth out or cover up any problems in the basic tracks, or to stylize the final sound of the recording.
(R,A)

SWING JOURNAL   The major Japanese jazz trade journal.
(R)

SWITCHER   Synonym for special effects generator. (*See* SEG.)
(V)

SYNC   1. Short for sel-sync. The operating mode of tape recorders that uses the sel-sync process of playback. 2. The operating condition in which two or more machines are running in synchronization with respect to some common measure of time (e.g., a SMPTE code recorded on each machine that is made to align with an external SMPTE reference; or mechanical sprocket holes). 3. (verb) To cause two or more machines to run in synchronization. 4. To align separate strands of sprocketed picture and sound (on magnetic film) so they will run in proper synchronization when played on a Steenback or a double-system projector, e.g., to sync dailies of a film.
(E)
(F,V)

SYNC BLOCK   A device used in editing to keep film and sprocketed
(F)

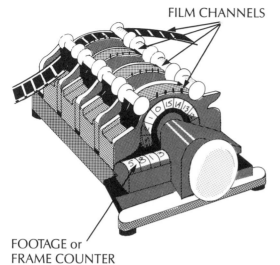

FILM CHANNELS

FOOTAGE or
FRAME COUNTER

SYNC BLOCK (35 mm).

sound tracks in sync. It can have two or more sprocketed wheels (called gangs) that rotate in unison, and a counter that displays footage and frame counts from a selected starting point. Also called synchronizer. (*See* A and B Rows.)

SYNC HEAD   1. Colloquially, the record head of a tape recorder, when used in sel-sync mode. **2.** The head on a Nagra or other synchronous recorder that records the sync signal onto, or plays the recorded sync signal back from, the recording tape. (*See* PUSH-PULL; NEO-PILOT TONE.)

(E)

(F)

SYNCHRONISM   The quality of being aligned in correct synchronization.
(F,V,G)

SYNCHRONIZATION   1. The precise alignment of picture and sound during projection and playback such that visual and audio events will be reproduced with the same time relationships they had in real life. **2.** The process by which this alignment is achieved.
(F,V,I)

SYNCHRONIZER   See SYNC BLOCK.

SYNCLAVIER   A sophisticated synthesizer made by New England Digital Corp., allowing detailed control of waveshape generation via direct video-monitor interface and other common systems. It can also record complete multi-track "master recordings" on hard disk, and is thus one of the so-called "tapeless recording studios" of the future.
(E,D)

SYNC MARK   A mark that the editor places on the head leaders for the workprint and each track of edited magnetic film. These generally put all tracks in editorial sync with one another, so that they will maintain synchronization when projected and reproduced on dubbers equipped with synchronous motors. The editor may also place a similar set of markings on the tail leaders of all reels of picture and magnetic film, to check that there has been no slippage in projection or playback.
(F,V)

SYNC PULSE   The signal recorded by the sync head of the Nagra, derived from the camera motor through a sync cable, or from the Nagra's own Crystal Sync generator, or the analogous tone recorded by any synchronous tape machine used in film or video production.
(F)

SYNC TONE   1. In reference to electronic drums machines and sequencers, a bi-phase modulated square wave generated in the machine. This can be recorded onto tape, and when played back into the machine will sync its signal output with the tape. Analagous to SMPTE and MIDI codes, but
(S,E)

differing in the frequencies and word lengths that various manufac-

(F)   turers use in their machines. **2.** The 60 Hz tone that motion picture cameras send to the Nagra or other sync recorder, and that controls the playback speed during transfer so that the magnetic film will sync with the workprint.

SYNC-WORD BITS   In SMPTE code,

(I)   an industry-defined sixteen-bit word used to identify the end of each frame of code. More precisely, these bits are: "0011 1111 1111 1101".

SYNDICATED TRACK   Music

(A)   produced for syndication by a producer or jingle house. Along with the right to use the music, the producer gives the buyer a guarantee of exclusivity (saying it will not sell the same music to another company in the same geographical area during the buyer's term of use), and perhaps a further guarantee to keep that music off the market for a period after the buyer's license expires.

SYNDICATION   **1.** The broadcast of selected network programming by

(A,V,B)   non-network stations, scheduled by these stations at times convenient for their audiences. One can syndicate a TV series that is currently running on network, or reruns of specials or series made and broad-

(R,T,B)   cast months or years earlier. **2.** The process undertaken by independent radio or television production companies who shoot and/or package complete programs or series, then license them to any broadcasters who wish to air them. The syndicators generally leave enough time within each program for the individual station to insert commercial spots.

SYSTEM REAL-TIME MESSAGES

(S)   MIDI signals that trigger the output of rhythmic devices such as drum machines. They consist of a single status byte, meaning "go!", and no data bytes.

- T -

TACH PULSE (E,I) A signal generated by the tachometer roller of an audio or video transport, one or more times per rotation. Because the tach roller is in contact with the tape in fast-wind modes as well as play or record mode, it can be used to get approximate tape-location data when SMPTE data cannot be read. Tach pulses sent by various decks to the synchronizer allow it to stop each deck near the SMPTE code designated by the engineer. Once in play or record modes, the decks will again interlock via the SMPTE data.

TACH ROLLER (E,I) Short for tachometer roller. A low-mass roller on a video or audio tape deck that is always in contact with the tape, and that drives the tape counter. It also generates an electric pulse with each rotation, which can be used to send tape location information to a synchronizer. (*See* TACH PULSE.)

TAG (A) A very brief, usually verbal, ending for a musical commercial. It can be spoken (example: for Shearson/American Express: "Minds over Money"), or sung (example: "Coke is it!").

TAIL (E) The end of a reel of tape or film.

TAILS OUT (or TAILS) (E) Describing a tape that has been played but not rewound, so that the recorded material nearest the outside of the reel is the end of the program. Professional users store tape tails out because this engenders less print-through. Opposite of heads out.

TAKE (E) A recorded performance of a composition, either partial or complete. Takes are normally numbered in the order in which they are played, until an acceptable complete take is recorded, or until the producer feels a good performance can be spliced together from parts of available takes.

TAKE SHEET (E,V) A sheet of paper on which the engineer makes notes about each take as it is recorded, such as complete or incomplete, good or N.G., which sections of a take are usable, etc.

TAKE-UP MOTOR   On a tape re-
(E)   corder, the motor that applies
take-up tension to the tape. This
motor also powers the fast-for-
ward mode. (*See* TENSION;
HOLD-BACK/TAKE-UP; SUP-
PLY MOTOR.)

TAKE-UP REEL   The reel onto which
(E,V)   tape is wound after it passes over
the audio or video heads.

TALENT   The actors, singers, and/or
(A)   narrators who perform in a radio
or television spot.

TALKBACK SYSTEM   The com-
(E)   munication system built into a
recording console that allows those
in the control room to speak to
musicians in the studio. A
microphone on the console is normally routed directly into the studio
amp and monitors, while a relay
mutes or reduces the volume of
the control room monitors to
prevent feedback. (*See* SLATE;
CUE SYSTEM.)

TANGENCY   The parameter of tape-
(E)   head alignment that determines the
geometric relationship between the
plane passing through the head gap
and the tape passing over the gap.
Ideally this plane should be exactly perpendicular to the plane
that is tangential to the tape passing the gap. Misadjustment of tangency will cause uneven head wear
on both sides of the gap. (*See*
ALIGNMENT, TAPE HEAD (il-
lustration).)

TAP (or DELAY TAP)   In a digital
(E)   delay, a point in the circuit after
one or more memory chips at
which the delayed input signal can

be obtained (via a patch point)
and routed to another destination.

TAPE   1. See MAGNETIC RECORD-
(E)   ING TAPE. **2.** Another name for
the tape recorder operating mode
normally called repro.

TAPE DELAY SYSTEM   Any delay
(E)   system that records the incoming
signal, then plays it back, the delay
produced by virtue of the time it
takes for a tape to pass from the
record head to the playback head.
Sometimes, the distance between
the heads can be varied to change
the delay time. More often,
however, the tape speed is varied
to achieve a shorter or longer delay.

TAPE HISS   Noise that is characteris-
(E)   tic of analog tape recordings,
produced by the random fluctuations in the positioning of magnetic particles along the tape, and
heard as low-level hiss during
playback. The noise, although
broadband, is most noticeable in
the high frequencies.

TAPELESS RECORDING STUDIO   Any
(E,D)   of the digital recording systems
that permit the recording of complete multi-track masters on computer hard disks or other mass-
storage media. The Fairlight and
Synclavier synthesizers are available with peripherals for tapeless
recording.

TAPE LOOP   A length of tape with
(E)   the ends spliced together. When
played, the sounds on the loop
repeat each time the loop passes
the heads. (*See* LOOP, various
definitions.)

TAPE OPERATOR (TAPE OP)
(E,V)   An assistant engineer whose primary job is to run the various tape recorders during a session, especially multi-track sessions. Video studios also employ tape ops.

TARGET MARKET
(A)   The demographically, geographically, or psychographically identified audience a commercial or campaign is intended to reach and motivate. More simply, the portion of the public the client believes is most likely to buy its product or service. (See PRIMARY MARKET; SECONDARY MARKET.)

TAX RETURN
(B)   The forms that every business must fill out and file yearly for the I.R.S. (Internal Revenue Service) and many state governments, detailing the previous year's financial results. The ins and outs of business tax laws are quite complex. Thus, to minimize payments, especially if a business has a significant cash flow or profit, legal and accounting advice is indispensable. Tax returns should be checked or prepared by professionals.

TBC   See Time Base Corrector.

TEASER
(A)   A very brief radio or TV announcment of some upcoming event.

TECHNICAL RIDER
(R,B)   A type of contractual rider in which one party specifies certain technical or engineering standards that will be met in the execution of his responsibilities to the other party. A concert promoter may insert a technical rider guaranteeing the starring act certain specifications for the house or monitor sound systems. A record company may guarantee an artist the ability to record an album digitally via a technical rider, etc.

TELECINE
(V)   British name for a film chain.

TELEPLAY
(V)   The script for a dramatic television show, live or taped.

TEMPERED TUNING (or SCALE)
(S,G)   The type of tuning used on most modern instruments, dividing each octave into twelve equal-pitch increments or semi-tones. Prior to Bach's time, most instruments were tuned by the "mean tone" system, in which thirds and sixths were made perfect at the expense of other intervals. The instrument had to be retuned for pieces in different keys. Tempered tuning works equally well in all keys, but has no perfect intervals.

TENSION, HOLD-BACK/TAKE-UP
(E)   The torque applied by the supply and take-up reel motors, which prevents the tape from spilling off the supply reel, maintains good tape-to-head contact, and winds the tape smoothly on the take-up reel.

TENSION SWITCH   See REEL SIZE CONTROL.

TERRITORY
(R,P)   As used in publishing and recording contracts, master purchase, or license agreements, etc., a single country or geographical area. In most contracts, for example, the United States and Canada are called the North American territory. (See SUB-PUBLISHING.)

(A) = Advertising • (B) = Business & Law • (C) = Computers • (D) = Digital • (E) = Engineering & Scientific •
(F) = Film • (G) = Music & General • (I) = Interlock & Sync • (J) = Jokes & Jargon • (P) = Music Publishing •
(R) = Record Industry • (S) = Synthesizers • (U) = Unions • (V) = Video

TESSITURA (G)   The relationship between a musical part written for a particular instrument or voice, and the range of notes that instrument or voice can produce. In producing jingles, for instance, a melody has good tessitura if the notes are in the strongest part of the lead singer's range.

TEST PRESSING (R)   The first actual pressing of a record, made from the stamper. This pressing is normally sent to the producer or label for a preview before commercial release pressings are made and shipped. If properly made, the test should sound exactly like the approved acetate.

TEST TAPE (E,G)   A laboratory-made tape with tones recorded at standard levels. Used in the alignment and calibration of the headstack and electronics. Also called a reference tape. (*See* FLUXIVITY, REFERENCE; SENSITIVITY.)

THEME (P)   One of the four use weights that determine the payment due to the publisher or copyright owner for a broadcast performance of a copyrighted song or recorded performance. The second lowest payment category, indicating that the work will be the theme of a single show or special. (*See* USE WEIGHT; PERFORMANCE CREDIT; CATEGORY.)

THREE-TRACK MIX (F)   A mix of all the soundtracks of a film, in which the sounds are divided into three groups, each group recorded on a separate stripe along the width of the 35 mm magnetic film. These groups are dialogue, music, and effects. Also called three-stripe. (*See* M&E TRACKS.)

THRESHOLD (E)   For any dynamic signal processor, the input level at which the device begins functioning. (*See* COMPRESSOR; EXPANDER; LIMITER; NOISE GATE; COMPANDER; GAIN-BEFORE-THRESHOLD.)

THRESHOLD OF HEARING (E,G)   The lowest level sound detectible by a listener with good hearing. Defined as 0 dB SPL, and usually specified for a 3 kHz tone, since the human ear is most sensitive in this frequency range. (*See* SPL; SOUND PRESSURE LEVEL METER; PHON; DYNE.)

THRESHOLD OF PAIN (E,G)   The very high sound level at which the listener begins to experience physical pain in his ears. Normally defined as 140 dB SPL. (*See* SPL; SOUND PRESSURE LEVEL METER; PHON; DYNE.)

THROAT (E)   The opening at which a driver attaches to a horn. Or the narrow end of the horn itself.

TIE LINES (E)   Signal paths or cables for line-level signals, routed between two separate control rooms, studios, or other locations. Used to interconnect devices in different locations, eliminating the need to move all the equipment into the same room.

TIE-TAC MICROPHONE (E)   A lavalier that can be pinned or clasped to the wearer's tie or other clothing.

TIGHT (G)   1. Colloquially, well-rehearsed or precise. Used to describe a performance or performing group. **2.** A subjective description of sounds picked up by a microphone in very close proximity. Very intimate, crisp, detailed, without ambient sound.

TIGHT-MIKE   To place a microphone very close to the sound source, either to minimize leakage from other sound sources or to get an intimate or tight sound from the desired source.

(E)

TILT   The parameter of tape-head alignment that determines whether the tape will be held against the head with equal pressure across its full width. Ideally, as the guides bring the tape into contact with the head, the "gap line" will be parallel to the cross-section of tape where the gap and tape meet. Incorrect tilt will cause one edge of the tape to make gap contact first. When full contact is achieved, that edge will have more pressure on it than the other edge, causing uneven head wear and tape slippage toward the edge under less pressure. This in turn causes tape to ride up or down along the gap. Also called zenith. (See ALIGNMENT, TAPE HEAD (illustration).)

(E)

TIMBRE   The specific tone color or quality of a sound, including its harmonic structure, envelope, and other identifying aural characteristics.

(E,G)

TIME BASE CORRECTOR   (TBC). An electronic device that repairs dropouts and other defects in the synchronizing signals of a video picture, then acts as an outside sync reference to which many

(V)

playback machines can conform. (*See* SPECIAL EFFECTS GENERATOR; KEY; FRAME; FIELD.)

TIME-BUYER   The ad agency employee who purchases time for the airing of spots on radio or television stations. One of the media buyers.

(A)

TIME CODE GENERATOR   An electronic device that produces SMPTE time code signals, which can be used to synchronize the frame rate of motion picture cameras and recorders, television cameras. VTRs, VCRs, etc.

(V,I)

TIME CODE   See SMPTE TIME CODE.

TIME QUEEN   A CD buyer whose primary consideration is the length of the program on a compact disc, not its musical or audio quality. According to some CD dealers, time queens will only buy discs over an hour long.

(R,J)

TIME SLOT   In broadcasting, the specific AM or PM time at which a program is scheduled to begin and end. For example, a certain program may have the 8-9 PM time slot.

(V)

TIMING   The adjustment of the overall exposure and color balance of each shot in a film. Done in the film lab using a machine made by the Hazeltine Corporation, timing is expensive, and therefore is normally reserved for the making of various answer prints. Once the answer print is approved, the paper tape containing the timing data will be used to create internega-

(F)

---

tives, master positives. Release prints can then be made quickly and cheaply. Analagous to scene-to-scene color correction in video post-production. (*See* RGB.)

TIMING CLOCK   A MIDI circuit that
(S)   outputs 24 pulses per quarter note (at the designated tempo). Slaved devices synchronize to this stream of pulses.

TIP SHEET   Slang name for any trade
(R,V,P)   magazine or periodical that publishes sales, radio or TV charts, pick hits, etc., or serves as an industry bulletin board to solicit songs for recording, announce available deals, etc.

TITLE   1. Any image that is
(F,V)   photographed in written or printed form and must be read from the screen by the viewer. This can include the actual name of the production; cast, creative, and technical credits; information that augments the plot or characters; or translations of dialogue into other
(B)   languages (subtitles). 2. A legal term indicating both ownership and the collective rights to determine the use, rental, licensing, and eventual sale of some designated tangible or intangible property. One may have title to a car or to the copyright of a composition.

TITLE STRIP   A label about 1″ × 3″
(R)   listing the titles of both sides of a single and the artist. The strip is used in juke boxes to allow customers to select records they wish to hear.

TONES   See REFERENCE TONE.

TOP-40   A radio programming format
(R)   in which the station plays only the 40 most popular songs in its geographical area. National top-40 shows play the singles currently in position 1 through 40 of *Billboard's* "Hot 100."

TORTOISING   The methodical se-
(J)   quencing and completion of small portions of an enormous production or task. Done to insure uniform quality in the final product, and to preserve the sanity of those involved in its creation. For example, the method by which this book was written.

TOUCH SENSITIVITY   General name
(S)   for any system by which a synthesizer measures the pressure or velocity with which a key is depressed, etc.

TOUR SUPPORT   Money spent by a
(R)   record company to help an artist cover the expenses of appearing as the opening act for a major star, or going on tour. A part of the promotion expense that is charged back to the artist's royalty account as a part of the recoupables.

TRACK   (noun) The recorded path of
(E)   a single channel of information on magnetic recording tape.

TRACK   (verb) 1. To physically move
(F,V)   the film or television camera toward, away from, or around the subject. Sometimes accomplished by mounting the camera on a dolly whose wheels are guided by metal tracks. 2. The shot that results from this movement. Short for tracking shot.

TRACK FORMAT   See FORMAT, TRACK.

TRACK LAYING   The editing and assembly of the various tracks of magnetic film containing dialogue, narration, sound effects, music, etc., in preparation for re-recording, mixing, or dubbing. Also called SOUND CUTTING.
(F,V)

TRACKING   1. In record promotion, the process by which the company gathers information about the radio play, chart position(s), and sales of a particular release. The tracker calls stations and record stores to get daily or weekly reports on airplay and consumer sales (as opposed to the number of copies shipped to stores). Tracking information is then used to make decisions about spending money for additional promotion, advertising, tour support, etc. **2.** The process of following the envelope of a signal's waveform, as in a level meter of any type. **3.** In describing the performance of a phonograph stylus or other transducer, the measure of its ability to precisely follow the instantaneous waveform of the applied signal, be it mechanical (e.g., a record groove), acoustic, or electrical. **4.** A synonym for overdubbing. **5.** In helical scan video playback, the parameter that determines whether the rotating heads are properly aligned with the individual tracks on which video data is written on the tape. This can be adjusted on most decks, and is internally accomplished by varying the time relationship between the reading of the control track and video data by their respective heads. **6.** Short for double-tracking or re-tracking.
(R)
(E)
(E)
(E)
(V)
(U)

An AFM and AFTRA performance category used in determining payments for recording sessions. If the performers are asked to do the same parts again, and this additional performance is recorded on separate tracks or bounced in with their original performance, the producer must pay each union member a full scale wage for each performance. If each performer tracks his original part twice, the producer will be responsible for three full payments to each. Done to give the effect of a larger group. (*See* DOUBLING.)

TRACKING ERROR   The measure of the limit of the ability of a transducer, electric circuit, or meter to precisely follow an applied signal or wave. It shows up as a difference between the waveform of the output and input signals—i.e., a difference in input/output level or frequency response. (*See* DAMPING FACTOR.)
(E)

TRANSCRIPTION LICENSE   Most often, a combined mechanical and performance license granted by a composition's publisher and the corresponding performing rights society to a company that syndicates music for background or environmental uses—e.g., Muzak, in-flight music, etc. There are several other types of transcription licenses, so be careful of the context.
(P)

TRANSFER   1. The copying of sound recorded on magnetic tape, records, or any other medium onto magnetic film. **2.** The magnetic film itself that results from this copying process. A "straight transfer" is made without any equalization or compression of the signal as it goes
(F,V)

(P,R) from the source to the magnetic film. **3.** In legal parlance, a synonym for an assignment or the process of assigning rights to another party.

TRANSFER CHARACTERISTIC   A (E) graph that displays the output of any device compared with its input. Can be displayed for various input levels, either broadband, or separately for various input frequencies, etc. (*See* SENSITIVITY.)

TRANSFORMER   An electric com- (E) ponent that contains two or more coils of wire in proximity, and is used to couple one circuit to another without permitting current flow from one to the other.

(E)   IMPEDANCE MATCHING TRANSFORMER: A transformer, the number of windings in each of whose coils is calculated to match the impedance of the device to which that coil is electrically connected. A signal passing through the input coil induces a voltage in the output coil. The energy transfer by such induction is more efficient than if the incoming signal were sent directly to the following device, the two having very different impedances.

TRANSIENT   A sudden, high-amplitude (E) signal peak that decays to the average program level very quickly. Percussive instruments create steep transients with every note. (*See* ENVELOPE (illustration).)

TRANSIENT RESPONSE   The measure (E) of the accuracy with which an audio system reproduces transients. For example, each hit of the snare drum in a digitally recorded rock cut may have a transient 12–15 dB above the average signal level. (*See* DISTORTION; CLIPPING; SATURATION.)

TRANSPORT   The mechanical portions (E) of a tape recorder or videotape recorder, including all parts that handle and guide the tape from the feed reel, past the various heads, and onto the takeup reel. (Illustration next page.)

TRANSVERSE SCAN   A type of (V) videotape recorder in which the tape passes by a rotating wheel on which the record and playback heads are mounted. The wheel rotates at right angles to the tape. This system is used in some broadcast-quality equipment, where higher-quality color is necessary, and the cost of running tape at higher speeds is not prohibitive. For example, 2-inch high-band VTRs record and reproduce via transverse scan. (*See* QUAD-RUPLEX.) (Illustration next page.)

TRAP   An acoustic or electronic device (E) intended to filter out or otherwise eliminate unwanted sounds or signals—e.g., a bass trap, a bias trap, etc.

TRAVELLING MATTE   A strip of (F) high-contrast black and white film with the image of a moving object that will be matted-in to another scene. If a camera negative and a positive matte (in which the shape of the object to be matted-in is clear, with everything else opaque) are double-exposed onto an interpositive, the resulting film will show the live action scene with the area to be matted-in blacked out. The foreground object can now be dropped into that area of each frame. (*See* ROTOSCOPING.)

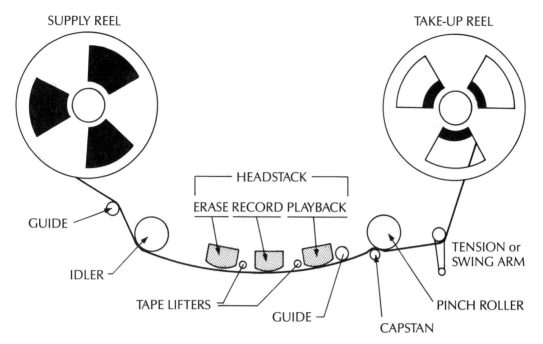

TRANSPORT. Open loop path process of the basic tape transport.

TREMOLO   A wavering quality in a
(G)   steady musical tone or sound,
caused by a cyclical change in its
volume level—above and below its
nominal level. Often confused with
vibrato.

TRIANGLE WAVE   An oscillator out-
(S,E)   put signal each cycle of which rises
linearly to a sharp peak, then des-
cends smoothly, repeating this in
positive and negative wave segments. The resulting waves look

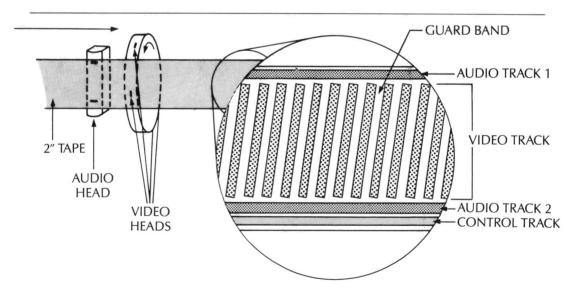

TRANSVERSE SCAN. The tracks are at a slight angle because the head rotates down as the tape moves from left to right.

like a series of normal and inverted triangles. Similar in sound to a sine wave, but with some mellow overtones.

TRIGGER (S)   A signal sent out by a keyboard, clock, or sequencer, telling a signal-generator or envelope-generator to begin its cycle. (*See* CONTROL VOLTAGE.)

TRIM (E) (F)   **1.** (noun). The attenuation control associated with the first stage of amplification in each module of a console, and by which the incoming level of a mic or line input can be lowered. **2.** (verb). To attenuate the incoming level of a signal. For example, "Trim the mic in module number three." **3.** A short section of exposed film, workprint, or magnetic film track that has been cut out of a shot or take included in an assembly or workprint.

TRIM BIN (F)   A bin or basket with small mounting nails mounted on its rim, used for saving the trims from various shots until the fine cut is completed.

TRUCK (F,V)   The vehicle or van in which video recorders, audio mixers, and other equipment is installed for mobile productions. Normally, sound or video trucks are permanently wired with several record and playback decks, and have the capacity for adding extra machines when necessary. Lighting, mics, stands, and other equipment may also be carried in luggage compartments, so that one vehicle is a complete mobile video and/or audio recording studio.

T-60   See REVERBERATION TIME.

TURNAROUND (G) (F,V)   **1.** In a song or arrangement, the measure or measures in which one verse or chorus ends, leading into the next section. Also, the short instrumental or vocal lines that accomplish this transition. **2.** A state in the pre-production of a feature film or television movie in which the project is abandoned by its current backers and producers, and is put up for sale (script, novel rights if any, and perhaps cast options, etc.) to another production company or studio.

TURNOVER FREQUENCY (E)   **1.** In a shelving equalizer, the frequency at which the amount of level change is 3 dB less than the maximum amount of change—i.e., the ultimate shelf height in decibels. The level at which the boost or cut begins to flatten out to form a shelf. (*See* SHELF EQUALIZATION.) **2.** In a passive filter, the cutoff frequency.

TV CUT-OFF (V)   Same as the safe-action area of a live or videotaped scene.

TWEEK (E,S,G)   To make a fine adjustment of an operating parameter—e.g., the azimuth of a playback head, or the tuning of a synthesizer.

TWEETER (E)   A loudspeaker designed to reproduce high frequencies.

TYLER MOUNT (F,V)   A mounting device used to suspend film or TV cameras in a helicopter, isolating the camera from vibrations. The resulting footage is sometimes called a Tyler shot.

- U -

UHF   Ultra High Frequency. The band
(V)   of television broadcast frequencies
reserved by the FCC for local and
community-access stations, services
giving continuous weather, stock
reports, etc. Channels 14 and up.

ULTIMATTE   The electronic device
that actually overlays one image
(V)   over another in chroma-keying,
etc.

ULTRA HIGH FREQUENCY   See
UHF.

U-MATIC   Sony Corporation's trade
name for the 3/4″ helical scan video
(V)   cassette format. Originally
developed for ENG applications,
it has become the world standard
for industrial and semi-pro
videotape productions of all types.

UNBALANCED LINE   A signal line
with two conductors: one that
(E)   carries the signal, the other at
ground potential. The ground conductor is often used as the shield.
Unbalanced lines are more subject
to the effects of ambient magnetic
or electric fields than balanced
lines.

UNDERCRANK   To run a motion picture camera motor at less than the
(F,V)   normal sync speed. The resulting
filmed action, when projected at
normal speed, will be sped up.
Opposite of overcrank.

UNDERSCORE   Using music to
provide emotional (and sometimes
(F,V)   informational) enhancement to on-
screen action, dialogue, or narration.

UNION STEWARD   A union employee
who acts as agent between union
(U)   performers and their employers,
especially where large groups of
musicians, singers or actors are involved—i.e., orchestras, opera companies, repertory companies. The
steward ensures that employers
meet all the terms of their contract
with the particular union.

UNIT   1. AFTRA uses a numerical scale
to compare the relative size of
(P)   various cities and markets. This
scale is used to compute payment
for singers. Example: Springfield,
Massachusetts is a 1-Unit Market,
Boston a 5-Unit Market. Singers
who perform on a commercial

---

aired in Boston get paid more (but not five times more) than singers on a Springfield area spot. (*See* PERFORMANCE.) **2.** One phonograph record, cassette, compact disc, etc. A store might place an order for 300 units of a certain album. A record company might have 100,000 units of this or that single pressed, etc. More generally, one example of any product intended for sale to the consumer.

(R,B)

UNITY GAIN   The operational condition in any electronic device or system where the output level exactly equals the input level. The gain—defined as the number of times the signal level is amplified from input to output—is thus 1.000.

(E)

UNSOPHISTICATED INVESTOR   See SOPHISTICATED INVESTOR.

(B)

UPDATE MODE   In console automation, the operating mode in which previously written automation data is read back to its respective input faders for alteration by the engineer. The position of each fader at the beginning of an "update take" is defined by the system as its null-point. If the engineer leaves these faders at their initial levels throughout the take, no data will be changed. Any fader movement above or below a null-point is read in dB, and that track's data changed to reflect the same dB change from the previously written signal level. This updated data must then be written into storage in order to be

(E)

read at a later time. (*See* NULL POINT; WRITE MODE; READ MODE; CONSOLE AUTOMATION.)

UPLOAD   In computers, to transmit data to a remote computer or peripheral device. (*See* DOWNLOAD.)

(C)

USER-ASSIGNED BITS   In SMPTE time code, 32 bits in each word (actually eight groups of four) have been designated as locations for user-defined information of any variety, from take numbers to comments for use in future editing.

(I,V,E)

USER INTERFACE   The way a particular computer and/or program appears to and is employed by the user. This can include the layout of a keyboard, use of other devices such as a "mouse," the screen layout a program establishes to accept or display data, etc.

(C)

USE WEIGHT   The parameter by which ASCAP or BMI assigns a broadcast performance of a copyrighted song or musical recording to one of four categories that determine the amount of payment due to the copyright holder. In order of increasing payment due, the four performance categories are: Background, Theme, Supertheme, and Featured. These categories are also used to develop an appropriate fee for a user seeking to purchase a synchronization license. (*See* CATEGORY; PERFORMANCE CREDIT.)

(P)

- V -

VAMP (G)   In a performance of a song, the ending. Either a continuing repetition of the last chorus intended to be faded out during the mix, or a coda section with solo lines, leading to a hard ending.

VARIABLE/SEMI-VARIABLE COSTS (B)   In any manufacturing process, variable costs are expenses that depend only on the number of items manufactured—e.g., the number of records pressed or jackets printed for a given release. Semi-variable costs depend partially on the number of items manufactured—e.g., the set-up charge a printer builds into every job to cover the time and cost of preparing the press for a run, no matter how small that run.

VARIETY (G)   The daily and weekly entertainment industry newspaper, with separate sections for charts and news in motion picture, theatrical shows and musicals, records, etc.

VARI-SPEED (E)   Short for variable speed. A device within a tape recorder that allows the record or playback speed of the tape to be changed from its nominal 7.5, 15, or 30 ips. Used mainly to match the musical pitch of a tape playback to the tuning of an instrument being overdubbed—e.g., a piano—that cannot easily be retuned to match the tape.

VARI-SPEED OSCILLATOR (E)   In tape recorders, an oscillator used to vary the frequency of the AC current driving an AC capstan motor and, hence, the tape speed. Recorders whose capstans are driven by DC motors often have DC voltage controls for vari-speed operation. These are often mistakenly called vari-speed oscillators.

VCA, VCF, VCO (E)   See VOLTAGE-CONTROLLED AMPLIFIER; VOLTAGE-CONTROLLED FILTER; VOLTAGE-CONTROLLED OSCILLATOR; CONSOLE AUTOMATION.

VCR (V)   Video Cassette Recorder. Cassette formats in current use are 1/4″, 8mm, 1/2″, Beta or VHS (home formats), and 3/4″ U-matic, a semi-pro and ENG format.

VDP   Video Disc Player.

VELOCITY OF SOUND   In air, sound travels at about 1,087 feet per second at 32°F and 30% humidity. This velocity changes by about 1 ft/sec, increasing as temperature goes down and decreasing as temperature goes up.
(E,G)

VENUE   The place where a performance takes place. Or loosely, any other vehicle by which an artist reaches an audience—e.g., a TV special, product endorsement campaign, concert tour, etc.
(G)

VERY HIGH FREQUENCY   See VHF.

VHF (VERY HIGH FREQUENCY)   The band of television broadcast frequencies reserved by the FCC mainly for networks and their local affiliates. Channels 2 through 13 on most sets. (*See* UHF.)
(V)

VHS   A system used for 1/2″ color videotape recording, generally for home use only.
(V)

VIBRATO   A wavering quality in a steady musical tone or sound, caused by a cyclical change in its musical pitch (or fundamental frequency)—above and below its nominal pitch. Often confused with tremolo.
(G)

VIDEO ASSIST   A small video camera/recorder system used in conjunction with a motion picture camera. The video camera is attached to the movie camera, taking its image from the motion picture lens. The resulting videotape allows instant replay of scenes and takes as they are shot. Any problems with lighting, camera movement, etc. can be corrected in subsequent
(F)

takes. The videotape can also be used for preliminary editing decisions.

VIDEO CASSETTE RECORDER   See VCR.

VIDEO DISC PLAYER   See VDR.

VIDEO JOCKEY   See VJ.

VIDEO MONITOR   Essentially a television set on which one can show images from a live video camera, or playback images from a VTR.
(V)

VIDEO TAPE RECORDER   See VTR.

VIDEOTEX   The international name for data transmission systems by which home television sets can display information sent from a remote computer via telephone lines. News, weather, and other information is available via Videotex. Various experiments have also been tried with at-home banking, shopping, etc. (*See* MODEM.)
(C,E)

VIEWER   A device for the rapid viewing of film. Usually table-mounted, with a small screen, the lightweight intermittent movement is driven by the sprocket holes of the film itself as it is hand-cranked from one reel to another using a pair of rewinds.
(F)

VINYL   A pliable plastic compound used in high-quality record pressings. It becomes soft at a relatively low temperature, and thus takes the impression of grooves from a stamper easily and accurately. However, pure vinyl discs scratch easily. For this reason—and
(R)

(A) = Advertising • (B) = Business & Law • (C) = Computers • (D) = Digital • (E) = Engineering & Scientific •
(F) = Film • (G) = Music & General • (I) = Interlock & Sync • (J) = Jokes & Jargon • (P) = Music Publishing •
(R) = Record Industry • (S) = Synthesizers • (U) = Unions • (V) = Video

cost—other mixtures are used by most record companies, especially for rock and other mass-produced releases.

VJ
(R,V)   Video jockey. Analogous to disc jockey. A person who selects and plays music videos and other tapes, either at a club or for a television station.

VLSI
(C)   Very Large Scale Integration. (See LSI.)

VOCAL BOOTH
(E)   An acoustically isolated booth in which one or more singers can perform while rhythm instruments are playing in the studio, but that keeps leakage of these instruments from reaching the mics located in the booth. The same booth can be used to house acoustic instruments being played at the same time as amplified ones in the studio, or vice versa.

VOICE-OVER (VO)
(E)   A spoken reading of copy mixed into a commercial over the music track, usually in a "donut" or other music-only portion of the spot. The voice can be that of a narrator, a well-known actor or personality, or the lead singer in the spot itself.

VOLTAGE
(E)   The difference in the electrical potential of two points in a circuit.

VOLTAGE CONTROLLED AMPLIFIER (VCA)
(E)   An amplifier whose gain is controlled by an external voltage having nothing to do with the signal being amplified. Used in some recording consoles for subgrouping, in automated mixing, etc. (See CONSOLE AUTOMATION.)

VOLTAGE-CONTROLLED ATTENUATOR
(E)   An amplifier (or resistive network) whose gain is 1.0 at maximum, and whose attenuation of an audio signal varies in proportion to an externally supplied DC voltage.

VOLTAGE-CONTROLLED FILTER (VCF)
(E,S)   A variable bandpass filter, the cut-off frequency of which increases or decreases in proportion to an externally supplied DC control voltage. Used in many synthesizers to change the timbre of the output signal.

VOLTAGE-CONTROLLED OSCILLATOR (VCO)
(E,S)   An oscillator whose output frequency varies in proportion to an externally supplied control voltage. The main tone-producing circuit of many synthesizers.

VOLUME
(E)   1. Colloquial term for sound pressure level. 2. Short for volume control. (See GAIN CONTROL.)

VOLUME UNIT
(E)   A unit of signal level corresponding to the ear's subjective judgment of changes in audio program level or loudness. (See VU METER.)

VTR
(V)   Video Tape Recorder. An open-reel recorder—e.g., the 1″ machines that are currently the professional broadcast standard.

VU METER   See METER, VU. (See also BALLISTICS; METER, PEAK READING.)

- W -

WA

(F,V) Wide Angle. Indicating that the designated shot will be made using a lens of short focal length. The shorter the focal length, the more panoramic the result on screen. Opposite of telephoto. "WA" and "LS" are used interchangeably in scripts to describe establishing shots.

WATT

(E) The basic unit of power or energy transfer. Defined as 1 joule per second. A joule equals 1 kg-meter^2/sec^2.

WAVEFORM

(E) For any audio signal or sound, the graph of amplitude with respect to time. Characteristic waves get their names from the general shape of their waveforms—i.e., sine waves, square waves, sawtooth waves, etc.

WAVEFORM MODULATION

(S) A voltage-controlled change in the timbre of a note or an entire patch, independent of the pitch or frequency being designated by the keystrokes.

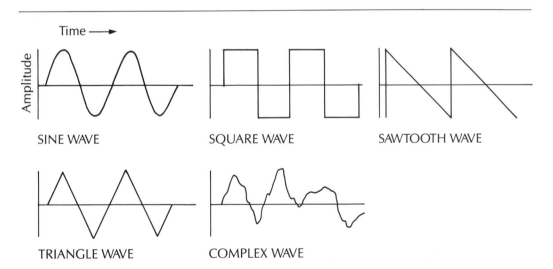

SINE WAVE SQUARE WAVE SAWTOOTH WAVE

TRIANGLE WAVE COMPLEX WAVE

WAVEFORM.

WAVELENGTH   The distance spanned
(E)   by one complete cycle of a sine
wave (or the fundamental frequency of any complex musical
tone) as it travels through an elastic
medium—e.g., air, or as it is recorded on tape, film, or a disc (not
a CD).

WAVELENGTH RESPONSE   For any
acoustical or electrical system, a
(E)   graph of amplitude vs. wavelength.
A modified type of frequency-
response curve. Used in the
measurement of performance of
head gaps, etc.

WEAVE JOB   A type of musical track
for a spot in which short segments
(A)   of lead vocal or instrumental lines
are interspersed between lines of
narration or dialogue. The music
weaves in and out, taking the
foreground whenever there is no
spoken copy.

WEBER   The basic unit of magnetic
(E)   flux. Defined as 1 volt-second.

WEIGHTING   In measuring frequency
response, introducing a predeter-
(E)   mined equalization to the signal
before taking the measurement.

WEIGHTING NETWORK   A filtering
(E)   network or active equalizer
precisely designed or calibrated
for use in weighting.

WEIGHTING (A,B,C)   See DECIBEL:
(E)   dBA, dBB, dBC.

WEIGHTING FORMULA   The equa-
tion(s) by which the performing-
(P)   rights societies determine the dollar value of the categories used in
calculating broadcast royalties payable to publishers and composers.

WEIGHTING, STATION   In the calculation of broadcast royalties and
(U,A)   residuals, the summation of all factors that determine how much a
specific radio or television station
must pay for broadcast performances, or how much its advertisers must pay as residuals to performers appearing in spots. Station
weighting factors include the
population and size of the station's
potential viewing audience, its current Arbitron or Neilsen rating, its
wattage, programming format, etc.
(*See* PERFORMANCE CREDIT;
UNIT.)

WET SOUND   A sound with reverberation added to it. For example,
(E)   "The guitar track is too wet."

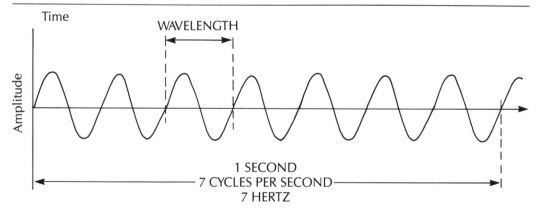

WAVELENGTH.

W-4 FORM   Employee Withholding Allowance Certificate. An I.R.S. form
(B) that must be filled out by union and non-union employees rendering creative or technical services in recording sessions, film or video shoots, etc. (i.e., musicians and singers, cameramen and crews, etc.) The employee gives the completed W-4 to the producer or employer, who computes the amount to be withheld and sends the form and a check to the I.R.S.

WHOLESALE   The price at which a record company (or manufacturer)
(B,R) sells its products to a distributor or retail store. Wholesale prices for the same product may vary with the quantity ordered or shipped, the total quantity of an order including many different records, a special agreement between the label and distributor, etc. Most record companies base artist and producer royalties on wholesale prices or total receipts. (*See* ROYALTY ARTIST.)

WILD SOUND   Any sound recorded when no film or videotape is roll-
(F,V) ing. Most often used to identify sound effects, room tone, crowd noise, which will be added to sync sound during the mix. Also called non-sync sound.

WIND SCREEN   A shield that allows all frequencies to pass through, but
(E) prevents blasts of wind from reaching a microphone's capsule. Usually made of open cell foam, layers of acoustically transparent material, etc, and attached to the mic itself. (*See* POP FILTER.)

WINDOW   1. A music-only passage in
(A) a commercial, during which a voice-over can be added. In various cities or single-production studios, the window is sometimes called a
(E) donut or a hole. (*See* DONUT). **2.** The frequency band in which a device is operational. For example, a telephone filter has a window from about 200 Hz to 2.4 kHz.
(V) (*See* BANDWIDTH.) **3.** Short for code window or time code window.

WINDOW DISPLAY   A very effective type of promotion for records.
(R) Most stores charge record companies for advertising in their front windows. The store generally accepts free copies of the record being advertised, which may not be returnable for credit.

WIPE   An optical effect in which **1.** one shot seems to "push" another
(F,V) off the screen, or **2.** the second shot "unrolls" across the screen, replacing the first. This can happen in any direction on screen. (*See* SPECIAL EFFECTS GENERATOR (illustration.))

WIPO   World Intellectual Properties Organization. (*See* BERNE UN-
(P,G) ION.)

WIRELESS MICROPHONE   A microphone—usually a lavalier—at-
(F,V,E) tached to a miniature FM transmitter, and that broadcasts to an FM receiver. Because the signal is

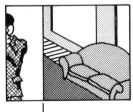

WIPE. (definition 1).

---

transmitted, no cable is necessary between the microphone and the audio recorder.

WOOFER (E)   A loudspeaker designed to reproduce low frequencies only.

WORD (D,C)   In any data-based operation, a group of bits that makes up a single complete parcel of information. In digital recording, each word contains 16 bits, whereas SMPTE synchronization words contain 80 bits of data.

WORD LENGTH (D,E)   The number of bits composing each word of digital data. The more bits in each digital audio sample, for instance, the greater the number of quantizing increments by which the incoming analog wave can be represented. This, in turn, affords greater accuracy in recording and reproduction of the original waveform. (*See* BYTE; QUANTIZATION; N-BIT.)

WORD PROCESSOR (C)   In computers, software that allows the computer to accept, edit, format, and then send data to a printer for finished text and/or graphic presentation. It enables the user to input long text programs, to electronically shuffle various parts of the text into a satisfactory order, then specify the format in which it will be printed, including margins, justification, characters, and line spacing, etc.

WORK MADE FOR HIRE (B,P, A,R)   1. A musical composition or finished master tape made by an employee as a part of his assigned duties, all rights to which belong to the employer. (F,V,R) 2. A composition or master tape specifically commissioned to serve in a defined context within a larger work. For example, the score and master tape for a jingle intended for use in a television spot. By industry convention, all motion pictures and television scores and all jingles or other advertising music were considered works made for hire until 1976. Since that date, with a revised copyright act and a growing awareness by film or TV producers and ad agencies of the free promotion a hit record gives a film or product, work for hire status has been negotiable between the composer/producer and the client.

WORKPRINT (F)   1. The first print made of the camera negative that is shot for a motion picture production, with all or selected takes included in their entirety, slates and all. Also called dailies. 2. The edited dailies of a film, in an assembly, rough cut, or fine cut. Usually marked with grease pencil to indicate planned optical effects or to carry negative-cutting instructions. Workprint is often loosely used to refer to all the edited materials, including magnetic film tracks, etc.

WORLD INTELLECTUAL PROPERTIES ORGANIZATION   See BERNE UNION.

WOW (E)   A slow variation in the musical pitch of recorded sounds caused by inconstant tape speed. A slower kind of FLUTTER.

WRAP (F,V)   1. Short for "wrap it up." An announcement that the day's shooting is completed, indicating that equipment can be dismantled and stored and all personnel may then (E) leave the set. 2. The parameter of

---

(A) = Advertising • (B) = Business & Law • (C) = Computers • (D) = Digital • (E) = Engineering & Scientific •
(F) = Film • (G) = Music & General • (I) = Interlock & Sync • (J) = Jokes & Jargon • (P) = Music Publishing •
(R) = Record Industry • (S) = Synthesizers • (U) = Unions • (V) = Video

tape-head alignment that determines how large an area of tape oxide is in contact with the front surface of the tape head—i.e., the surface containing the gap. Also called contact. The correct wrap is different for heads of different frontal design. The combination of wrap and tape tension determines whether the tape makes adequate contact at the gap itself. Called insertion in the U.K. (*See* ALIGNMENT, TAPE HEAD (illustration).)

WRITE
(C)   To put information or data onto a disk or other storage medium. Opposite of read.

WRITE MODE
(E)   In console automation, the operational mode in which the system scans channel fader levels (and perhaps other parameters), making continuous note of the engineer-specified initial conditions for each channel and all changes made by the engineer in real-time during a mix-

down. The scanned data is continuously written into storage, either on one track of the multi-track tape itself, or onto floppy disk. If stored to floppy disk, the multi-track tape and floppy disk must carry identical time codes for later reproduction of the mix by the system when operating in its read or update mode. (*See* CONSOLE AUTOMATION; READ MODE; UPDATE MODE.)

WRITE OFF
(B)   To deduct the cost of an acquisition or service from a person's business income. A percentge of the cost is subtracted from one or more years' books, P&L, or tax reports. The item deducted may be called a write-off. (*See* AMORTIZE.)

WRITER
(P,G)   Loosely, the lyricist or composer of a song (correctly called its author). Legally, writer only applies to the bookwriter of a dramatic or literary work.

- X -

XLR CONNECTOR A three- (or more) pin grounded and lockable audio connector designed for professional use, especially in balanced lines.
(E)

X-Y MIKING A coincident stereo miking technique that employs two cardioid microphones, diaphragms placed one over the other, but each aimed 45 degrees left or right of the nominal direction of the music source. (*See* SPACED PAIR; BLUMLEIN PAIR; M-S MIKING.)
(E)

-Y-

Y CONNECTOR (E)   A single-input, dual-output connector that sends incoming signals to two destinations. Also called a split feed.

YES (B,J)   When used to indicate agreement to a verbal contract, potentially the most dangerous word in the language. Use wisely and sparingly. (*See* NO.)

-Z-

ZENITH (E)   In tape head alignment, another name for tangency. (*See* ALIGNMENT, TAPE HEAD (illustration).)

ZERO FRAME (F,V)   The first frame of a roll of film or video tape, appropriately numbered 00:00:00:00.

ZONE, IN THE (E,G)   Short for "in the twilight zone." Used to describe situations in which an electronic or computer-based device malfunctions without apparent cause or obvious cure. For example, if the console automation system refuses to recreate a stored mix properly, you're in the zone.

ZOOM (F,V)   1. The apparent movement of the camera toward or away from the action, either to zero in on an important detail, or to enlarge the viewer's field of view beyond the central action. The zoom is achieved optically in the camera lens, and does not actually involve a movement of the camera. (*See* DOLLY; TRACK.) 2. The actual operation of a zoom lens to achieve such movement on-screen. (*See* TRACK.)

Standard Units and Measures

ATMOSPHERE (STANDARD) A unit of pressure. 1 atmosphere (atm.) = 101,325 newtons per square meter.

BAR A unit of pressure. 1 bar = 100,000 newtons per square meter.

BEL (symbol B) A dimensionless unit used to express the ratio of two power values. Defined as the logarithm in base 10 of the power ratio. The decibel (symbol dB) is more commonly used, and equals 1/10 bel. Thus, the corresponding number of decibels is defined as 10 times the log of the power ratio.

CANDELA (symbol cd) The luminous intensity of 1/600,000 of a square meter of a radiating cavity at the temperature of freezing platinum, 2,042 degrees Kelvin).

COULOMB (symbol C) The standard international unit of electric charge. Defined as the quantity of charge that passes through any cross-section of a conductor in 1 second when the current is exactly 1 ampere.

DYNE The unit of force in the cgs system. Defined as the force necessary to give an acceleration of 1 centimeter per second per second to a mass of 1 gram.

ELECTRON VOLT (symbol eV) A unit of energy. Defined as the energy acquired by an electron when it passes through a potential difference of 1 volt in a vacuum. $1 \text{ eV} = 1.602 \times 10^{-12}$ erg.

ERG A unit of energy. Defined as 10^{-7} joule. Also defined as the amount of work done when 1 dyne is applied through 1 centimeter. Hence, 1 foot-pound = 13,560,000 ergs.

FARAD (symbol F) The standard international unit of electrical capacitance. Defined as the amount of capacitance produced when a charge of 1 coulomb produces a potential difference of 1 volt between the terminals of a capacitor.

FOOTCANDLE (symbol fc) A unit of luminance. Defined as 1 lumen per square foot.

GAUSS (symbol G) A unit of magnetic flux density or induction. The ratio of the flux in any cross-section to its area, where the cross-section is normal or perpendicular to the direction of flow. 1 gauss = 1 maxwell per square centimeter.

HENRY (symbol H) A unit of inductance. Defined as the inductance of a circuit in which a current of 1 ampere produces a flux linkage of 1 weber.

HERTZ (symbol Hz) The standard international unit of frequency. 1 Hz = 1 cycle per second.

HORSEPOWER (symbol hp) A unit of power. Equals 33,000 foot-pounds per minute, or 550 foot-pounds per second.

JOULE (symbol J) The standard international unit of energy. The work done by 1 newton acting through 1 meter. 1 joule = 1 watt-second = 10^7 ergs = 10^7 dyne-centimeters.

KELVIN   (symbol K) The scientific unit of thermodynamic temperature. Defined as 1/273.16 of the Kelvin scale temperature of water at its triple point. (The triple point is the temperature at which a substance achieves three-phase equilibrium.)

KILOGRAM   (symbol kg) A unit of mass. Based on a platinum cylinder kept at the International Bureau of Weights and Measures in Paris. 1 kilogram = 1,000 grams = 2.205 pounds.

LAMBERT   (symbol L) A unit of luminance. A surface of 1 lambert luminance emits 1 lumen per square centimeter.

LITER   (symbol l) A unit of volume. 1 liter = 10^{-3} cubic meter = 1,000 cm³ = 0.03531 cubic foot = 61.02 cubic inches = 1.057 U.S. quart = 0.22 imperial gallon.

LUMEN   (symbol lm) A unit of luminous flux. Defined as the flux passing through a unit angle of 1 steradian from a point source of light emitting 1 candela.

LUX   (symbol lx) The standard international unit of illuminance. Defined as 1 lumen per square meter.

MAXWELL   (symbol Mx) A unit of magnetic flux. The flux through a square centimeter normal to a field at 1 centimeter from a unit magnetic pole.

METER   (symbol m) The standard international unit of length. 1 meter = 100 centimeters = 3.281 feet = 39.37 inches = 1.094 yard.

MHO   A unit of conductance. The conductance of a conductor whose resistance is 1 ohm.

MICROMETER   (symbol Greek letter mu, μ). One millionth of a meter. Formerly called a micron.

MIL   A unit of length. 1/1,000 of an inch.

NEWTON   (symbol N) A unit of force. The force that will impart an acceleration of 1 meter per second per second to a mass of 1 kilogram. 1 N = 10^5 dynes.

OERSTED   (symbol Oe) A unit of magnetic field strength. The magnetic field produced at the center of a plane circular coil of 1 turn and a radius of 1 centimeter carrying a current of 5π amperes.

OHM   (symbol Greek capital letter omega, Ω) A unit of resistance and impedance. The resistance of a conductor in which a constant current of 1 ampere produces a potential difference of 1 volt between its ends.

PHON   A unit of loudness level. The pressure level in decibels of a pure 1,000 Hz tone.

TESLA   (symbol T) A unit of magnetic flux density. The flux density of a uniform field that produces a torque of 1 newton-meter on a plane current loop carrying 1 ampere and having a projected area of 1 square meter on the plane perpendicular to the field. 1 T = 1 N/ampere-meter.

VOLT   (symbol V) A unit of voltage. The voltage between two points of a conducting wire carrying a constant current of 1 ampere, when the power dissipated between these two points is 1 watt.

WATT   (symbol W) A unit of power. Equals 1 joule per second. 1 W = 10^7 ergs per second = 44.27 foot-pounds per minute.

WEBER   (symbol Wb) A unit of magnetic flux. The flux passing through an area of 1 square meter placed normal to a uniform magnetic field whose flux density equals 1 tesla. 1 Wb = T·m².

Selected Bibliography

Alkin, Glyn. *TV Sound Operations.* (London, 1975: Focal Press.)

Alten, Stanley. *Audio in Media.* (Belmont, CA, 1981: Wadsworth.)

Anderson, Gary. *Video Editing.* (White Plains, NY, 1984: Knowledge Industry Publications.)

Anderson, O.J. *Business Law.* (Totowa, NJ, 1964: Helix.)

Anderton, Craig. *Electronic Projects for Musicians.* (Saratoga, NY, 1980: Guitar Player Books.)

———. *MIDI for Musicians.* (Berkeley, CA, 1982: Music Sales.)

Backus, J. *The Acoustical Foundations of Music.* (New York, 1969: W.W. Norton.)

Baskerville, David. *Music Business Handbook and Career Guide,* 4th ed. (Denver, 1985: Sherwood.)

Bateman, Wayne. *Introduction to Computer Music.* (New York, 1980: Wiley.)

Beranek, Leo L. *Acoustics.* (New York, 1954: McGraw-Hill.)

———. *Music, Acoustics and Architecture.* (New York, 1962: McGraw Hill.)

Berk, Lee Eliot. *Legal Protection For the Creative Musician.* (Boston: Berklee Press.)

Black, Henry Campbell. *Black's Law Dictionary.* (Chicago: West Co.)

Boden, Larry. *Basic Disk Mastering.* (Berkeley, CA, 1979: Mix.)

Borwick, J., ed. *Sound Recording Practice.* (1977: Oxford University Press.)

Browne, Steven. *The Video Tape Post-Production Primer.* (Burbank, CA, 1982: Wilton Place Communications.)

Campbell, Russell. *Photographic Theory For the Motion Picture Cameraman.* (London, 1970: Zwemmer.)

Carlson, Verne and Sylvia. *The Professional Lighting Handbook.* (New York, 1967: Verlan Industries.)

———. *Practical Motion Picture Photography.* (London, 1970, Zwemmer.)

Chamberlin, Hal. *Musical Applications of Microprocessors.* (Rochelle Park, NJ, 1980: Hayden.)

Cheshire, David. *The Video Manual.* (New York, 1982: Van Nostrand Reinhold.)

Connelly, Will. *The Musician's Guide to Independent Record Production.* (Chicago, 1981: Contemporary Books.)

Cooper, Jeff. *Building a Recording Studio,* 4th ed. (Calabasas, CA, 1984: Synergy Group.)

Crittenden, Roger. *The Thames and Hudson Manual of Film Editing.* (New York, 1981: Thames of Hudson.)

Crombie, David. *The New Complete Synthesizer.* (London, 1986: Omnibus.)

Crowhurst, Norman. *Basic Electronics Course.* (Blue Ridge, PA, 1972: Tab Books.)

Csida, Joseph. *The Music/Record Career Handbook.* (New York, 1980: Billboard.)

Dann, Allan and John Underwood. *How To Succeed In the Music Business.* (London, 1978: Wise Publications.)

Davis, Clive. *Inside the Record Business.* (New York, 1975: Ballantine.)

Davis, D. and Davis, C. *Sound System Engineering.* (Indianapolis, 1974: Howard Sams & Co.)

Dearling, James. *Making Money Making Music.* (Cincinnati, 1982: Writers Digest.)

Devarahi, *The Complete Guide to Synthesizers.* (Englewood Cliffs, NJ, 1982: Prentice-Hall.)

Dranov, Paul. *Inside the Music Publishing Industry.* (Elmhurst, IL, Music Business Publ.)

Eargle, John. *Sound Recording.* (New York, 1980: Van Nostrano.)

———. *The Microphone Handbook.* (Plainview, NY, 1981: Elar.)

———. *Handbook of Recording Engineering* (N.Y., 1986: Van Nostrand Reinhold.)

Ennes, Harold E. *Television Broadcasting.* (Indianapolis, 1979: Howard Sams.)

Everest, Alton. *The Master Handbook of Acoustics.* (Blue Ridge, PA, 1981: Tab Books.)

Faulkner, Robert. *Hollywood Studio Musicians.* (New York, 1971: Aldine-Atherton.)

Feist, Leonard. *Popular Music Publishing in America.* (New York, 1980: National Music Publishers Assoc.)

Fink, D. G., ed. *Color Television Standards.* (New York, 1955: McGraw-Hill.)

Frater, Charles. *Sound Recording For Motion Pictures.* (London, 1974: Tantivy-Barnes.)

Friedman, Dean. *The Complete Guide to Synthesizers, Sequencers and Drum Machines.* (Berkeley, CA, 1983: Music Sales.)

Fuller, Barry J. et al. *Single-Camera Video Production.* (Englewood Cliffs, NJ, 1982: Prentice-Hall.)

Gross, L.S. *The New Television Technologies.* (1983: William Brown.)

Grove, Dick. *Arranging Concepts Complete.* (Los Angeles, Dick Grove School.)

Hagen, Earl. *Scoring For Films.* (New York, 1971: Criterion Music.)

Hall, Donald. *Musical Acoustics.* (Belmont, CA, 1980: Wadsworth.)

Helmholtz, H. *On the Sensations of Tone.* (New York, 1954: Dover.)

Hindemith, Paul. *Elementary Training For Musicians,* 2nd ed. (London, 1949: Schott.)

Hubatka, Milton, Frederick Hull, and Richard Sanders. *Audio Sweetening For Film and Television.*

Iazzi, Frank. *Understanding Television Production.* (Englewood Cliffs, NJ, 1984: Prentice-Hall.)

Ingrahm, Dave. *Video Electronics Technology.* (Blue Ridge, PA, 1983: Tab Books.)

Iuppa, Nicholas. *A Practical Guide to Interactive Video.* (White Plains, NY, 1984: Knowledge Industry Publications.)

Jacob, Gordon. *Orchestral Technique.* (London, 1982: Oxford University Press.)

Jordan, Thurston. *Glossary of Motion Picture Terminology.* (Menlo Park, CA, 1968: Pacific Coast.)

Keyboard Magazine. *Synthesizer Basics.*

——. *Synthesizer Techniques.*

Kinsler, L.E. and Frey, A.R. *Fundamentals of Acoustics.* (New York, 1962: Wiley.)

Knowledge Age editors. *The Video Age.* (White Plains, NY, 1982: Knowledge Industry Publications.)

Lambert, Dennis with Ronald Zalkind. *Producing Hit Records.* (New York, 1980: Schirmer Books.)

Lazendorf, Peter. *The Videotaping Handbook.* (New York, 1983: Harmony Press.)

Legalvision, Inc. *The Entertainment Business Video Primer Series, 5 Videocassettes.* (New York, 1984–85 Legalvision. Inc.)

Lindey, Alexander. *Lindey On Entertainment, Publishing and The Arts,* 4 Vols. (New York, 1985: Clark Boardman.)

Lipton, Kenny. *Independent Filmmaking.* (New York, 1982: Straight Arrow.)

Mackay, Andy. *Electronic Music.* (Oxford, 1981: Phaidon.)

Macrae, Donald. *Television Production.* (Ontario, Canada, 1982: Methuen.)

Marner, Terence St. John. *Directing Motion Pictures* (London, 1972: Tantivy-Barnes.)

Marquis. *Music Industry Directory,* 7th ed. (Chicago, 1983: Marquis Who's Who Inc.)

Martin, George. *All You Need Is Ears.* (New York, 1982: St. Martins.)

——. ed. *Making Music.* (New York, 1983: Morrow.)

Miller, Arthur and Walter Strenge, eds. *American Cinematographer Manual,* 6th ed. (Hollywood. 1984: American Society of Cinematographers.)

Miller, Ellen. *Video, A Guide For Lawyers.* (New York, 1984: Law-Arts.)

Miller, Fred. *Music In Advertising.* (New York, 1985: Amsco.)

Nakajima, H., T.T. Doi, J. Fukuda, and A. Iga. *Digital Audio Technology.* (Blue Ridge, PA, 1983: Tab Books.)

Nisbett, Alec. *The Technique Of the Sound Studio.* (Plainview, NY, 1978: Sagamore.)

Nimmer, Melville B. *Nimmer On Copyright,* 4 vols. (Albany, NY, 1982: M. Bender.)

New York University Law School. *Complete Guide To the New Copyright Law.* (Dayton, OH, 1978: Lorenz Press.)

Olson, H. *Music, Physics and Engineering.* (New York, 1967: Dover.)

Oppenheim, A.V. (*Digital Signal Processing* (Englewood Cliffs, NJ, 1975: Prentice-Hall.)

——. *Applications Of Digital Signal Processing.* (Englewood Cliffs, NJ, 1978: Prentice-Hall.)

Peresic, Zoran. *Special Optical Effects.* (New York, 1980: Focal Press.)

Pincus, Edward. *Guide to Filmmaking,* 3rd ed. (New York, 1982: Signet.)

Pohlmann, Ken C. *Principles Of Digital Audio.* (Indianapolis, 1985: Howard Sams.)

Practising Law Institute. *Counseling Clients In the Entertainment Industry.* 2 vols. plus suppl. (New York, 1980: Practising Law Institute.)

——. *Legal and Business Aspects Of the Music Industry: Music, Videocassettes and Records.* (New York, 1980: Practising Law Institute.)

——. *Patents, Copyright, Trademarks and Literary Property.* (New York, 1981: Practising Law Institute.)

Rachlin, Harvey. *Encyclopedia Of the Music Business.* (New York, 1981: Harper and Row.)

Ragan, Robert. *Step-By-Step Bookkeeping.* (New York, 1984: Sterling.)

Rapaport, Diane. *How to Make and Sell Your Own Record,* rev. ed. (New York, 1982: Putnam.)

Roberts, Neal A. et al, ed. *Music Industry: Contract Negotiations and the Law* (Toronto, 1980: New York University Press.)

Robinson, Richard. *The Video Primer.* (New York, 1983: Perigee Books.)

Roederer, Juan. *Introduction to the Physics and Psychophysics of Music,* 2nd ed. (New York, 1979: Springer-Verlag.)

Rossing, Thomas. *The Science of Sound.* (Reading, MA, 1982: Addison-Wesley.)

Runstein, Robert and David Huber. *Modern Recording Techniques,* 2nd ed. (Indianapolis, 1986: Howard Sams.)

Shemel, Sidney and William Krasilovsky. *This Business of Music,* 5th ed. (New York, 1985: Billboard.)

——. *More About This Business of Music.* (New York, 1979: Billboard.)

Siegel, Alan. *Breaking Into the Music Business.* (Port Chester, New York, 1983: Cherry Lane.)

Skiles, Marlin. *Music Scoring For TV and Motion Pictures* (Blue Ridge, PA, 1976: Tab Books.)

Spottiswoode, Raymond et al, eds. *Focal Encyclopedia Of Film and Television Technique,* 2nd ed. (New York, 1969: Amphoto-Focal Press.)

Stokes, Geoffrey. *Starmaking Machinery: The Odyssey Of an Album.* (Indianapolis, 1976: Bobbs-Merrill.)

Strawn, John. *(Digital Audio Signal Processing.* (Los Altos, CA, 1985: Kaufmann.)

Struczynski, J. Michael. *The Complete Book of Scriptwriting.* (Cincinnati, 1982: Writers Digest Books.)

Swain, Dwight. *(Scripting For Video and Audiovisual Media.* (London, 1981: Focal Press.)

Taubman, Joseph. *(Performing Arts Management and Law,* 7 vols. (New York, 1983–84: Law-Arts.)

Thomas, T. *Music For Movies.* (London, 1977: Tantivy-Barnes.)

Tobler, John and Stuart Grundy. *The Record Producers.* (London, 1982: BBC.)

Traylor, J. G. *Physics Of Stereo/Quad Sound.* (1977: Iowa State University Press.)

Tremaine, H. *The Aduio Cyclopedia.* (Indianapolis, 1974: Howard Sams.)

UCLA Extension. *The Recording Contract—1980.* (Los Angeles, 1980: UCLA Extension.)

Vale, Eugene. *The Technique Of Screen and TV Writing.* (Englewood Cliffs, NJ, 1982: Prentice-Hall.)

Viera, John D. *The 1985 Entertainment, Publishing and the Arts Handbook.* (New York, 1985: Clark Boardman.)

White, Gordon. *Video Recording.* (Boston, MA, 1972: Butterworth.)

——. *Video Techniques.* (Boston, MA, 1982: Butterworth.)

Wiegand, Ingrid. *Professional Video Production.* (White Plains, New York, 1985, Knowledge Industry Publications.)

Wiese, Michael. *Film and Video Budgets.* (Boston, MA, 1984: Butterworth.)

——. *The Independent Film and Videomakers Guide.* (Boston, MA, 1984: Butterworth.)

Wilkie, Bernard. *(Creating Special Effects For TV and Films.* (London, 1977: Focal Press.)

Winckel, Fritz. *Music, Sound and Sensation.* (New York, 1967: Dover.)

Woodward, Walt. *An Insider's Guide To Advertising Music.* (New York, 1982: Art Direction.)

Woram, John. *The Recording Studio Handbook.* (Plainview, NY, 1982: Elar.)

Wurzel, Alan. *Television Production.* (Berkeley, CA, 1981: McGraw Hill.)

Zettl, Herbert. *Television Production Handbook.* (Belmont, CA, 1984: Wadsworth.)